Building Intelligent Information Systems Software

Introducing the Unit Modeler® Development Technology

Thomas D. Feigenbaum

AMSTERDAM • BOSTON • HEIDELBERG • LONDON
NEW YORK • OXFORD • PARIS • SAN DIEGO
SAN FRANCISCO • SINGAPORE • SYDNEY • TOKYO

Morgan Kaufmann is an imprint of Elsevier

Acquiring Editor: Todd Green
Editorial Project Manager: Lindsay Lawrence
Project Manager: Priya Kumaraguruparan
Cover Designer: Maria Inês Cruz

Morgan Kaufmann is an imprint of Elsevier
225 Wyman Street, Waltham, MA 02451, USA

British Library Cataloguing-in-Publication Data
A catalogue record for this book is available from the British Library

Library of Congress Cataloging-in-Publication Data
A catalog record for this book is available from the Library of Congress

ISBN: 978-0-12-805101-6

For information on all Morgan Kaufmann publications
visit our website at www.mkp.com

Working together
to grow libraries in
developing countries

www.elsevier.com • www.bookaid.org

Building Intelligent Information Systems Software

Introducing the Unit Modeler® Development Technology

This book is dedicated to my wife, Jessica, whose support, patience, and understanding have been without limits through the process of writing this book. It is also dedicated to my girls Kyra and Raegen, just because you guys are so awesome. I hope someday you will be able to read this book and better understand what your father has been working on.

Contents

About the Author

Tom Feigenbaum holds a bachelor's degree in physics from Duke University and a master's degree in physics from the University of Illinois. Early in his career, Feigenbaum worked as a systems engineer for TRW, Space and Technology Group in Los Angeles, CA. While at TRW, Feigenbaum worked in the area of space based electro-optical systems design and analysis. Feigenbaum also served as a part-time physics instructor for Indiana University-Purdue University Indianapolis (IUPUI). Feigenbaum currently is the founder and Chief Executive Officer of KeLabs-Knowledge Engineering Laboratories. KeLabs is the developer of the Unit Modeler Technology.

Prior to establishing KeLabs, Feigenbaum founded Problem Solving Concepts, Inc. (ProSolv). ProSolv initially developed educational software for physics and math. Later, ProSolv became a developer of cardiology image management and reporting software. The company then changed its name to ProSolv Cardiovascular (also the product name). ProSolv introduced some important innovations to the field of digital image review and reporting, a field that was in its infancy at the time it was introduced. In particular, it ran on standard computers with no hardware acceleration. In addition, it offered unlimited customizability for each sites reports, a feature which was uncommon at the time but essential for its practical implementation. It also helped bring the price of this new digital era technology within reach of many smaller laboratories.

ProSolv entered a market that was dominated by major corporations such as GE, Siemens, and Philips. The company successfully competed with these major corporations and expanded its customer base to more than 300 installations throughout the United States, Japan, Australia, and the European Union. The company's product was used by many of the most prestigious institutions, such as The Mayo Clinic, Cleveland Clinic Foundation, Johns Hopkins, Indiana University Heath, and NASA. In December 2006, ProSolv was acquired by Fujifilm Medical Systems U.S.A., a wholly-owned subsidiary of Fujifilm. The acquisition was an integral component to Fujifilm's strategy to become a leader in the international health care market.

Feigenbaum has had a lifelong obsession with the field of artificial intelligence. After selling ProSolv he was able to focus on ideas and pursuits in this area. The Information Unit Model was the product of this time. KeLabs was formed to create the technology necessary to implement the Unit Model.

Foreword

In the 21st century, all scientists and engineers will write their own algorithms. The time, when computer programmers were hired to write programs for someone else, has gone. This means that there now is a dearth of tools designed to teach scientists and engineers how to write their own computer programs. All existing tools have been written for programmers. We need tools for scientists, medical doctors, and students; tools that will make it possible for individuals without explicit training as computer scientists to translate their creative ideas into software. Simply put, we all will be writing analytical software just as we all have been using calculators, word processors and email for nigh onto 30 years. The main reason for doing this is that we all solve problems at work, in school and at home. Problems solving is arguably the most fundamental human cognitive ability. We all also now know that computers have come to play a unique role as an "extension of our human intellect." Those of us, who are already writing computer programs, know this very well.

The technology being developed by Feigenbaum will really be a game changer. For decades, we have been hearing about how robots and artificial intelligence will take over and do everything for us, but this possibility still resides in a very remote future. Until this comes to pass, we humans must make better and better use of our innate cognitive abilities by integrating them with powerful computers. This can only be done by developing software specifically designed to handle each individual task and problem. The tools that Feigenbaum is developing will fill-in this currently critical gap. Having such tools will be indispensable during the next several dozen years.

We have been told for years that the field called "artificial intelligence" would deliver products like this, but this specialty went astray when it focused on other issues such as 'expert systems'. One can say that Feigenbaum singlehandedly brings the AI focus back to where it belongs. Computer tools are getting better and better as evidenced by Google search. But Google search provides only one-step help. We need a tool that will allow each user to implement a multiple-step solution in the form of a program. Feigenbaum is proposing just this. This tool will occupy a central role in his technology. Feigenbaum has already accomplished a lot in software development. His wide experience and his successes to date encourage me to believe that this project will provide an important breakthrough in this critical area.

Dr. Zygmunt Pizlo
Purdue University, 2015

Preface

The Information Unit Model is a technology for creating intelligent information systems software. It is a comprehensive set of applications that address a wide spectrum of the needs of software development in general.

The Unit Modeler technology holds the promise of transforming the way information-based applications are built. It introduces a new language that is simple, general and consistently applied to any area of human endeavor. It is a language that is optimized for building intelligent information-based applications and incorporates the ability to control critical software technologies necessary for the practical implementation of these systems.

Anyone can learn the language of the Information Unit Model and how to apply it with the Unit Modeler Development Environment. You do not need a programming background to learn the necessary skills and concepts. The doors to advanced software development are open to entirely new groups of people.

The Unit Modeler is a point-and-click environment requiring no syntax. Built-in intelligence guides and assists you in the tasks of development. Libraries of reusable content are accessible and ready to be incorporated into your application; much of your application is assembled from preconstructed resources rather than being built from scratch.

The ability to share your work with others, incorporate it into the body of publically available content, or sell it, is unique and unmatched. Workspaces allow you to work together with others and to codevelop and distribute your creations. Workspaces serve as a personal place of development where you can track your work and access it, as well as a host of other utilities, from anywhere.

The bottom line for developers is that, compared to existing technologies, the Unit Modeler is easier to learn, has shorter development timeframes, allows you to create more capable applications, and can lead to the realization of possibilities that would otherwise just not be practical. For businesses and organizations this means lower development expenses, less risk, increased productivity, efficiency, and innovation. For educational institutions this means having your students see more, do more, and learn more.

The Unit Model is not intended to ever replace programming. Programming languages of today are incredibly powerful for a multitude of purposes, all of which are far outside the scope of the Unit Model. You would not use the Modeler, for example, to create a driver, an operating system, or a high-end graphics application, such as a game. Generally, if speed and size are the ultimate requirement, the Unit Model should not be your first choice.

The Unit Model's focus is on building Intelligent Information based software applications that incorporate advanced software technologies. If your application needs to access, process, transform, visualize, analyze, archive, or display information, then the Unit Modeler can open up new doors of possibilities. When your application is reliant upon cognition based processes, the Unit Model is an ideally suited solution.

By reading this book you will learn the concepts of the Information Unit Model and how to apply it (Parts 2 and 3). You will be introduced to the Unit Modeler Development Environment, the package where models are built (Part 4). You will be presented with several examples that demonstrate a variety of techniques of the Unit Model and show the kinds of applications you can build (Introduction and Part 5). You will find out how the applications you build can be distributed, sold, and/or shared via Workspaces (Part 6).

The book is meant to help guide and train you to becoming a modeler. Along this pursuit and as a purchaser of this book you will receive a 3-month free trial subscription to the Unit Modeler software. You will also have exclusive access to run, explore and modify the examples described in this book within a workspace called 'Elsevier Book Examples'. You will be able to create and practice building new applications on your own. You will be able to create workspaces where you can distribute and sell your applications. After reading the book and working through a few examples, you should know how to start independently creating models on your own.

For a free, three-month trial subscription to the Unit Modeler® software, visit the following website: "*http://www.KeLabs.com/Elsevier*"

Acknowledgments

Very few projects of any substance are ever completed by one person alone. The Unit Modeler technology is no exception. I have had the extreme luck and privilege to work with a group of smart and talented people each and every day. Without their dedication, perseverance, and thoughtful contributions, the Unit Modeler technology would not nearly be the tool it is today. I would like to especially recognize Joe, Kurtis, Peter, and Justin. You guys dug deep to see a vision through. It is often pointed out that the journey can be as good as the destination. I have truly enjoyed brainstorming with you on how to best overcome the challenges that we faced along the way and, of course, all of the blue sky sessions. It is one thing to enjoy what you work on, quite another to enjoy who you work with. I have enjoyed both.

I have also had the privilege, not once, but twice to have worked professionally with my father. Not only has his domain expertise provided invaluable guidance to products such as the Echo Test and Teach software described in this book, but his passion and determined spirit have been inspirational to all those with whom he has interacted.

Introduction

The Unit Modeler technology is a new and unique environment in which to develop, codevelop, distribute, and run applications. It focuses on applications that fall within an area referred to as information-based applications, which is also called information systems, intelligent computing, knowledge-based programming, big data, and other names.

Unit Modeler technology strives to make computers more practical and powerful for solving the problems of people across many fields. It is a technology whose focus is on building pathways for all that lead to creation of intelligent software applications, by making the process of developing them more intelligent.

Unit Modeler technology has many components:

- The Unit Modeler Development Environment, which introduces a new development language and a new approach to the discipline of software development.
- Workspaces, which are cloud-based utilities for codeveloping, distributing, and maintaining applications.
- Public Libraries of reusable resources for automatic inclusion into your application, shortening development times and expanding possibilities.
- Server for creating robust network architectures and secure, private enterprise solutions.

First and foremost, however, is the Information Unit Model, which is a new modeling language with which to describe information and knowledge. It is simple to learn, natural and intuitive to use. Complex organizations of knowledge, knowhow and information are described efficiently and capably in terms of the Unit Model. The Information Unit Model is general and can describe any area of human knowledge and experience. It can describe a mathematical formula, a principle of physics, an algorithm, a visualization, an animation, and even a computer application. Models can be used to create advanced, intelligent computer applications that would otherwise be out of reach. The examples presented in this book have been selected to demonstrate these types of models.

The following eight requirements always have and always will guide Unit Modeler technology:

1. The process of creating applications must be natural, intuitive, and accessible to both programmers and nonprogrammers.
2. A developer need only concentrate on the developer's domain, what the developer knows, not on the computer and the intricacies of the programming

languages that control it. Information-based systems developers should not have to be intimately familiar with computer technology.

3. Work should be reusable. Nothing should ever have to be done twice. Whether this comes for free or for a fee, it must be a technically possible.

4. Reusable work must be easily found and easily incorporated into other applications. For users, reusable work must be dynamically loaded, and for developers reusable work must not require header files, resource files, or other complexities.

5. An environment must be established that supports the needs of groups of users—from single-person groups to multidepartment enterprises.

6. A development environment should incorporate intelligence that can continue to learn and do increasingly smarter things. Anything the computer can do for us, it should do. It should provide guidance and assistance. It should be smart enough to anticipate our intentions.

7. Any complex task or information structure can be made simple through encapsulation. Encapsulation hides complexities revealing only the relevant parts. Encapsulation is a requirement for reuse. A system that can encapsulate anything can always continue to get easier to use and able to build ever more powerful applications.

8. Understanding someone else's work should be easy and straightforward. It is seldom that software is developed by only one person.

INFORMATION-BASED APPLICATIONS

Information-based applications are a genre of software that almost everybody is familiar with, although they may not have heard this term applied to the genre. The reason is that there are few, if any, general-purpose development tools, other than the Unit Modeler, that are squarely focused on just this type of application. The Unit Modeler technology is unique in this focus.

Information-based applications are needed virtually everywhere and serve a variety of functional purposes:

- Data analytics
- Data visualization
- Decision support
- Dashboard displays
- Research and analysis
- Database frontends
- Quality assurance
- Quality management systems

There are two aspects to information-based applications. As the name implies, the first is the part that works with information. Information, as we all know, can be manipulated and processed in many ways. It can be transformed, filtered, sorted, and calculated, and can undergo a wide range of other operations. Information-based applications are ones that perform these functions. These are the cognitive duties of the application.

However, if information just remained in the memory of the computer, it would not be useful. The second aspect of information-based applications is that which makes the information useful by interacting with various computer hardware devices and peripherals. Any application performs several tasks that require the control of computer hardware, such as displaying the information to a monitor arranged in a way that is optimized for its audience. There are many other areas of software technology that also make useful, modern, intelligent computing solutions. All of these interactions with computer technology are areas that can require a great deal of expertise when being implemented in a programming environment.

An important goal of the Unit Modeler is to make control of these computer technologies available to a developer without having to get into all of the details and minutia of programming. The Unit Modeler has encapsulated these areas so that the intricate details are hidden. They can be added to your application through guided assists and prebuilt components. A modeler/developer should never have to lose focus from his/her domain. The system should have the internal intelligence to do everything else. As a user developer once noted:

> "This ISDE [Intelligent Software Development Environment] really puts the emphasis on the model/knowledge/problem you are working on. I was also really impressed with the default forms—again, taking the focus away from details (e.g., visualization) and putting the focus back on the model."

Before leaving the topic of information-based applications, it is helpful to define two related terms. *Information* and *knowledge* are often used together and as if they are synonymous. I would like to point out a distinction, however, that is useful when describing items in this book: Information represents static things. A list of numbers or a database of customers represents information. Knowledge, however, represents the things we know that work on information. An algorithm that calculates the average of the list is knowledge. A process that finds all customers who would be interested in a certain product would also be knowledge.

This distinction will be maintained throughout this book.

INTELLIGENCE

The phrase *intelligent software* is a common and often-used term. It is used throughout this text, as well as in the title. But what is meant by the word *intelligent*? It can conjure up many different definitions depending on to what it is applied. Therefore, it is important to establish a common understanding of what *intelligent* means and in what manner it will be pursued. It is, at a minimum necessary to establish a definition for its use within this text.

The Oxford Dictionaries describes intelligence as "the ability to acquire and apply knowledge and skills".

Intelligent software is software that has a good understanding of a multitude of areas and is able to apply this understanding to solving problems; to figure things out, calculate, predict, manage, and analyze. Intelligent software wants to be able to learn and apply the material of any subject and at any level of complexity. It should transfer to the computer the ability to increasingly do the tasks that we now do as humans.

Just as important, intelligent software should never be static; it must have the ability to continually expand its base of knowledge. It is interesting that when a computer does something that we think would make it intelligent, it does not seem so intelligent after it is actually able to do it. The luster of the skill just seems to dissipate. Perhaps because we know how it is done, but perhaps also because our own knowledge is always expanding so we have high expectations. The lesson is that intelligent software cannot remain static or bounded.

The term *intelligent* therefore describes a pursuit, not a destination and to make the continual progress this pursuit requires, we need a few things. First, we need the ability to describe the content of any field in a consistent, intuitive, and efficient manner. We are unable to do this right now. The closest we have come is, perhaps, the language of mathematics. But this language is not efficient for information outside its own sphere.

Second, we need the ability to convey the description of any given field of knowledge and information to the computer. The computer must understand these descriptions and must be able to save, present, and apply their knowledge and information. Traditionally, this would be accomplished by implementing our descriptions in a programming language such as C++, Basic, or any one of many others. But not everybody knows programming and it is riddled with inherent difficulties. This is a huge extra step that should not be necessary.

If we want intelligent software, then we need the people who are intelligent in any particular area to be closer to its design and creation. And after describing the content of a field, the computer must recognize and understand this description automatically. Creation of intelligent information-based software should have virtually nothing to do with computers. A creator should be able to concentrate on the creator's domain and nothing else.

If we are to achieve this goal, we must have a framework, a means of communication, a general model—that is, a language that is optimized and specifically designed for the purpose of defining knowledge and information; a language that is much more natural to use than existing programming languages; a language that encapsulates and simplifies all of the software technology capabilities that intelligent information-based applications require.

Third, we must be able to reuse the work of others. We must be able to more effectively build off of what has been built before—not just the sweat, but also the expertise. Any content that we put into the computer should coexist and work with any other. A way must exist to package areas of work into components that can be incorporated into other applications or components. These components must also be easily accessible both when applications are being designed and when they are being run.

Successful implementation of these requirements will yield a technology that is highly efficient at creating applications with an endless reach of intelligent function.

DIFFICULTIES OF CURRENT TECHNOLOGIES

We live in an information age in which the application of knowledge upon information is becoming increasingly demanding and demanded. The creation of information-computing applications is becoming increasingly important. Even though software applications have advanced and become faster, more powerful, and more intuitive, the technologies used to create them, that is, programming languages, have not. Certainly, the tools and the constructs of programming languages themselves have evolved, but programming is much the same as it has been for decades, and this technology has some significant drawbacks.

Programming languages are extremely powerful but at the expense of being very complex; consequently, they can be inefficient to use to develop certain types of applications. In fact, their complexity is so great it limits their ability to be used and mastered. A limited number of people can use them in the first place, and those who can are often limited in their ability to efficiently do so. The highly syntactical nature of the languages can make them frustrating and far less than enjoyable to work with. We have a shortage of skilled programmers in no small part because of these factors.

Another limiting factor to programming code is the difficulty of being shared in a "plug-and-play," "snap together" manner. The codes are too syntactically sensitive. Ideally, functional areas of code would be nicely organized, readily available, and easily accessible, and able to be incorporated seamlessly—even automatically and dynamically—into our applications. The concept of prefabricated components would be standard in the absence of this limitation. Very little would have to be redone that had been done before.

In addition, software should become more intelligent. It should be able to speak the language of any subject in a consistent, intuitive, and concise manner. It should be able to hold onto and reuse the expertise and efforts of those who have come before us and of our colleagues today. It should be more intelligent and know more about more subjects such as math and science, with the ability to apply this knowledge. The expanse of this knowledge should always be growing. It should be easy to share our work and contribute to collective learning efforts.

The promise that digital technologies offer to process, create, and work with information calls for a better way. The language of computers must be much more efficient and intuitive in describing reality and the applications we want to create. They must act more intelligently. There is a great deal of untapped potential for the application of software technology.

Consider, for example, the very simple application presented in Figure 1.1. It is a form that will add two numbers. The code required to create this application is presented in two languages in Figure 1.2: HTML and C++. The Unit Model implementation is also presented.

There are three different languages involved in the code in Figure 1.2: HTML for markup, Cascading Style Sheets (CSS) for style, and JavaScript for scripting purposes. The JQuery library is used in the JavaScript code to make use of existing encapsulations of common tasks in JavaScript, like accessing a particular input element.

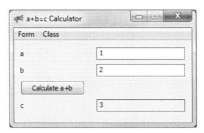

FIGURE 1.1 A Simple Calculator Application

```html
<html>
    <head>
        <!-- Load the jQuery library -->
        <script src="http://ajax.aspnetcdn.com/ajax/jQuery/jquery-1.8.2.min.js"></script>
        <script type="text/javascript">
                function calculateC()
                {
                    // Parse the two values as floats.
                    var a = parseFloat($("input[name=a]").val(), 10);
                    var b = parseFloat($("input[name=b]").val(), 10);

                    $("input[name=c]").val(a + b);
                }
        </script>
        <style type="text/css">
            label
            {
                float: left;
                width: 100pt;
            }
        </style>
    </head>

    <body>

        <h1>a+b=c</h1>
        <form>
            <label for="a">a</label>
            <input type="number" name="a" />

            <br />

            <label for="b">b</label>
            <input type="number" name="b" onchange="calculateC();" />

            <br />

            <button onclick="calculateC();">Calculate a+b</button>

            <br />

            <label for="c">c</label>
            <input type="number" name="c" readonly="readonly" />
        </form>
    </body>

</html>
```

FIGURE 1.2 HTML Code to Implement the Simple Calculator in Figure 1.1

```
//////////////////////////////////////////////////////////////////
//
// Dialog
//

IDD_SIMPLECALCULATOR_DIALOG DIALOGEX 0, 0, 201, 79
STYLE DS_SETFONT | DS_MODALFRAME | DS_FIXEDSYS | WS_POPUP | WS_VISIBLE | WS_CAPTION | WS_SYSMENU
EXSTYLE WS_EX_APPWINDOW
CAPTION "Simple Calculator"
FONT 8, "MS Shell Dlg", 0, 0, 0x1
BEGIN
    LTEXT        "a",IDC_STATIC,7,9,8,8
    LTEXT        "b",IDC_STATIC,7,28,8,8
    EDITTEXT     IDC_A,78,7,116,14,ES_AUTOHSCROLL
    EDITTEXT     IDC_B,78,26,116,14,ES_AUTOHSCROLL
    LTEXT        "c",IDC_STATIC,7,60,8,8
    EDITTEXT     IDC_C,78,58,115,14,ES_AUTOHSCROLL | ES
    PUSHBUTTON   "Calculate a+b",IDC_BUTTONCALC,7,41,56
END
```

```
class CSimpleCalculatorDlg : public CDialog
{
private:
    double a, b, c;

public:
    CSimpleCalculatorDlg(CWnd* pParent = NULL);

    // Dialog Data
    enum { IDD = IDD_SIMPLECALCULATOR_DIALOG };

protected:
    virtual void DoDataExchange(CDataExchange* pDX);

    // Implementation
protected:
    // Generated message map functions
    DECLARE_MESSAGE_MAP()
    afx_msg void OnBnClickedCalculateButton();
```

```
void CSimpleCalculatorDlg::DoDataExchange(CDataExch
{
    CDialog::DoDataExchange(pDX);
    DDX_Text(pDX, IDC_A, a);
    DDX_Text(pDX, IDC_B, b);
    DDX_Text(pDX, IDC_C, c);
}

BEGIN_MESSAGE_MAP(CSimpleCalculatorDlg, CDialog)
    ON_BN_CLICKED(IDC_BUTTONCALC, &CSimpleCalculatorDlg::OnBnClickedCalculateButton)
END_MESSAGE_MAP()

void CSimpleCalculatorDlg::OnBnClickedCalculateButton()
{
    // Update the variables from the controls on the dialog.
    UpdateData(true);

    // Calculate the value
    c = a + b;

    // Update the controls from the variable values. This
    // is to make sure the value of c gets updated.
    UpdateData(false);
}
```

FIGURE 1.3 The Simple Calculator Using C++ and the MFC Framework

Snippets of the primary resource, header, and source files are included. Note that the entire solution for this project includes a few more files for starting the application.

The C++ example illustrates just how much text is involved in writing programs in text-based languages. Three snippets of files are shown in Figure 1.3—this is not even the complete source code for such a simple example. Modern Integrated Development Environment (IDEs) will assist with putting much of this together, but the code on its own is not always easy to understand. Even this code has the benefit of having been commented by the developer.

From here, an even more difficult exercise is trying to make modifications to the solution. Suppose we want to move the calculate button or display the result as a rounded number. Multiple files will likely have to be edited, and there are many opportunities for syntactic mistakes to be made.

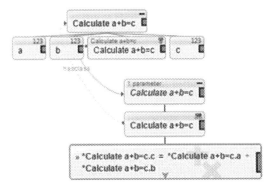

FIGURE 1.4 A Model Equivalent to the Code Examples Shown in Figures 1.2 and 1.3

The model shown in Figure 1.4 achieves the same end product as the code in Figures 1.2 and 1.3. Differences between models and standard programming languages are readily apparent.

A BRIEF TOUR OF UNIT MODELER TECHNOLOGY

Unit Modeler technology is a comprehensive suite of components and capabilities. Perhaps the easiest way to introduce these parts is through a brief tour of the technology. In this tour, you will see the architecture of the technology and examples of tools and reusable components that are in the standard libraries of the Unit Modeler and commercial applications built with the Modeler.

THE UNIT MODELER DESKTOP

Your experience with the Unit Modeler technology begins with your personal desktop (Fig. 1.5). You can customize your desktop with the resources that you use most often. Here you will find a list of applications and workspaces, plus common packages and workspace tools.

In the desktop in Figure 1.5, the icons labeled Development, Data Analytics, Math, and Data Set Generators are all packages. A package is a suite of applications that address a particular area of computing.

The Development Package is actually the focus of this book. Everything described in this book was built with the Development Package.

STANDARD LIBRARY COMPONENTS

The standard libraries include many resources for you to use as applications or components that you can include in your application. They also serve as examples of

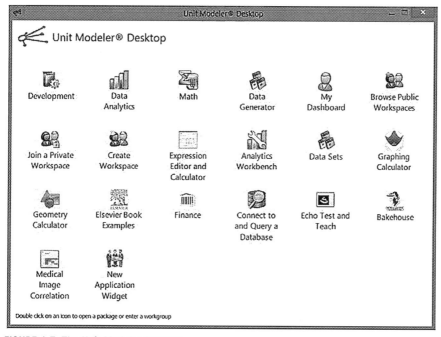

FIGURE 1.5 The Unit Modeler Desktop

what you can build with the Unit Modeler and how you construct applications in the Unit Modeler.

Data analytics package

Data Analytics is a package containing many tools that are all integral to performing analytics on data sets. This includes importing data, cleaning and preparing data, and tools and applications for doing statistics and data mining. There is a large list of examples that demonstrate the use of the tools. Figure 1.6 is an example showing the use of the Simple Linear Regression tool.

Any application that requires a linear regression calculation can reuse the underlying model of this tool.

Figure 1.7 shows the Categorical Summary Bar Graph tool. It provides totals for different categories of data. The data can be imported from a spreadsheet file or selected from another form.

We will reuse this tool in the Checking Account example presented in Part 2 Modeling Fundamentals (A Simple Example).

Analytics workbench

The Analytics Workbench (Fig. 1.8) is a tool for doing all manner of statistics on imported data files. All of the individual tools within the statistics, data mining,

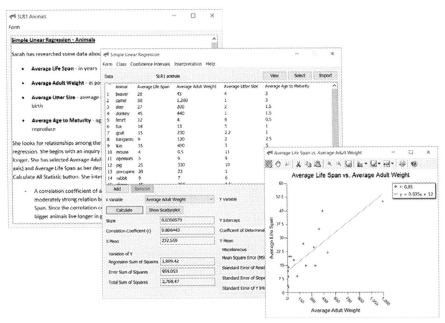

FIGURE 1.6 An Example from the Data Analytics Package

This example illustrates the use of the Simple Linear Regression tool.

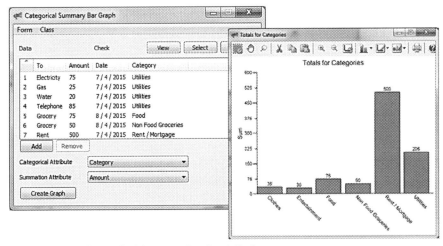

FIGURE 1.7 The Categorical Summary Bar Graph Tool

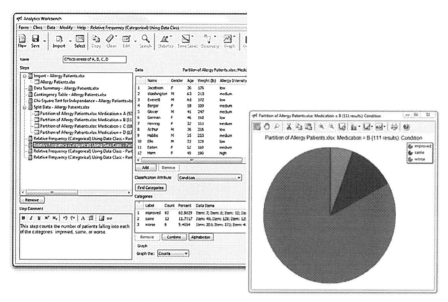

FIGURE 1.8 The Analytics Workbench Tool

and data processing domains can be applied. You can save your analyses for later recall. The Analytics Workbench is more than just a mini application; it, too, can be incorporated into other applications, as will be seen in the commercial application Echo Report Simulator within this tour (see "Commercial Applications" below).

You have a few options as to where you save your work. You can save it to your computer or to a workspace. If you save the work to your computer, you may also add it to the File Organizer (Fig. 1.9). The File Organizer is a built-in feature of the Unit Modeler Client software. Workspaces are a cloud-based environment, one feature of which is as a repository for files.

Expression editor

Expression Editor (Figs. 1.10 and 1.11) is a multipurpose tool that is also part of the Math package that allows you to create and evaluate expressions. It is much like the Windows calculator but can also include many other math operations such as vectors, matrices, logic, set theory, and more. It acts as a calculator, but its primary purpose is to create units that represent the expression.

Data sets

The Data Sets workspace contains a list of data sets that were created by tools within the Data Generators workspace. Anyone can use these data sets for research and education. Data Sets is a publically available workspace. These sets of data are also

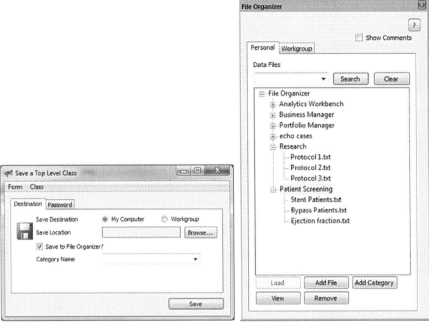

FIGURE 1.9 **The Save Dialog and the File Organizer**

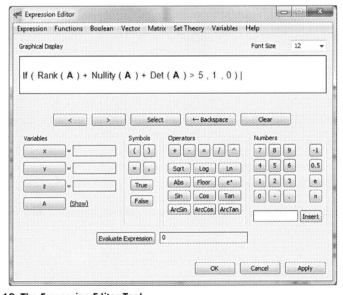

FIGURE 1.10 **The Expression Editor Tool**

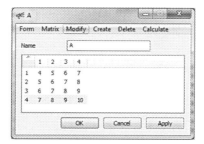

FIGURE 1.11 The Matrix as Used in the Expression Example of Figure 1.10

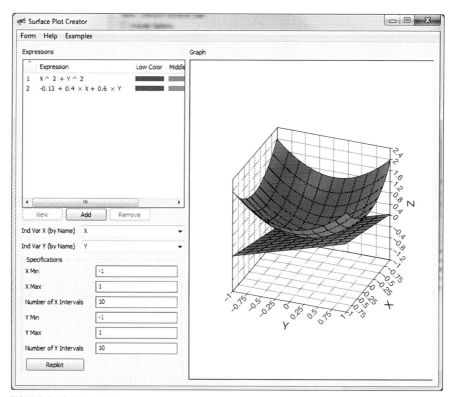

FIGURE 1.12 The Surface Plot Creator Tool

In addition, the Surface Plot Creator tool allows you visualize expressions of two variables. The 3D image can be rotated to view the graph from any angle.

useful when you are developing a new application and need to test it on data with certain characteristics.

Surface plot creator

This tool (Fig. 1.12) allows you to enter a mathematical expression and to then graph it. There are two versions: one for expressions of a single variable and one

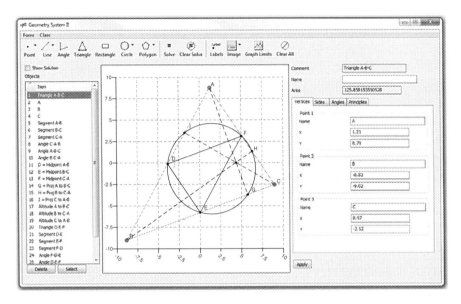

FIGURE 1.13 The Geometry Calculator Tool

An example showing an interesting fact: For any triangle ABC, the midpoints of the sides (D, E, and F) and the altitude feet (G, H, and I) all lie on a circle.

for expressions of two variables. It is interesting to note that this tool reuses the Expression Editor mentioned above as a means to enter the expressions. This is an example of reuse.

Geometry calculator

This tool (Fig. 1.13) allows a user to create a system of geometric elements such as points, lines, circles, rectangles, and triangles. It will calculate all of the quantities relevant to these shapes, such as lengths, angles, and areas. You can even import a picture, and calibrate and identify shapes on top of the imported picture. The Geometry Calculator tool highlights many aspects of the Unit Modeler, such as interactive graphics and autonomous calculation of variables. This tool is located within the Math package.

The Geometry Calculator tool allows you to specify any set of known values for the items in the system. It will solve for the unknown values (=). The domain called *Systems* is a general domain that can help setup models that solve for unknown values by applying the principles of a domain, math, and a general algorithm for the solving of unknown values.

Database query and connect

This is a set of tools that allows a user to connect to and query a database (Fig. 1.14). The Database tool (Fig. 1.15) allows creation of complex queries via a point-and-click

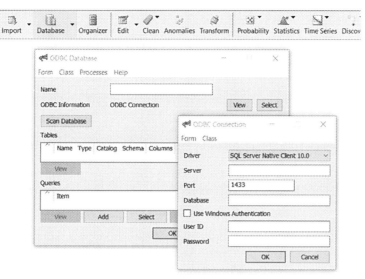

FIGURE 1.14 Forms That Allow You to Specify a Database to Connect to

Enter the information that identifies the database and authorizes you to connect to it.

FIGURE 1.15 The Database Tool '

This tool automatically scans and recognizes tables and their relationships. It is aware of each table's columns and their types.

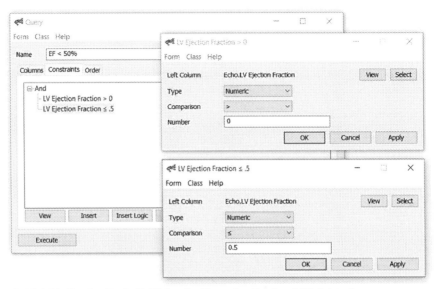

FIGURE 1.16 You Can Easily Build Queries Through a Point-and-Click Interface

interface (Fig. 1.16). It does not require any knowledge of SQL (Structured Query Language) (Fig. 1.17). You can run the queries you build immediately (Fig. 1.18) or you can save them and include them in an application you are building.

The Database tools are located in the Data Analytics package toolbar.

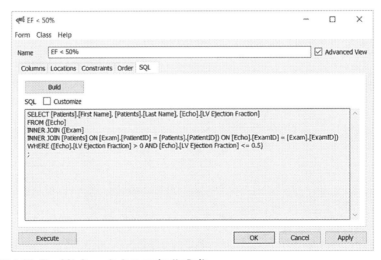

FIGURE 1.17 The SQL Query Is Automatically Built

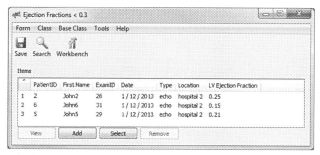

FIGURE 1.18 Clicking Execute Automatically Returns Results

Notice that the Analytics Workbench application described earlier is embedded in the results form.

COMMERCIAL APPLICATIONS

ASE echo test and teach

The American Society of Echocardiography (ASE) is the largest international organization for cardiac imaging and a leading advocate for setting practice standards and guidelines in this area. The ASE is committed to improving the practice of ultrasound imaging of the heart and cardiovascular system for better patient outcomes.

The Echo Test and Teach application (Fig. 1.19) is a unique training tool for sonographers and physicians who quantitate and interpret echocardiograms. This tool was originally developed in collaboration with Dr. Harvey Feigenbaum of Indiana University, considered by most as the father of echocardiography. ASE is developing content for the application in order to help meet its mission statement goals of promoting excellence in cardiovascular ultrasound and its application to patient care through education and innovation.

The Echo Test and Teach application simulates everyday activity performed by healthcare professionals reviewing cardiac ultrasound examinations. It is used for training and quality assurance purposes. There is a user mode, which is the actual simulator, a design mode, where simulated cases are created, and an analytics mode where results can be aggregated and analytics performed (Fig. 1.20).

The Echo Test and Teach application presents a list of Simulation Cases from which a user can choose one to load. A case consists of a set of images that are deidentified and a set of measurements and interpretations that the user must make. The user may also be asked standardized questions such as true/false and multiple choice. When the user has done what is asked, the user submits the user's responses and goes on to the next slide.

From a technical perspective this tool utilizes quite a few of the benefits of the Unit Modeler technology including, video display, interactive graphics, analytics, reporting, network communication and client–server architecture.

Summary results can be viewed that aggregate all of the individual results (Fig. 1.21). They can be viewed in a spreadsheet with summary statistics, such as mean, standard deviation, and variability. Or they can be viewed graphically.

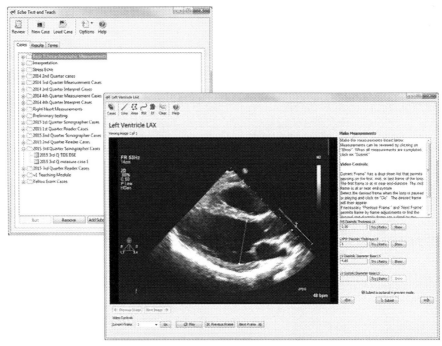

FIGURE 1.19 The Echo Test and Teach Application

Users practice measuring certain features of medical images. Their results are compared to those of the expert who created the practice case.

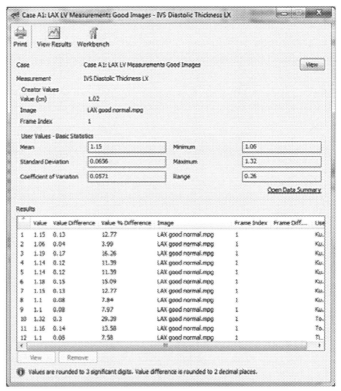

FIGURE 1.20 A User's Results Are Stored for Later Analysis

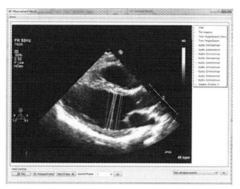

FIGURE 1.21 Administrators Can Compare the Measurements of All Users

All of the statistics are calculated using tools from the statistics library. Notice that the summary report includes a toolbar button link to the Analytics Workbench, which we looked at earlier. The application also tests a user's interpretation of the images. Users select interpretations from a tree of standard phrases. The tools pictured in Figure 1.22 are used to collectively analyze the users' selections.

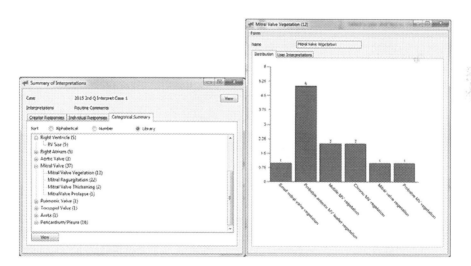

FIGURE 1.22 The Echo Test and Teach Application

This application can also test users on interpretations and then analyze these responses.

Medical image correlation

Fujifilm Medical Systems U.S.A., Inc., is a leader in the field of medical imaging and informatics. It needed an application that would assist various laboratories in

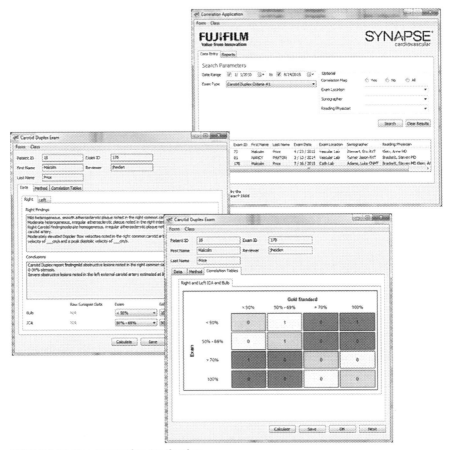

FIGURE 1.23 The Correlation Application

This application is used to aid the evaluation of quality assurance activities in medical institutions.

correlating data to determine whether certain quality control standards have been met? Certain information within medicine can be ascertained by multiple types of exams. Some exams are more accurate than others, and some have greater risks and are more expensive. Nevertheless, the results of these different exams can be correlated to see how they compare for quality control purposes. The Correlation Application (Fig. 1.23) helps laboratories perform this task and analyze the results.

The Correlation Application contains more than 20 different reporting areas. A challenge, once again, was that while all of these report categories are commonly used across the industry, their contents may be slightly different for each institution. The underlying database tables and fields are slightly different and even the way an institution creates reports can be different. Therefore, the Correlation Application could not "hardcode" the reports, but rather had to be able to configure and modify each one based on each site's details.

FIGURE 1.24 The Configuration Tool for the Correlation Application

Any part of any report can be configured to address the specific implementation details of the 1000s of potential customer sites. In this image, you see the ability to define the specific elements of each report, as well as the database tables and fields where a particular measurement value is stored.

This requirement places an additional burden on the software, because now the design could not just address the needs of 20 specific reports but had to consider the wide range of variability amongst 20 reports implemented at 1000s of institutions. This required encapsulating the commonalities among all of these sites and exposing the differences within configurable screens (Fig. 1.24).

Encapsulation is a cornerstone capability of Unit Modeler technology and why the technology has been effective in addressing the requirements of this application. Encapsulation is addressed in detail within this book.

Bakehouse purchasing application

The Bakehouse is a small bakery in Bloomington, Indiana. It produces more than 100 products with hundreds of different ingredients. Tracking orders and costs is extremely important to its bottom line. The bakery had attempted to accomplish this using spreadsheets, but with only limited success and convenience. The number of spreadsheets was piling up in a directory and there was little analysis that the bakery was able to do. Certain spreadsheets had so many columns that they were unwieldly.

The Bakehouse's situation is not unique. These are common problems when using spreadsheets to track information. The owner knew there was a better way, but assembling or contracting a programming team was just out of the question because of the cost and effort involved in such an approach.

The Purchasing application pictured in Figure 1.25 streamlined the process for The Bakehouse and provided a number of features that could not be implemented

FIGURE 1.25 The Purchasing Application

The Purchasing application can be used to track vendor orders and pricing. The application shows some of the features that can be included in Unit Modeler forms.

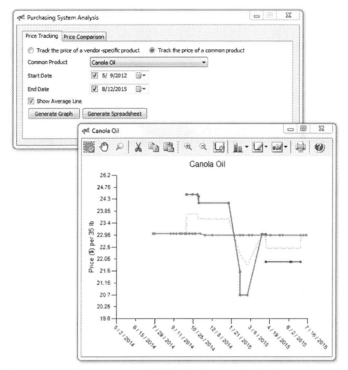

FIGURE 1.26 Analysis of the Data Stored Within the Purchasing Application

using the spreadsheet method. The Bakehouse has now improved its operations and is able to get a better handle on its costs and the efforts to reduce them.

The Purchasing application demonstrates how the Unit Modeler can overcome some of the limitations of spreadsheets. It can easily track multiple spreadsheets' worth of data and combine the data to work in an integrated fashion. Analytics can be readily applied because of this (Fig. 1.26). User interfaces/forms can be created that provide efficient methods for a user to enter and interact with the data.

An analysis package was built specifically for the application to conveniently provide access to The Bakehouse's most often used and desirable analyses. All of the analysis and graphing tools were created by reusing components within the standard library.

WORKSPACES

Workspaces (formerly Workgroups) are a very important and powerful component of the Unit Modeler Environment. Workspaces serve three purposes: they act as a (a) device for distributing the applications that you develop; (b) forum where multiple people can work together on a project; and (c) cloud-based storage location so that you can access files from anywhere.

Within the limits of your subscription level, you can create your own workspaces and join those of others. The three icons below are tools for browsing, joining, and creating workspaces. Workspaces that you join will appear as icons on your desktop.

Browse Public   Create   Join a Private
Workspaces   Workspace   Workgroup

Note: Workspaces were formerly called Workgroups and the term *Workgroup* may appear in several screenshots, as in the icons above.

Elsevier book examples workspace

An example of a workspace is the Elsevier Book Examples workspace (Fig. 1.27) where you will find working copies of all of the examples provided in this book. You can see and play with the models. This workspace is private to readers of this book.

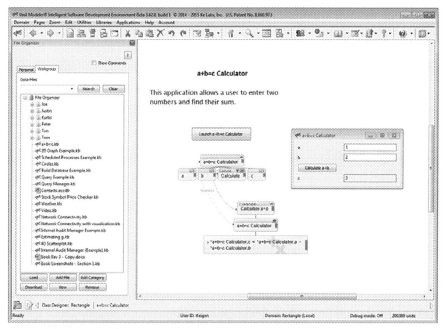

FIGURE 1.27 The Elsevier Book Examples Workspace

The workspace File Organizer is docked on the left side of the screen. To load an example, just double click on it. Its home page will appear in the whiteboard area.

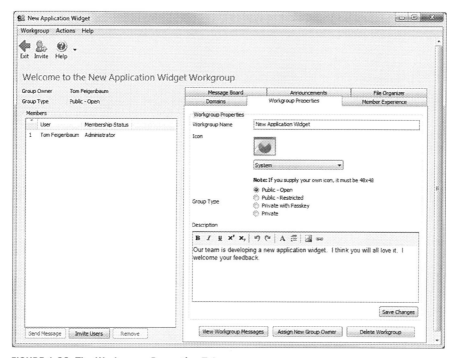

FIGURE 1.28 The Workspace Properties Tab

You can join this workspace by double clicking the Join a Private Workspace icon. The name you to enter is *Elsevier*. The password is described in the Appendix.

Creating a workspace is easy. Double click on the Create Workspace icon. Then fill out some descriptions and elect the type of workspace this will be (Fig. 1.28).

The workspace console allows you to configure certain properties of the Workspaces and what the experience will be for those who join your workspace. The experience is defined by what they see after they join and what permissions they have to see and modify various features of the workspace.

If you chose the Public–Open for the Group Type, your workspace will appear in the list of Public Workspaces. If you also configure the user experience so that users see an application startup, then the icon acts just like an application icon. Distributing your work can't get much easier. Not all public workspaces are free; you can also define a workspace as a subscription workspace.

You can change the properties of your workspace at any time, so it is wise to initially make your workspace private until you are finished developing your application. Then you can make it public.

Workspaces have an owner, administrators, and members. The administrators can control all aspects of the workspace, including the members' privileges and experience. The owner has ultimate authority over the space.

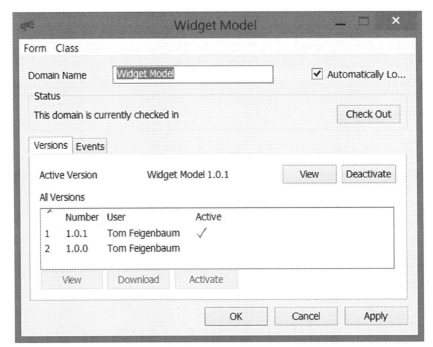

FIGURE 1.29 Workspaces Have a Built-in Feature Called Domain Manager

This tool tracks all domain submissions. You can compare one version to another in a tool called the Merge tool.

A workspace contains a file organizer, which is a repository for files of all types, including spreadsheets, documents, pictures, and movies. They are cloud based so they can be available at home, school, or work, and can be shared among all members of the space.

Workspaces include a domain manager, which is the equivalent of a source code management tool. Domain Manager (Fig. 1.29) tracks the history of submissions so you can track all of the changes to your files. It also includes a compare feature so you can exactly identify what has changed from one submission to the next.

THE DEVELOPMENT PACKAGE

The Development Package icon loads the Unit Modeler ISDE. As you can see from the screenshot in Figure 1.30, the Unit Model is a highly visual environment. There is no syntax and almost everything is accomplished via guided point-and-click operations. On the left part of the screen is a feature called the Development Resource Center (DRC). The DRC provides hundreds of assists that can help you with almost

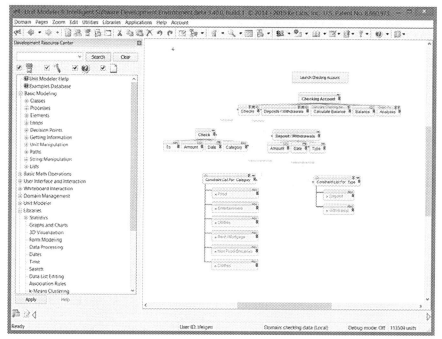

FIGURE 1.30

The Unit Modeler Development Package with the Development Resource Center docked on the left side.

anything you need to do. The assists in the DRC bring a world of computer technology to your fingertips and you do not need to know anything about programming. They make available for reuse a vast amount of work that has already been completed.

Modeling fundamentals

2

Modeling is the process of creating models. When you develop something with the Unit Modeler Platform, you ultimately are creating models. Models embody information, knowledge, knowhow, and applications themselves. They are the output of your work.

To create models with the Unit Modeler, you will need to understand the following topics:

- The Information Unit Model language
  - * The Information Unit
  - * Structures (classes and processes)
- The General Modeling Process, that is, the approach to applying the Information Unit Model

The language of building models is the Information Unit Model. The Unit Model (for short) is a simple, natural, and intuitive language. The basic concepts are very few and can be described and explained in just a few pages. Although simple, the basic building blocks of all models are extremely versatile and general and can be used to describe any area of information and knowledge.

The Unit Model looks at everything as if it is composed of many pieces of information that are related to each other via some relationship. These pieces or units of information are called *Information Units* and their relationships with each other are called *Paths*. Units and paths are the fundamental building blocks of every model. Every model is composed of networks of these two items.

Networks of units form two common types of configurations or structures; classes and processes. Classes are used to represent things that can be characterized by some set of attributes (such as size or color). Processes are a series of steps, each of which performs some function. All models are composed of classes and processes. Classes and processes are, in turn, all constructed of units and paths.

The General Modeling Process (GMP) describes how to apply the Information Unit Model language. How do we approach creating an application? What high level, beginning steps must we take? What is the basic approach to building models? This is the topic of the section on the General Modeling Process. Here you will see how to apply the Unit Model language to building actual applications. Ultimately, the General Modeling Process is about how to map the facts of a situation to sets of classes and processes.

Next we explore reuse of existing models so that we can build ever-more-capable applications. Reuse of models is discussed in general, followed by the specific ways in which reuse takes place in a model, how it is implemented.

Lastly, we explore the domain library where the reusable domains are accessible. These domains determine what it is that we can reuse. Later in Part 5, Additional Examples and Tutorials section, we will look at several models that are built upon the components of this library.

WHAT IS A MODEL

Models are a collection of Information Units that address some specific area of information and knowledge. Models can serve many different purposes. They may act as an application themselves, they may serve as a repository of data, or they may be designed as resources to be reused by other models.

Every system or application can be described by a model and every model is constructed of the same simple set of basic elements and structures. All utilities that operate on these basic structures can be applied to every model. This makes models fundamentally simple and powerful in a way that is difficult to achieve.

An application model will generally have a process that is run when the domain it is saved in is loaded. This process may do any of several things which make the application accessible to the user. It might, for example, show a form or modify the menu and toolbar.

A utility or support model is one that provides components that can be reused in other models. These components will generally be added to the domain's Domain Class, described in Part 4 Section Special Units, Domain Class, so these reusable components can easily be found. When this is done, the utilities will also be available in the Development Resource Center (DRC). Support models might also provide pages that offer some assistance.

Models are saved in domain files. A domain file may contain multiple models or just one. Domains reside on servers and local computer drives. Models or, more specifically, the domain files they are saved in, are loaded and run by the client software. The client software is described later in Part 7, The Client Software.

An important property of models is that they can be constructed using other models. For example, one model may reuse some part of another model, which in turn may reference another model. When a model is referenced by another model, the content in the new model will automatically be loaded when needed. A developer does not have to worry about any includes or other merging. This is called *dynamic loading* and is an important feature of the Unit Modeler technology.

THE INFORMATION UNIT MODEL

The Information Unit Model is unique in the language it employs, and is also unique in its general approach to the design of software and to solving information-based problems. A formal definition of the Unit Model will be presented, but we will first walk through an example of applying the Unit Model to a particular project.

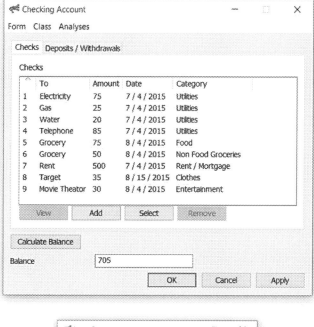

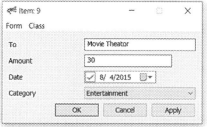

FIGURE 2.1 The Checking Account Application

A SIMPLE EXAMPLE: CHECKING ACCOUNT

To demonstrate the use of the Information Unit Model, we will begin with something simple and familiar. Let's say we want to build an application that tracks our checking account activities (Fig. 2.1). We want it to track the checks we write, our deposits, and our withdrawals. We want the application to calculate how much money is in our account. We also want to do some analysis on what we are spending our money on, for example, food, clothes, rent/mortgage, and so on.

Step 1 in applying the Unit Model is to define the domain and the goals of the project. In this case, both are described fairly well above.

- **Goals:** The goals are that we want to track three types of transactions—checks, deposits, and withdrawals—and calculate the balance of the account. We also want to apply analytics to the data we collect to help us understand our spending. Among other things, we will want to track the categories that the things we are purchasing fall within, such as food and clothing.

- **Domain:** The domain is that of a checking account and our interactions with it. We will not be considering any other type of account, such as a savings account. For now, we are only concerned with the checking account. There are no interfaces in this application to external sources (like the bank), in this simple example. The technology that could be used to connect our bank, Web Services, will be discussed in Parts 3 and 5. Information will be manually entered, which requires a user interface.

Step 2 is to break down the domain and identify its different parts. Then we need to identify the things that describe/define these parts. In this case, we have a checking account that has checks, withdrawals, and deposits. The checks have an amount and a date. We can more conveniently convey this information in the following table.

Parts

1. Checking Account
   a. Balance
   b. Checks
   c. Deposits
   d. Withdrawals
2. Check
   a. Amount
   b. Date
   c. To
   d. For
3. Deposit
   a. Amount
   b. Date
4. Withdrawal
   a. Amount
   b. Date

Actions

1. Add a new check, withdrawal, and/or deposit
2. Calculate the balance
3. Do analytics

We have now begun to structure our model. As we will learn in the next section, Parts 1 to 4 above are referred to as classes and their lettered subitems are referred to as attributes of the classes. The actions 1 to 3 are referred to as processes.

Classes and processes are the language of the Information Unit Model. Much of what the Unit Modeler describes is in terms of classes and processes. There are two tools that are specifically designed to facilitate the construction of classes and processes call Class Designer and Process Designer.

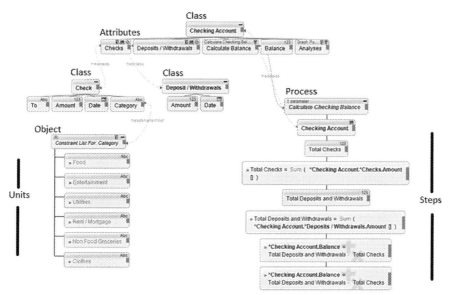

FIGURE 2.2 The Model of the Checking Account Application

Once having created the classes and processes (which should take less than 10 minutes), the model will emerge as shown in Figure 2.2, which correlates directly with the table above.

If we right click on the Checking Account class above and select Show Object Form, then the form we saw earlier in Figure 2.1 will appear, enabling us to enter checks, deposits, and withdrawals, and calculate our balance.

A few notes and observations about the model:

- Checks is a list of class Check.
- Deposits/Withdrawals is a list of class Deposit/Withdrawal.
- By convention, deposits are positive and withdrawals negative.
- The Check's Category attribute can have a value of any of the items listed.
- The "Calculate Balance" attribute is a process attribute. The process that this attribute represents will do the balance calculation.
- The analyses attribute is a list of processes.
- In the process, you will notice the use of stars (*). Wherever one is used, you can read it as "the contents of."
- The lines indicate various relationships between the various pieces of information, such as, hasclass and hasconstraint list, iselementof. These lines are referred to as paths.
- The rectangles of information are referred to as Information Units.

Another goal was to perform some analyses upon our data. A common type of analysis would be to categorize our expenses so that we could know what we are spending our money on. The Categorical Summary tool (Figs 2.3 and 2.4) for this purpose is available in the Statistics Library.

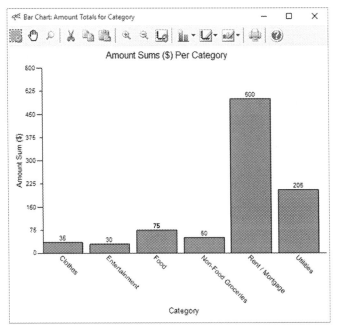

FIGURE 2.3

The Categorical Summary Bar Graph Tool shown in Figure 1.7 was incorporated into the Checking Account application.

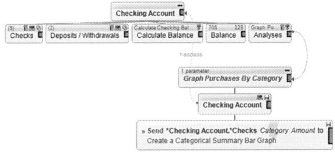

FIGURE 2.4

The Categorical Summary Tool is a part of the Statistics Library and adding it is a simple process.

With this simple example, we have demonstrated some important aspects of the Information Unit Model:

1. The essence of creating an application is in identifying the classes and the processes that exist in the application's domain. Every problem/project can be approached in this same manner.

2. Once having built the structures, creating the user interface is automatic. We did nothing to create the windows that we used.
3. A developer can now concentrate on their domain, not the computer.
4. Libraries of resources are available for reuse, for analytics and other things.
5. The Unit Modeler can save immense amounts of time in creating applications. Programming from scratch would have taken a great deal of time. The model presented above can be created in minutes.

We can now present the Information Unit Model in a more formal sense.

THE INFORMATION UNIT

In Figure 2.4, above, there are grayish rectangles with rounded corners. These are called *Information Units*. All of the models, their structures—both classes and processes—are composed of these Information Units. Although we have seen them in use, we have not defined them specifically.

An Information Unit, as its name suggests, is a representation of an individual piece of information. The classes, the attributes, the process, steps in the process, and the list of check categories were all made up of Information Units and they were all connected by lines.

All Information Units have the following properties (Fig. 2.5):

1. A comment to help identify what the unit represents. In general, Comments have no impact upon the model other than to help us understand it. The exception are those few occasions when displaying form controls.
2. Elements, which represent a list of other units or text characters.
3. An operator, which carries out a function upon the elements of the unit.
4. Units have relationships with other units. Equivalently, units have paths to other units.

Elements

Each information unit can contain any number of elements. Each element is a reference to one or more other information units. There are different categories of elements. These categories include:

- **Simple Elements** (Fig. 2.6)—These elements directly reference another information unit.
- **Complex Elements**—These elements indirectly reference one or more other information units.
- **Character Elements**—These elements reference text characters.

We will come back to complex elements in the section Other topics, Complex elements.

Operators

Each information unit has an operator (Fig. 2.7). The operator defines what the information unit does when it is shocked. Shocking a unit's operator is equivalent to

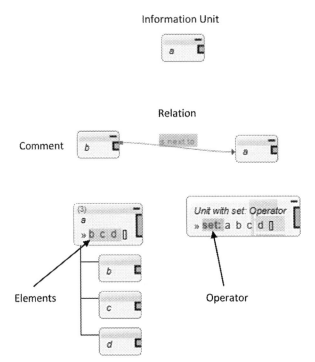

FIGURE 2.5 **Components of the Information Unit Model**

FIGURE 2.6 **A Unit with Simple Elements. Units b, c and d Are Elements of Unit a**

calling a function with the elements as parameters in a traditional programming language. Shocks and program flow are addressed in more detail within this Part 2 under the section Processes.

There are two categories of operators: those that operate only on elements of the Unit Model and those that encapsulate code that is required to control computer hardware and networks. The first are referred to as *Unit Model operators*. The latter are referred to as *real operators*. The Unit Model operators allow you to move and manipulate pure information. The real operators allow for control of computer technologies such as the screen, hard drives, networks, and databases.

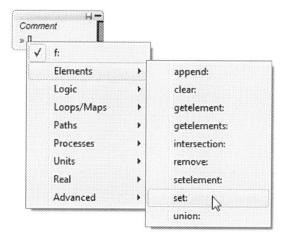

FIGURE 2.7 Setting a Unit's Operator

FIGURE 2.8 A Path Between Units a and b

The relationship between them is "is next to." Unit a is the source and unit b is the destination.

The real operators represent encapsulations of computer technology and the software that controls it. This is why when you develop with the Unit Modeler, you do not have to do any coding. This simplification allows for rapid development of applications that fall in the area of information-based computing because these operators are finely tuned to provide the versatility that is demanded of such applications.

Paths and relations

Information units have relationships to each other. A path (Fig. 2.8) is a characterization of this relationship. Each path is composed of the following pieces:

- **Source**—This is the information unit corresponding to the source of the path between the two information units.
- **Relation**—This is the relationship between the source and destination information units.
- **Destination**—An information unit corresponding to the destination of the path between the two information units.

A unit can be the source and/or destination for an unlimited number of paths. Each source information unit has a list of all relations it has with other units. You can

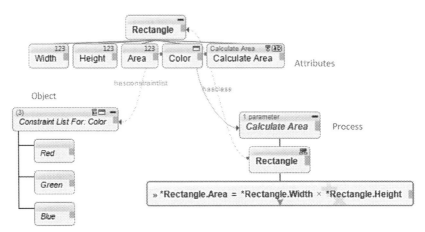

FIGURE 2.9 An Example Showing the Structures of the Unit Model

assemble information units and paths in an infinite number of ways to represent any area of knowledge.

Information units and paths are the fundamental concepts of the Information Unit Model. The structures, which are described next, are all built with units and paths.

STRUCTURES

We introduced in some of the examples above the notion of structures, both Classes and Processes. Now we look at these structures in a more formal sense. We begin with definitions:

- **Classes**—A class represents anything that can be characterized by a set of attributes. It can be a specific object or general category of objects.
- **Processes**—Processes are used to implement algorithms, tasks, principles, and many other functions. A process brings action and change to a model.
- **Objects**—Objects are a catch-all category for things that are neither classes nor Processes.

The Rectangle example pictured in Figure 2.9 illustrates each of these structures.

Classes

A class is a structure that represents a particular object or set of objects that all have the same characteristics. These characteristics are referred to as the attributes of that class. Programmers will recognize a class as being similar to the class as defined in object-oriented programming languages.

For example, a car can be modeled as a class that has attributes of model, color, manufacturer, and fuel mileage (Fig. 2.10). There is a car in the general sense and

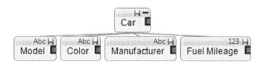

FIGURE 2.10 A Class Representing a Car

there are specific cars, like the blue Chevy and red Ferrari. The Chevy and Ferrari are called *instances of the car class* and the original car class is called a *base class*.

Classes can be used to model far more than just physical objects. Anything that is part of a general category of person, place, or thing and that has a set of common characteristics can be modeled by a class.

Attributes

An attribute is a unit that contains information that describes the class to which it belongs. An attribute can represent a number, date, text string, another class, a process, a list of any of the former, and other types of information.

Types

What an attribute represents is referred to as its type. The complete list of types is shown below. The icons that indicate the type of a unit are shown in the upper right hand corner of the unit display.

- ✓ boolean
- ⬚⬚ class
- a+bi complex number
- ⬚ date
- ⬚ file data
- √x+z expression
- ⬚ holder
- ⬚ list
- ⬚ matrix
- 123 number
- ⬚ process
- ⬚A richtext
- Abc text
- ⬚ time
- ⬚ timestamp
- ⬚ unit

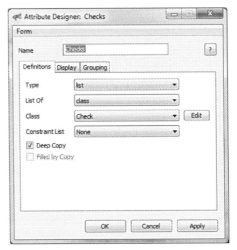

FIGURE 2.11 Attribute Designer

Types and definitions attached to attributes are useful because they help the engine act intelligently.

1. The engine uses this information to automatically create forms.
2. Smart Selection—When having to make selections in the construction of your model, the engine can provide visual guidance steering you toward options with sensible possibilities. Smart selection depends upon types to help it make this determination.
3. Warnings—Unit Displays can contain warning symbols when dubious selections exist. These warnings depend, in part, upon the types of the units involved.

Fully defining a unit configuration can require up to five pieces of information about a unit. Each of these pieces of information is referred to as a definition. The majority of configurations require two to three definitions. Attribute Designer is a tool that will guide you through these definitions. To access Attribute Editor, right-click on the attribute you wish to define and select **Edit attribute…**. You can also define the unit via options in the unit's right-click menu, as shown in Figure 2.11.

If, for example, an attribute has type class, its element will be a class. In this case, the attribute may have a further definition that defines what type of class it can hold. Figure 2.11 shows Attribute Designer for the Checks attribute of the Checking Account example discussed earlier.

In addition to attributes, parameters, variables, and objects can also be typed (Fig. 2.12).

Types may be added or removed quickly by right-clicking on the unit and selecting the desired type from the **Type** menu list (Fig. 2.13).

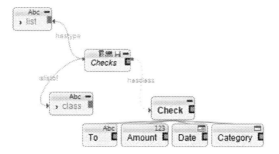

FIGURE 2.12

The type and other definitions of an attribute, variable, or parameter are attached to the unit by paths to special vocabulary units.

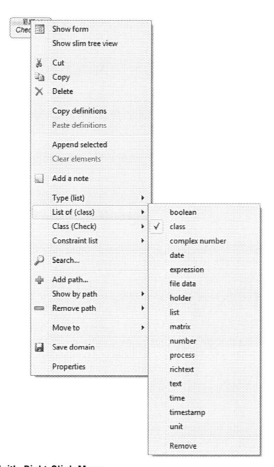

FIGURE 2.13 A Unit's Right-Click Menu

The specific options in this menu will vary depending upon the type of unit.

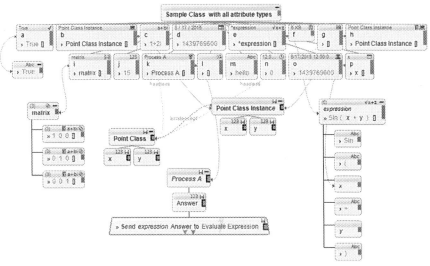

FIGURE 2.14

An example class with attributes representing all of the possible types.

The sample class shown in Figure 2.14 has an attribute representing each of the types below and in the same order. The default form for this sample class is shown in Figure 2.15

Boolean
Units that are typed as boolean are expected to contain either the "True" unit or "False" unit from System Vocabulary (or a reference to these units).

Class
Units that are typed as class are expected to contain a class (i.e., a unit with an "isa class" path off of it) or a reference to class. If a unit should contain a particular kind of class inside of it, class typing can be added as well. Class typing is defined by adding a "hasclass" path from the unit to a base class that is used to determine what kind of class can be stored inside the unit. In the sample class shown in Figure 2.14, attribute b is typed as a class and specifically a Point class.

Complex number
Units that are typed as complex are expected to contain or reference a numeric text string, which may or may not be complex.

Date
Units that are typed as dates are expected to contain or reference a numeric text string. The number stored inside a date unit (referred to as the date value) represents the number of seconds that have passed since 12:00 AM on January 1, 1970 (dates before January 1, 1970 are stored as negative numbers). Observe that each day in the calendar can be represented with 86,400 different numeric strings (24 hours/day × 60 minutes/hour × 60 seconds/minute = 86,400 seconds in a single day).

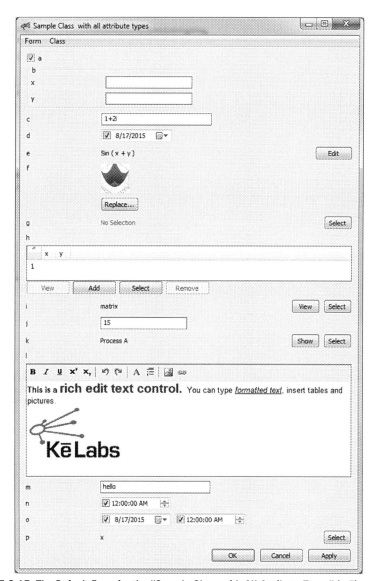

FIGURE 2.15 The Default Form for the "Sample Class with All Attribute Types" in Figure 2.14

Expression

Units that are typed as expressions are expected to contain or reference a set of other units, which together (in the order in which they are stored in the expression unit) form an expression compatible with the Evaluate domain.

File data

Units can also hold file data. File data is converted from binary and stored as a text string inside the unit using the EncodeFile operator. Although the file data is stored

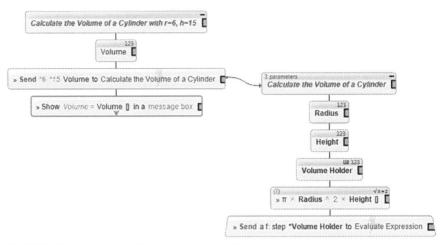

FIGURE 2.16 Example of the Use of a Parameter Typed as Holder

as text, it is unsuitable for reading or modifying with operators. The most common use for encoding file data into units is so images can be displayed on form controls such as buttons, trees, and toolbars.

Holder

Units that are typed as holders are expected to contain or reference a unit typed to hold a particular type of information. To determine the type of information that the holder unit should contain, a "holdstype" path is added to one of the type units. For instance, if a unit should contain a unit that holds a date, that unit would be typed as a holder via a "hastype holder" path and a "holdstype date" path.

A common reason to type a unit as a holder is when that unit is an output parameter on a process (i.e., a parameter that sends some form of information back to the process that shocked it). Consider the process "Calculate Volume of a Cylinder" shown in Figure 2.16. "Volume Holder" is an output parameter, which is typed as a holder of a number. In other words, "Volume Holder" is expected to contain a unit typed as a number. Once the process "Calculate Volume of a Cylinder" has finished calculating the volume, this numeric string can be passed back to the process that shocked it via the numeric unit passed into the calculation process. In this example, once "Calculate the Volume of a Cylinder with r = 6, h = 15" is finished shocking "Calculate Volume of a Cylinder," it displays the message "Volume = 1696.460032939."

List

Units that are typed as list are expected to contain or reference a list of units (zero to an infinite number of units).

If a unit's list should be made up of a particular kind of unit, list typing can be added as well. List typing is defined by adding a "islistof" path from the unit to one

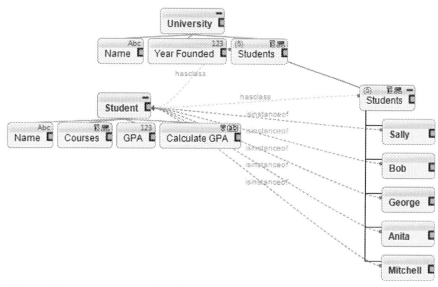

FIGURE 2.17 Example of an Attribute Typed as List

Students is a list attribute with type class Student.

of the type units (text, number, class, and so forth), which is used to determine what kind of list is stored inside the unit (Fig. 2.17).

Matrix
Units that are typed as matrix are expected to contain a matrix (i.e., a unit with an "isa matrix" path off of it). In the Unit Modeler, a matrix is defined using lists of numbers (which may or may not be complex). The number of lists determines the number of rows in the matrix. The number of entries per list determines the number of columns in the matrix.

Number
Units that are typed as number are expected to contain or reference a numeric text string.

Process
Units that are typed as a process are expected to contain or reference a single process (i.e., a unit with an "isa process" path off of it).

Generally, attributes typed as a process should contain a process that has a single parameter typed to contain an instance of the parent class of the attribute.

Rich text
Units that are typed as richtext are expected to contain or reference RTF markup that can be used to display rich text in a rich text control. Rich text is a format used to store text that includes formatting such as different fonts, bold, and italics.

Text

Units that are typed as text are expected to contain or reference a text string. Text string elements appear differently than unit elements when units are expanded.

Time

Units that are typed as time are expected to contain or reference a numeric text string. The number stored inside a date unit represents the number of seconds that have passed since 12:00 AM.

Timestamp

Units that are typed as timestamps are expected to contain or reference a numeric text string. Just like the date type, the number stored inside a timestamp unit (referred to as the timestamp value) represents the number of seconds that have passed since 12:00 AM on January 1, 1970 (dates before January 1, 1970 are stored as negative numbers). Timestamps can be found by adding a unit typed as date to a unit typed as time. The timestamp domain provides other utilities for constructing, modifying, and modifying timestamps.

Unit

Units that are typed as a unit are expected to contain or reference a single unit. The type of that single unit is not relevant; the unit can be a class, process, step, attribute, or something else. The only invalid content for a unit typed as unit is a text string or a list of units.

Constraint lists

Sometimes the value for an attribute, no matter what type it has, will be limited to a certain set of options. Defining an attribute's constraint list (Fig. 2.18) allows you to impose this limitation. The Attribute Designer tool allows you to define a constraint list for an attribute.

If a constraint list is known at design time and will never change, then it can be represented by a unit that is a list of other units, as seen in Figure 2.18. Sometimes, however, the constraint list cannot be known upfront and may change over time. In these cases, the constraint list can be represented by a process as in the Figure 2.19.

Types of classes

Classes have different purposes and play various roles in models. Some of the most common roles are described below.

Base classes and instances

A base class (Fig. 2.20) is a class that models some general category of object. The attributes typically have no specific values other than default values.

If we create an instance of a base class and put in values for its attributes, it can be used to represent a specific occurrence of the class. For example, if you create a base class "Car" that represents a car, an instance can be made to represent a specific car, such as a blue 2014 Ford Taurus. Instances can be made by right-clicking on a class and choosing **Create instance**, or by using the create instance assist.

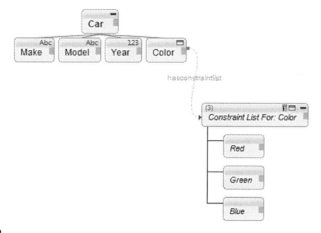

FIGURE 2.18

In this example, the attribute Color has a constraint list of Colors, which is a list of three units: Red, Green, and Blue.

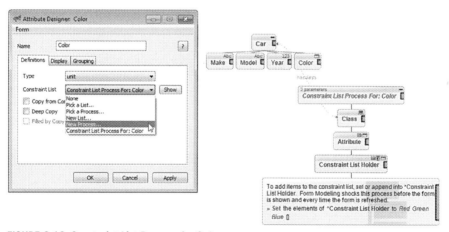

FIGURE 2.19 Constraint List Process for Color

Note that the constraint list process for color was automatically generated by selecting the **New Process...** option from the Constraint List dropdown. Only the Red, Green, and Blue elements of the last step were entered by the developer.

Copying classes/creating a class instance

Copying a class and creating an instance of a class are exactly the same, except that when creating an instance, an "isinstanceof" path is added from the copy to the original unit. It is more common to create instances as it is often required to know the base class of an instance.

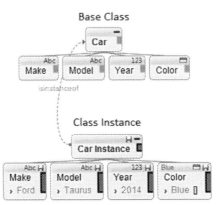

FIGURE 2.20 Example of a Base Class and an Instance of the Base Class

When you make an instance of a class, new units are created for the class and each attribute. Identical paths are added between the new class unit and the new attributes. Any paths that exist on the original units will also be added to the new units. This includes attribute definitions.

If the attributes of the original class have any elements, then one of two things will happen, depending upon whether the attribute is marked as deep copy or not:

1. *Not marked as deep copy*—The new attributes will reference the same units that the original units referenced.
2. *Marked as deep copy*—A copy of the units referenced by the elements will be made and be added as elements of the new attribute.

Deep copy acts in a nested fashion. If an attribute marked for deep copy holds a class as its element(s), then those classes will, in turn, be deep copied.

Class attributes can also be marked as "Filled by copy." If an attribute marked this way is empty, the attribute is automatically filled with an instance of the specified class.

If any unit holds an element that references a unit that is already being copied, the new attribute's element will reference the copied unit.

Base classes are an important concept in the Unit Model. Base classes can describe a great deal of knowledge, which you can reuse simply by creating an instance of it.

Top-level classes

When modeling certain areas, the classes that define the model will form a hierarchical structure. When this is the case, one class will be at the top of this hierarchy. This class is called the *Top Level Class* (Fig. 2.21). A top-level class could, also be a base class and/or a class instance.

Processes

Processes make models dynamic. Anything that changes in a model is the result of a process being run. Processes can perform many different tasks, such as performing a calculation, displaying information, and setting values.

FIGURE 2.21 Model of a Contact Manager Application

The Contact Manager has two attributes which represent lists of classes (Company and Contact). The Contact Manager class is the top-level class for this model.

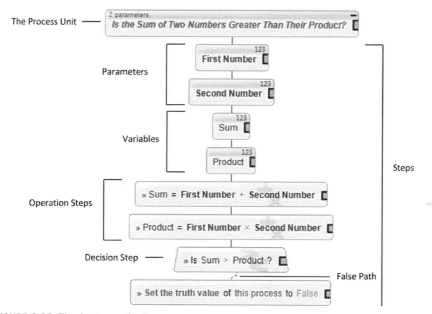

FIGURE 2.22 The Anatomy of a Process

The parts of a process

Although processes have many different purposes and can look very different, all of the units that make up a process serve a common set of roles (Fig. 2.22).

The process unit. The main unit at the top of the process is called the *process unit*. Its comment is always in red. The process unit has a path "isa" "process" and this is how it acquires this definition.

Parameters. Parameters are a way to pass information to a process and a way to receive information from a process.

Parameters are variable steps that are also elements of the process unit itself. When a step shocks a process that has parameters, it sets the elements of each of the parameters. The elements sent to the parameters of a process are also known as arguments.

Variables. Variables are steps in the process that are used to hold temporary values. They have a fact operator and are typed. They are typed so that smart selection will know how to interpret them.

Operation steps. Operation steps take action when they are shocked. The action an operation step takes depends on its operator.

Truth values. Every unit has a property referred to as its *truth value*. The truth value of a unit may be either True or False. By default it is always True. The truth value of a unit can be set by its own operator or another step that uses the Set Truth Value operator.

The truth value of a step determines which path a shock will flow through next. If the operator is True, then the shock will travel down the True path (>). If the operator is False, making the step's truth value False, then the shock will travel down the False path (! >).

The truth value of the process unit is important because a step that shocks this process will have its truth value set to the value of the process unit. In Figure 2.23, "My Process" shocks the "Is the Sum…" process. The subprocess has steps that set the truth value in the process unit. When this process ends, the shock step in "My Process" will have its truth value set to the truth value of sum process.

Error paths. While processing a shock, the Unit Modeler may encounter malformed steps that display an error to the user, such as a "divide by zero" error. In many cases, this is desirable for you as the developer, but may not be desirable for your enduser to see. In these cases, you may find that you would like to keep the user from seeing

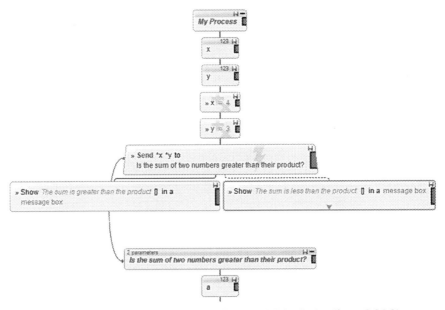

FIGURE 2.23 Process Demonstrating the Use of True and False Paths. Figure 2.24 Shows how Steps can Set the Truth Value of a Process.

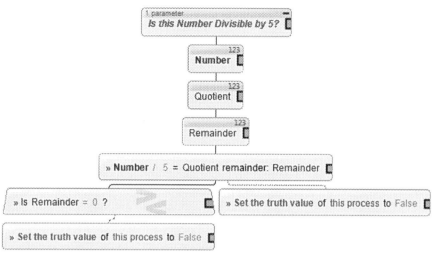

FIGURE 2.24 Example of Handling an Error Path

the error and handle it yourself. Even though it's generally better if you do your error checking upfront, at times it can be difficult to determine if an error is going to occur. An example of this is determining if a divide by 0 error is going to happen in a long, complicated equation.

The Unit Modeler provides a method for you to suppress these errors and handle them through the error path. Error paths are connected to steps just like True and False paths are. The error path is designed by the ?> relation and is drawn with a dotted red line. If an error occurs in a step or process, that error is thrown up the stack of shock steps. If any of the shock steps handle the error, the shock flow will follow that error path. This allows you to catch errors that occur deep within subprocesses of a process that you shocked. If more than one of your shock steps in the stack handles the error, only the first error path encountered is followed.

In the process shown in Figure 2.24, if the argument for Number is nonnumeric, the step that calculates the quotient and remainder of its division by 5 will "error out." This is caught by adding an error path to a step that sets the truth value of the process to False if this should occur.

Return values. In some cases we want a process to do more than just return True or False. We may also want it to set the value of one or more variables. Perhaps we want a process to calculate $Cos(a)^2 + Sin(b)^2$ and set the value of c to the result. We can accomplish this by having an extra parameter on the process that will hold the unit we want to set (Fig. 2.25).

In Figure 2.25, the first two parameters are numbers. The answer parameter will actually hold the third argument sent by the calling process, in this case z. The shocked process (Sum a, b) can access this unit by getting the element of the Answer parameter.

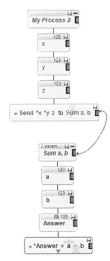

FIGURE 2.25 Example of a Process Returning a Value to a Parent Process

Shocks and process flow

Shocks are an important aspect of the Unit Model. The term *shock* is borrowed from the analogy of electrical circuits. For a unit to activate its operator (and carry out whatever operation defines it) it must receive a pulse of energy. A shock delivers this hypothetical pulse to a unit.

When a process or step unit receives a shock, it does the following (Fig. 2.26):

1. Executes its operator.
2. Shocks the next appropriate step.

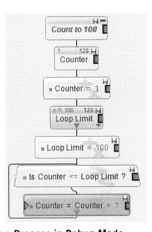

FIGURE 2.26 Walking Through a Process in Debug Mode

The step highlighted in green is the active step.

The next step that is shocked is determined as follows:

1. If the operator's truth value is True, the True path is followed (>). If a True path does not exist, the process returns.
2. If the operator's truth value is False, the False path is followed (! >). If a False path does not exist, the process returns.
3. If the operator generated an error, error paths handle the error message. If no process handles the error, the error is displayed to the user.
4. If the step is terminal (it has neither a True nor False path off of it), the truth value of the process is returned to the shock step that shocked the process. If a shock step did not shock the process, shocking is complete and the program returns to normal operation.

Categories of processes

Just as classes played different roles in a model, so, too, do processes have different purposes and common roles. There are several types of processes you will build over and over. These process types include utilities, tools, launch processes, and directives. Any particular process may be multiple of these types.

Action processes. Classes can have attributes typed as a process or a list of processes. The processes that are the elements of these attributes are referred to as *Action processes* (Figs 2.27 and 2.28). These processes are intended to take some action upon the class and its attributes; as such, Action processes have one parameter: the class the action will be executed on. The processes in the checkbook example were both Action processes.

Utility processes. Processes that serve a general purpose and that can be reused by others outside of the domain in which it exists are called *utility processes*. You can expose this utility to others by adding the process to the Utilities attribute of the Domain class. You do this by right-clicking on the process unit and selecting "Add to Utilities." It will now show up in the DRC and other places within the development environment.

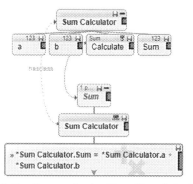

FIGURE 2.27 "Sum" Is an Action Process for the Class "Sum Calculator"

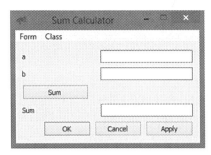

FIGURE 2.28 When a Class's Form Is Shown, Action Processes Will Be Shown as Buttons By Default

Tool processes. Tool processes are those that are interactive with the user in some way. Tool processes typically perform some kind of task or provide some type of assistance to a user. Tool processes usually do not have any parameters; users can just shock them and go.

If you launch the DRC, you'll find hundreds of commonly used tools. A domain's tool processes should be stored in the "Tools" attribute of the domain class of said domain. This makes the tools easier for other users to find and use.

Launch processes. A launch process is a process that shows a form of some kind for a user. Commonly, these processes copy a top-level class into a scratch domain and display a form for that class. A subject domain typically has one main launch process. The launch process serves as an "entry point" for users trying to use the domain's applications.

A domain's launch processes should be stored in the "Launch Processes" attribute of the domain class of said domain. This makes the launch processes easier for other users to find and use.

Directives. A directive process, or directive, is a process that gets automatically shocked when the domain it is housed in gets loaded into the Unit Modeler. These processes do not take any parameters.

A process's directive status (also called "directive state") can be changed by right-clicking on the process and choosing **Edit...**. This will launch Process Designer for the process. To toggle the process's directive status, go to the **Options** tab and check the **Directives** checkbox. You may also set a process's directive via the setdirective operator.

Directives can also be manually shocked (either by a user or by other processes) if need be.

A domain's directive processes should be stored in the "Directives" attribute of the domain class of said domain. This makes the directive processes easier for other users to find and use.

Objects

Objects (Fig. 2.29) are Units that represent something that is not a class, a number, or a text string. An object is most often used to represent a list.

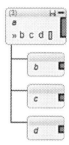

FIGURE 2.29 Unit a Is an Object

It represents a list of b, c, and d.

Domains

The term *domain* has multiple meanings. The first and most common definition is as a reference to some area of knowledge, such as math, science, and law. The other definition, as used in the context of the Unit Modeler Development Environment, refers to the file created when a model is saved. All of the units, structures, and paths of a model are saved in domain files. Just as a text editor saves .txt files, the Unit Modeler saves domain files.

Domain categories

Although all domains store units, the units that they store can represent different categories of information. The domains then take on different types. A partial list of domain types is listed below.

Domain types

The four domain types are:

1. Application domain
2. Definition domain
3. Data domain
4. Scratch domain

An application domain is one that holds units which represent an application. An application domain will generally have a directive process that will set up the environment for that application. This directive could, for example, show a form for the application, or add a menu item that shows a form, or any other function that is desired.

Definition domains store all units, structures, and paths that are constituents of a model. Definition domains generally contain fundamental classes, processes, and various other unit types. The main classes of definition domains are often copied and the new instances are used to do work within a specific problem. For example, a Project Management application might have a definition domain containing a class called project. The project class may have attributes of description, type, start date,

FIGURE 2.30 A Unit in a Domain and a Unit in No Domain

end date, and others. The Project Manager application will create an instance of the project class when a new project is added.

Data domains hold units that represent data. Data domains generally do not have any processes. They have no knowledge, just information. You can specify whether a domain is to be designated as a data domain by setting the type attribute on the domain class. A consequence of designating a domain as a data domain, is that it will load units differently. When a unit is referenced with a standard domain, all of the units in that domain are loaded. This is done because it is efficient to load units in bulk and it is quite likely that many other units within the domain will be loaded soon anyway. Data domains load units incrementally, one class at a time.

During any session of the Unit Modeler application, units get created. These units are added to whatever domain is set as the current working domain. If the units are meant to become additional components of a model, then the units need to be saved in the same domain as the model's other units.

If, however, units are going to represent results of an analysis or calculation, or visual objects in a visualization display, then they have only temporary importance and do not need to be saved with the models' domain. Before creating these types of units, it is important to set the domain to either the empty domain ("< >") or to a scratch domain.

The purpose of creating a scratch domain is so that units belonging to the scratch domain can easily be unloaded from memory. This is important because after a while, as more and more units are created during a session, the quantity of units starts to use up RAM. This memory issue can be partly alleviated by unloading units that are no longer needed. Entire domains can be unloaded at once via the UnloadDomain operator or units can be unloaded in groups via the UnloadUnits operator.

A unit can have no domain assigned to it. This is the empty domain, represented as < >. To make it very obvious when units are in the <> domain, the Unit Modeler displays them with a yellow background (Fig. 2.30).

Dynamic loading

Dynamic loading is another extremely important property of the Unit Modeler technology. Reuse means that one model may reuse another model and that that model could reuse yet a third model. This can go on indefinitely. This is very powerful, but because the reusable library of components could grow indefinitely and be ever changing, dynamic and on-demand loading of content is essential. It means an unlimited expanse of material can be accessible and updates are a nonissue.

When a unit within a domain is referenced and it is not currently loaded, the engine can go out and find it. It will first look on your local computer, then it will look in any workspaces you are currently joined to, then it will look on the server you logged into, and then it will look amongst all servers that are part of the wider network. Once found, the unit will be automatically loaded.

A consequence of dynamic loading is that there is sometimes a small delay in program operation as new domains are found and loaded into your session. After that, operation will have no delay.

Other topics

Discussed below are a few topics that were skipped earlier.

Stars (*)

Often it is necessary to differentiate between a unit and its elements. Sometimes you want that unit and other times you want its elements. To reference the elements of a unit, you can add a star (*) in front of the reference. Figures 2.31–2.33 show examples of setting the elements of a unit with no *'s and a single *.

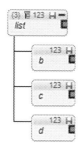

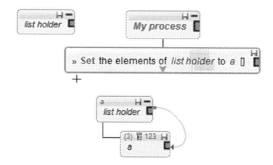

FIGURE 2.31

In this example, the unit list has three elements: b, c, and d. The set step in My Process will set the elements of list holder to the unit a, as shown in Figure 2.32.

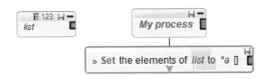

FIGURE 2.32

In this example the set step references the elements of a (*a). So the list unit will now have b, c, and d as its elements, as shown in Figure 2.33.

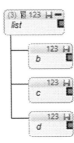

FIGURE 2.33 The List Unit After Shocking the Set Step in Figure 2.32

A double * can also be used, for example, **a. Figure 2.34 demonstrates the results of a set step with ** reference.

There are several ways stars can be added to an element. The first option is to let Smart Selection take care of it. When units are properly typed, Smart Selection can know what * levels should be used and can automatically set them. Selection mode also provides options with the various star levels. So left-clicking on [elements]

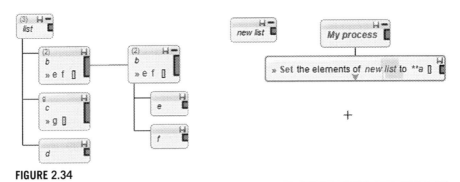

FIGURE 2.34

The first * in the set step references b, c, and d, but the second * references the elements of b, c, and d, which are e, f, and g (Fig. 2.35).

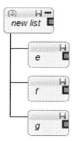

FIGURE 2.35 The Result of Shocking the Set Step in Figure 2.34

(Fig. 2.36) will put you in select mode and if you hover over Unit A, a popup menu will appear with various options.

Note that using these right-click menu items only adds and removes stars from the front of a complex element reference. In other words, if we had a complex element reference to *University.*Faculty.Office Number, selecting **Add** * from the right-click menu would add a star in front of this complex expression. To add or remove stars before "Faculty" or "Office Number," you must either reselect your complex element via Smart Selection or manually correct the reference path via **Edit element path...**, found below **Remove** * in the right-click menu.

Complex elements

We earlier defined elements and described three types: simple, complex, and virtual. An example of simple elements was provided, but the details of complex elements were skipped. Now that we have been introduced to paths and stars, we can revisit complex elements.

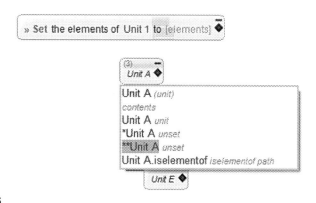

FIGURE 2.36

After left-clicking on *[elements]* and hovering over Unit A, Smart Selection will present a number of reasonable options (Fig. 2.37).

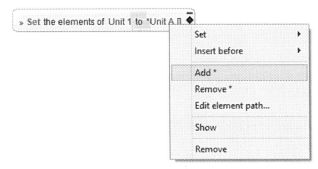

FIGURE 2.37

Another way to add and remove stars is by right-clicking on a unit reference and selecting the **Add** * or **Remove** * menu items.

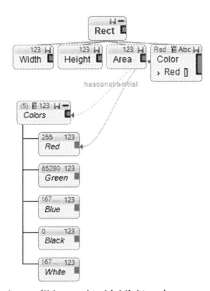

FIGURE 2.38 The class above will be used to highlight various complex elements and the units they reference

Complex elements reference (a) the elements of another unit, (b) path destinations of another unit, or (c) combinations of the former. Any combination of stars and relations is possible. Complex elements indirectly reference other units and they can be used to reference multiple units at the same time (Figs 2.38 and 2.39).

Complex Element	What it Represents
*Colors	Red, Green, Blue, Black, White
Rect.Color	Color
Rect.*Color	Red
Rect.**Color	255
Rect.Color.hasconstraintlist	Colors
Rect.Color.*hascontstraintlist	Red, Green, Blue, Black, White

FIGURE 2.39 Examples of Complex Elements and What They Represent

Basic operations within a process

Although processes can perform an unlimited variety of functions, there is a limited set of common tasks that they almost always carry out.

The basic modeling techniques are a set of skills that are used most often in creating processes. These techniques cover many areas and provide the foundation for all modeling activities.

Setting and removing elements. Information Units use elements to reference other units. There are many operators that allow you to edit a unit's elements. These include set, append, clear, getelement, remove, and setelement.

Basic math operations. There are several categories of basic math operations that you may want to use in your processes. The most common are the simple arithmetic operators for adding, subtracting, multiplying, dividing, and raising numbers to an exponent. These operators are named $a = b + c$, $a = b-c$, $a = b*c$, $a = b/c$, and $a = b^\wedge c$, respectively.

There are also a category of mathematical functions that operator on a single input. These mathematical functions include Abs, Round, Log, and trigonometric functions such as Sin, Cos, and Tan.

Decision points. Decision points are steps in a process that ask certain questions and return True or False based on the result of the step. There are many operators that act as decision points including $=?$, $<$, $!=$, $<=$, $>$, $>=$, IsEmpty, IsNumber, sameas-, and SameText.

Looping over the elements of a unit. One of the most common tasks in the Unit Modeler is to loop over the elements of an Information Unit. This is commonly done when you need to examine or execute a task on each of the element in an Information Unit. Although there are many ways that you can loop over the elements of a unit, the most common method is to use the loop operator. This operator loops over each element in the information unit individually, placing the current element in a loop variable. The loop operator keeps an internal counter so it knows which element is next to loop over. You can reset this internal counter using the reset operator.

Shocking a process. Shocking processes from other processes can be accomplished via the shock operator.

Setting truth values. In many cases, you will find the need to have a process you have created return a truth value, just like a decision point step. You can do this by using the settv operator.

Showing a form. There are many utilities for showing a form, but the most common is called "Show Object Form." This will either generate and show the default form for a unit/structure or show the custom form.

All of the form-showing utilities are located in the Form Modeling domain.

Creating and evaluating expressions. Search the DRC for expression. You will find an assist that will add steps that create an expression and steps to evaluate it.

Mapping elements. Mapping elements allows you to find specific elements or sequences of elements within a unit. Virtual atoms and virtual sequences are special types of elements used by the mapelements operator.

String manipulation. Character strings can be created and modified just as in any programming language. Strings are units with alphanumeric character elements. All of the element operators will work on character elements. You can use them to set, edit, append, and replace characters in strings. There are also some special operators for other operations such as finding substrings and other comparisons.

There are many assists to help you add string manipulation to your application.

User interface and interaction.

Prompts It is often necessary that a model to either give or receive immediate input from the user. Some examples of these interactions include displaying simple message boxes, Yes/No prompts, prompts for text, getting a file path, getting a save path, and getting a color.

Unit selection Other times, you may need to prompt the user to select unit(s) as input. The select operator is what allows you to prompt the user to make these selection(s).

Copying structures. The copy operator can be used to copy any structure, including processes.

This operator will always perform a deep copy. If you've ever created a class in Class Designer, you may have noticed that there is an option to make an attribute have the "deep copy" property.

If an attribute is marked as a deep copy attribute, then when its parent class is deep copied, the elements inside the attribute get deep copied as well (and the deep copy travels recursively down the structure).

When you use the "copy" and "paste" operators from the toolbar and Whiteboard menus, deep copy is automatically applied.

Note that performing a deep copy of a class with the copy operator will create a class instance.

Creating new units. You can create new units with the create operator.

Adding and removing paths. Adding and removing paths can be done using the pathadd and pathdelete operators.

There are also several utility processes for adding and deleting paths (or multiple paths at once), which can be found in the Utilities domain or applied via assists.

Virtual elements

Virtual elements are used by the mapelements and mappaths operators. A virtual atom is designated by a single _ and a virtual sequence is designated by two underscores: _ _. A virtual atom must always contain a single information unit while a virtual sequence can hold any number of information units.

References in processes

A good rule of thumb for modeling processes is that the steps in a process should try to make as many references inside the process as possible. For this reason, among others, elements that reference units outside of the process will appear in italics and the unit holding these elements will have a warning on it (Fig. 2.40).

The elements of the highlighted expression shown in Figure 2.40, reference the Rectangle 2 class directly, as indicated by the turquois line connecting the two. This is why the elements are italicized and why there is a warning indicator on the expression unit. The expression should have referenced the area, width, and height through the parameter of the expression as shown in Figure 2.41.

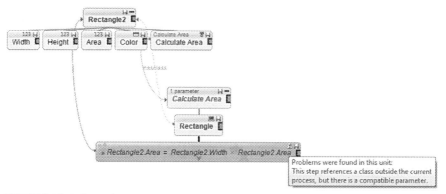

FIGURE 2.40 Referencing the Rectangle 2 Class Directly

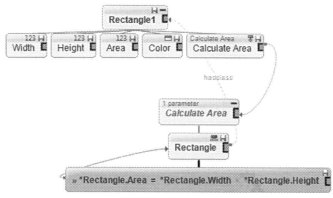

FIGURE 2.41

The proper way to reference the rectangle's attributes is through the Rectangle parameter.

Compose and decompose

Complex elements are composed of multiple parts. These parts are modeled by the Element class, which the compose and decompose operators use. These parts are as follows:

- **Base Unit**—The base unit defines the starting point for traversing the paths and elements.
- **Contents Of**—The contents of is represented by the stars in front of an element. These stars indicate if the element points to the base unit, or the contents of the base unit.
- **Paths**—An element can have multiple paths off it. Each path represents a section of the element delimited by periods (.). When the Unit Modeler sees a new path, it gets the destination of that path.
- **Type**—Each element has a type. This indicates whether the element is virtual, a target, a character, or a plain unit.

The compose and decompose operators allow you to dynamically set a unit's elements to a dynamically defined complex element.

THE GENERAL MODELING PROCESS

Now that we have addressed the vocabulary and grammar of the Information Unit Model, we need to spend some time looking at composition. How do we approach creating an application? What high-level, beginning steps must we take? What is the basic approach to building models that do what we want? This is the topic of this section on the General Modeling Process (GMP). Here you will learn how to apply the Unit Model language to building actual applications.

To some degree, modeling is an art. There is not often only one design to solve a problem. Solutions can, however, vary in their complexity and organization. The following discussion is a general approach to building models that will aid in finding the "simple" solution and keep the model well organized.

Every model has two major components, its structural component and its functional component. The structural component consists of the classes, their attributes and the interconnections of these classes. The functional component pertains to the processes that do things in the model.

Every good model has a soundly designed structural component. Such a design is simple, fit for purpose, and understandable. If it is designed according to established standards of GMP, then it will be able to reuse the multitude of resources within the core domains. This will significantly simplify the functional component of the model. If not, then much of the core functionality will have to be built from scratch.

The functional component makes the model dynamic and performs all of the things that make the model useful. The section "Functional Design: Modeling Processes," below, addresses how to create processes within the Unit Modeler environment.

STRUCTURAL DESIGN

The structures of a model make up its backbone. The functional aspects of the model will all depend upon these classes. Even though there is not one set of classes that will properly define a model, there is a common approach that is helpful, particularly for people new to modeling. There are only a few steps, which are listed below. The message of each step will be illustrated through examples:

1. Understand your domain and what you want it to do, and what you don't necessarily want/need it to do (Intentional Limitations). Identify the components and elements of your domain/application.
2. Design the classes. The classes and their attributes will be composed from the components and elements you found in the first step.
3. Build your processes. While you are building, check the DRC to find any reusable models that can save you time and effort.

Step 1: Define the domain

Define the scope of the domain. Identify what it is intended to do, what subject material will be included, what restrictions and what assumptions it makes, and how comprehensive it wants to be. The goal of defining a domain is not to be too simple or too complex (although you can accomplish either), but rather to have the domain achieve what you'd like it to do.

A domain consists of many components. Identify and list those components that are relevant to the domain in both the breadth of its coverage and its intended goals.

Step 2: Identify the Unit Model structures

After you have made a comprehensive list of components and principles, as described in Step 1, these components and principles need to be translated into Unit Model structures (i.e., classes, processes, attributes, and objects). The following rules of thumb can be applied to this list to identify what they are and their relationships to other units.

- If one unit characterizes another unit, then the first unit is an attribute of the second, and the second unit is a class.
- If there are many possible units that could be elements of another unit, then that second unit is a list.
- If a unit has a value, then it is an attribute and probably either a number or text.
- If a unit is described in the plural (e.g., dogs, houses, patients), then it is a list and will be a list of classes. The specific class (base class) for the list is the singular of the list (dog, house, patient).

EXAMPLE: A+B=C CALCULATOR

We wish to create an application that will allow a user to enter two numbers and find their sum (Fig. 2.42).

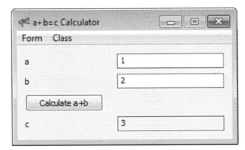

FIGURE 2.42 The a+b=c Calculator Example

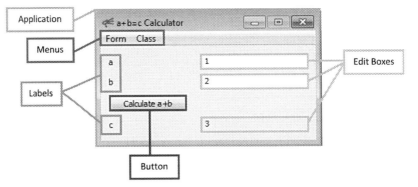

FIGURE 2.43 Parts of the a+b=c Calculator Example Identified

General Modeling Process

Our first step is to identify the components of the application (Fig. 2.43).

The parts of the calculator are:

1. The application itself
2. Variable "a"
3. Variable "b"
4. Variable "c"
5. The calculate process
6. Labels representing the name of the variables
7. The edit box with the 1 in it
8. The edit box with the 2 in it
9. The button with "Calculate a + b"
10. The edit field with the 3 in it that is also greyed out
11. The Menu with items Form and Class
12. The minimize, maximize, close buttons

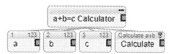

FIGURE 2.44 The Model of the a+b=c Calculator Application

We now need to take this list of items in our domain and translate them into a model. This means we must translate this list to the structural and functional components of our model.

First, everything listed from 6 on describes a user interface element that appears on the form. We do not need to consider these in our model. If we make our model properly, they will be built for us. This leaves us with:

1. The application itself
2. Variable "a"
3. Variable "b"
4. Variable "c"
5. The calculate process

So now the task is to identify which of these items are classes, which are attributes (and which class they belong to), which are processes, and which are objects. We can use our rules from above. The application takes three numbers and sets the third one equal to the sum of the first two. These three variables are all numbers and they are therefore attributes of a class. They are a part of the application, so they are attributes of the Application, which is itself a class. We therefore have the model shown in Figure 2.44.

The application is modeled as a class. The numbers are attributes of this class and each are of type number. The fourth attribute, entitled Calculate, has a type process. The calculate process is an action that acts upon the three variables: a, b, and c. It gets information from a and b, and sets information into c. It is, therefore, an attribute of that class. A process attribute will, by default, be shown as a button on the class's form. When the button is clicked, the process that is the element of the Calculate attribute will be shocked with the class itself as a parameter.

FUNCTIONAL DESIGN: MODELING PROCESSES

The functional aspect of a model consists of its processes. The functional model is not predominantly concerned with the internal workings of a process but rather its purpose, where and when it will get shocked.

Continuing the example
Step 3: Create the processes

Identify the tasks that you wish to have carried out and build a process for each task. An important design principle with processes is to try and keep the parameters easy to work with. Generally, a process should be associated with a class and take that class as its parameter.

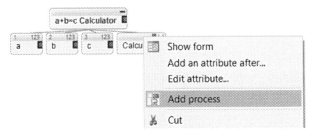

FIGURE 2.45 Right-Click on a Process Attribute to Add the Action Process

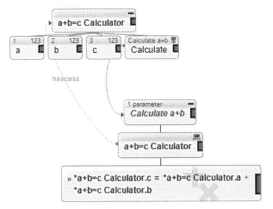

FIGURE 2.46 The Last Thing to Do Is to Add the Step That Adds the a and b Attributes and Sets the Value of c

We must now create the Calculate process and set it as the element of the Calculate attribute. There is an option in the right-click menu to do this: Add process (Fig. 2.45).

This option will create the process, set it as the element of the Calculate attribute, and add a parameter to the process with a class type a + b = c Calculator. We then have only to add one step that sets the value of attribute c to a + b (Fig. 2.46).

How do processes get shocked?

There are several places within an application that processes can get shocked.

- **GUI Interaction**—Processes can be shocked because of a user's interaction with some component of the graphical user interface (GUI). Perhaps they clicked on a menu item, a toolbar button, or a button on a form. Each of these actions would cause the engine to shock a process that is identified to respond to these actions.
- **Subprocesses**—Processes can be shocked by steps within other processes. In this case, the process is referred to as a subprocess.

- **Directives**—Directives are processes that get shocked when a domain is loaded. Perhaps you want a form to be shown upon loading a domain. This is the case for a domain that is acting as an application. A directive process that shows the form would do this. This directive may also modify the application menu or toolbar so that the form can be reshown if it is closed.
- **Watches**—An additional way that processes can get shocked is through a Watch. A Watch is device that a developer can setup to have a process run when something changes. A Watch therefore has a Watch process and a list of Units to watch for changes. Watches have many useful purposes. Watches are usually associated with a form.
- **Form processes**—Forms have several different processes that are associated with them, such as a process when it opens and when it stores, among others. All of these have defaults, but you can design your own if you want.
- **Timers/scheduled processes**—Timers are yet another source for shocking a process. Timers are defined by a developer and their function is to shock a process at a particular time or time interval. The process in this case is referred to as a timer process. Timers can be useful in a number of ways.

In the example above, we created a process that was an attribute of the class. It was interpreted by the Form Modeling core domain that this attribute should appear as a button, which when clicked would shock the process that is the element of that attribute. So the Calculate process is one which would be shocked by GUI Interaction.

Ideally, all processes (other than subprocesses) would be added to a model as process attributes of the model's classes. This structure has the following advantages:

1. It is easy for someone else to understand the model, because everything related to a class can be immediately seen by just looking at the class.
2. Attributes are understood by the engine and by Form Modeling. So the benefits of such things as automatically showing up in a form as a button are there.
3. Simplicity. Watches, form processes, and timers are not as straightforward to implement as process attributes.
4. It is a good modeling technique. Classes have process attributes because there are generally a set of processes that are in some way associated with the class. Perhaps these processes perform calculations or create visualizations. They all act on the class and therefore belong to the class as attributes. Therefore its one and only parameter is to hold the particular class that it is working on. It will be able to find out everything it needs from this class.

Despite these advantages, sometimes it will be necessary to use watches, form processes, and timers. Use of watches and form processes is discussed in Part 4 Custom Forms and timers is discussed in Part 3 Scheduled processes/timers.

Reuse of models and the domain libraries

3

Models that are meant for reuse must be accessible to those who would wish to use them. This requires a central library of content. KeLabs is maintaining such a library. The library of domains is accessible from within the ISDE (Intelligent Software Development Environment), which is described in Part 4.

There is a portion of this library that is open source and is also open to public contribution. Continuing the growth of this library is one of the primary objectives of this book and of KeLabs. We call these efforts the Collective Learning Project. To learn more about this project and how you and/or your institution can contribute to it, visit the KeLabs website at www.kelabs.com.

There are generally three categories of domains within the library. The first deals with the manipulation of information contained within the Unit Model structures. These tools and assists will help you work with classes, their attributes, lists, lists of classes, and other information structures and components.

The second category deals with computer technologies and further encapsulates the activities associated with real operators. Real operators are encapsulations of a carefully chosen set of software technologies (i.e., lower-level C++ code). The library domains further encapsulate these operators and provide guided assists for using them to do everything from creating forms to visualizations to databases.

The third category of library domains is referred to as subject domains. These address areas such as math, analytics, the sciences, and finance. Subject domains have the greatest potential for growth as there is no limit to the subjects that can be encapsulated and included in the libraries for reuse. The purpose of the discussion of subject domains is to present how the Unit Model can be applied to these areas.

ENCAPSULATION

Encapsulation is the process of hiding complexity and making things simple. Encapsulation is one of the most important topics in computer science because if you look all the way down in the computer to see what it is doing, it would be overwhelming and astounding. Processors today are executing billions of operations per second. If programming tools did not introduce layers of simplification that progressively hid more and more of the details of this activity, it would be impossible to get anything done.

There are more specific reasons to encapsulate domain areas. First, so that models can be easily understood by those who might need to understand them in the future, such as a colleague or even yourself. Second, to prepare the model for reuse by other developers. A properly encapsulated model meant to be reused will present itself in a simple manner for this purpose.

There are some tasks that are required often, but where each performance is somewhat different. Situations like this lend themselves to encapsulation because each time the task is performed, there are some similarities and there are some differences. All of the things that are similar can be encapsulated; that is, a developer reusing this domain would not have to worry about those details. The parts of the task that are dissimilar are exposed to the developer.

Anything can be encapsulated in the Unit Model and therefore any area of work can be reused. Any process, any structure of information, any presentation of this information can be encapsulated. This is one of the most important properties of the Unit Model. It ensures that we have a path to continual expansion of our capabilities and that our applications can become increasingly intelligent.

The goal is that no one should ever have to do anything that has been done before. We would more effectively build upon the work of the past, enabling us to achieve much more in the future.

One model may be encapsulated and incorporated, so what once was an entire application is now just a component in another application.

When a domain is encapsulated, it can be presented such that upon reuse of the model, the reusing domain can have a list of different options to configure the domain in reuse.

Encapsulation can require more effort than just getting something done. It requires understanding not just one situation but a series of situations and seeing patterns among them. Although it may be more difficult than solving one specific problem, it has a big impact, because if properly encapsulated, it can be reused. It can be placed in a common repository where others can access the encapsulated area and reuse it in their own work. We can build off the shoulders of others. By encapsulating your work, you have just freed others from having to repeat it, and you will be sharing some of your knowledge and know-how as well.

Of course, for this to happen there must be a mechanism by which these encapsulations and the models in which they exist can be distributed to others. There are many options with which domains can be distributed. They can become part of the core login server's domain set, they can be hosted by any third party server that is registered with KeLabs, they can be added to workspaces, or they can just be emailed/messaged to a colleague.

Within the Unit Modeler, there are several examples and layers of encapsulation:

1. **Operators**—Operators are encapsulations of certain programming capabilities. The capabilities are encapsulated for reuse by making them the operators of units. Operators are actually encapsulations of C++ code. That is what is ultimately called when an operator is activated. The operators enable the Unit Modeler and can be structured to hide a vast amount of the detail that is required when writing something in a programming language like C++. C++ was

designed for uses far outside of the Unit Model. Operators represent the lowest level of the Unit Model. You do not need to know any of the C++ behind these operators. The set of operators provided in the Unit Modeler cover a wide range of software technology areas and allow you to do what models require in those areas. They are not, however, as general as the C++ code that is behind them. If your application requires this level of control, then there will be some limitation to the Unit Modeler's utility.

2. **Reused processes**—A process that is reused is an encapsulation. The process has parameters, which is the only thing a developer needs to know about when calling this process. All of the other steps internal to that process are completely irrelevant to a developer and their inherent complexities are hidden. To encapsulate process steps, you must identify the units (variables, parameters) that change from one situation to the next and those that do not. Those that do not can be hidden and the rest can be exposed through parameters of the process. There are many tasks that are commonly used across all domains that are developed. Utilities, for example, such as finding all instances that have color attribute of red. These tasks have been encapsulated and are available as assists and utilities in the Development Resource Center.

3. **Classes**—The notion of a base class is an encapsulation itself. A multitude of objects can be represented by a single class. A class is a generalization of many instances of that class. They model the properties of many objects by collecting their common characteristics into a single knowledge structure. Thus reducing a description of many things to a description of one thing is encapsulation. A class can be reused to represent multiple instances of that class. To design the class, one has to be familiar with the commonalities of all the instances that are embodied in the base class. Thus a very complex situation is reduced to a very simple one-encapsulated.

4. **Groups**—Classes themselves can be aggregated into groups, which are themselves modeled by classes. Once again, this is a form of knowledge encapsulation, which can go on endlessly and, therefore, models can become easier and smarter. Nothing would have to be created from scratch. Things would just be "assembled."

5. **Objects**—An object can be an encapsulation when it represents a list. Instead of having to remember all of the items or to identify all of the items, only the list unit need be remembered.

6. **Information Unit**—The Information unit is an encapsulation of all knowledge.

MAX CALCULATOR ENCAPSULATION EXAMPLE

The Max Calculator model allows users to enter in X-Y pairs and it includes a button that calculates the maximum value of the X and Y values. Figure 3.1 shows the class structure for this model.

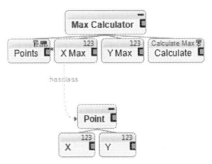

FIGURE 3.1 Max Calculator Class Structure

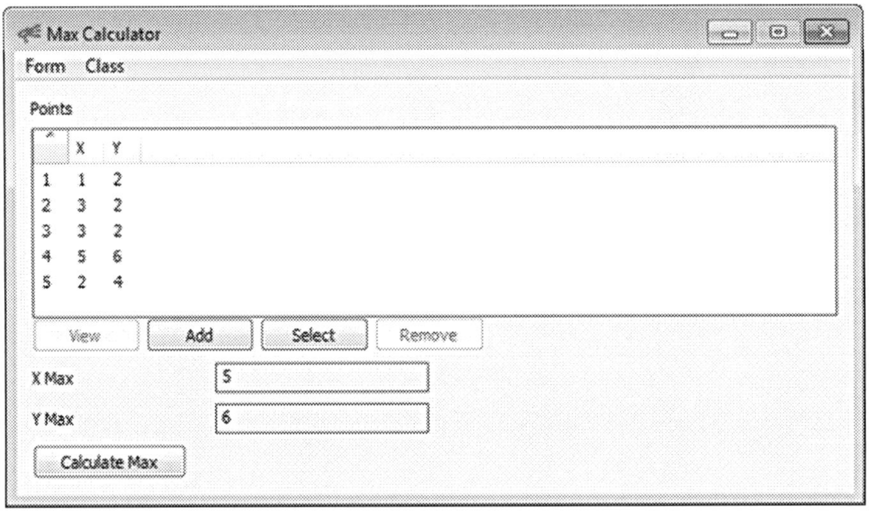

![Max Calculator Form screenshot showing Points table with X and Y columns containing rows: 1 1 2, 2 3 2, 3 3 2, 4 5 6, 5 2 4. View, Add, Select, Remove buttons. X Max 5, Y Max 6, Calculate Max button]

FIGURE 3.2 Max Calculator Form

Figure 3.2 shows the resulting form, including data.

The process behind this calculator will be used in this chapter to demonstrate encapsulation of processes. Encapsulating processes is important for many reasons, including:

1. Encapsulation simplifies existing processes to make them more readable.
2. Encapsulating components of processes automatically creates reusable processes.
3. Identifying and fixing process bugs is much easier when processes are encapsulated into individual pieces that have a specific purpose.

Figure 3.3 shows the process associated with the Max Calculator example.

In the majority of cases where a process takes this much room to display, there are components that can be encapsulated. You can often visually identify the components

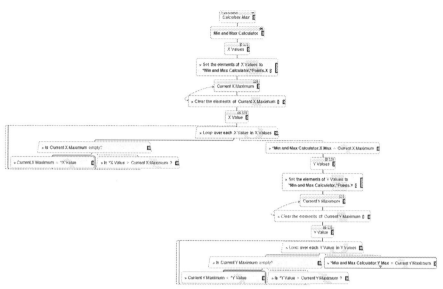

FIGURE 3.3 Unencapsulated Calculate Max Process

that are good candidates for encapsulation. In this example, there are two main loops to this process. The first loop calculates the X Maximum while the second loop calculates the Y Maximum. Since both of these calculate a maximum, there must be a reusable process that we can encapsulate.

The branches that calculate the X and Y maximums do almost the exact same things. The only difference is the list of values and answer holder that they are working with. Using the encapsulation tool, we can encapsulate all of these steps into one process that will calculate the maximum of a list of numbers. This results in the utility process shown in Figure 3.4.

Now, our Calculate Max process has been simplified to just two steps and we've also created a utility process that is reusable by other domains. Had we had this utility when we started (it can be found in the DRC [Development Resource Center]), then our task would have been much simpler as well. Figure 3.5 shows the power of encapsulation.

TEST CREATOR: ENCAPSULATION EXAMPLE

The Test Creator domain was created as a general purpose tool for creating surveys and tests. It is a good example of the encapsulation principle applied to classes. Applying this principle to classes is arguably one of the more difficult things to do. It involves determining what properties of a particular object class are common to all objects and what properties need to be exposed because of their differences.

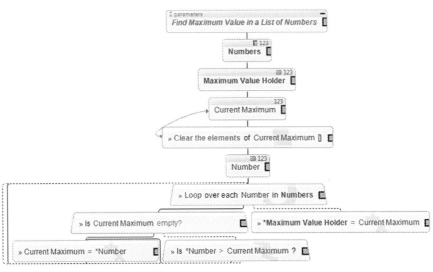

FIGURE 3.4 General Maximum Utility Process

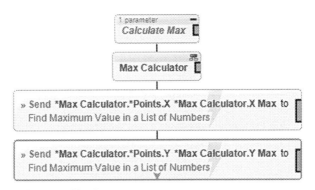

FIGURE 3.5 Final Calculate Max Process

We first look at some examples of what test creator can do, and then investigate the model behind test creator. Figure 3.6 is an example of a survey-type test created using the Test Creator tool.

There are many other possible tests that could be created. Figures 3.7 and 3.8 show the Test Creator model. As you can see, a test is composed of a list of questions. There are various types of questions, e.g. yes/no, multiple choice, numbers. Each type of question has some text associated with it and either a set of choices that enable a user to make a selection (Fig. 3.9) or a text field in which to type.

Multiple choice questions have a list attribute for the choices (see Fig. 3.10). Any number of possible answers can be entered.

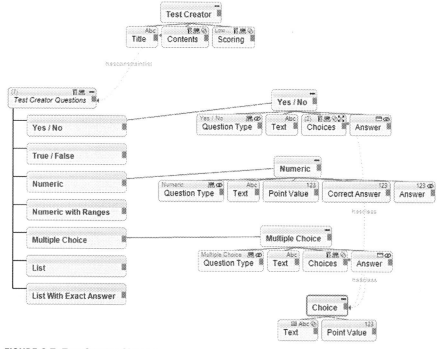

FIGURE 3.6 Investment Risk Tolerance Survey

FIGURE 3.7 Test Creator Classes

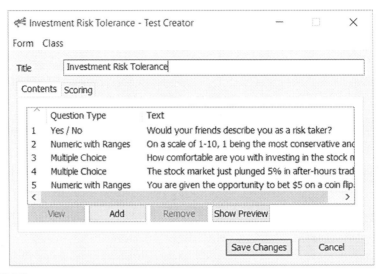

FIGURE 3.8

Showing the form on the Test Creator class, will show the design mode form for the Investment Risk Tolerance test.

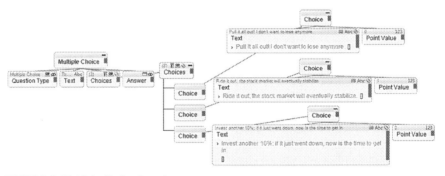

FIGURE 3.9 Multiple Choice Question

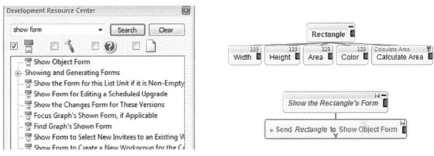

FIGURE 3.10

The Show Object Form assist adds a step to the Show the Rectangle's Form process.

REUSE OF MODELS

Reuse of models is one of the most important aspects of the Unit Model technology. It can save you development time and effort, as reuse enables you to build off of the work of others, taking advantage of the design, the testing, and the lessons learned from mistakes made by other developers. It also brings within your reach the expertise of others that might otherwise be hard to come by.

But how specifically does reuse happen? There are two steps to reusing models: first, you must be able to find and access the models you wish to reuse, and second, once having found them, you need to actually incorporate them into your model.

FINDING REUSABLE COMPONENTS

There are a number of resources to help you find and access other models within the Unit Modeler technology.

1. The DRC is the main tool. The DRC is a one-stop shop for finding and accessing other models.
2. View pages for a domain.
3. Show the class and response processes for a shown form.

MECHANISMS FOR REUSING COMPONENTS

In a very specific sense there are a couple of ways that reusable models can be incorporated into other models.

Assists in the Development Resource Center

Assists are tools that provide guided assistance in creating a process. Many of the assists will add steps to a process that shock existing processes in the library. For example, the assist in Figure 3.10 adds a step to shock the Show Object Form, which is a process within the Form Modeling domain.

Creating a class instance

Creating an instance of a class, makes a copy of it (Fig. 3.11). All of the machinery behind that class, including all of its definitions, will come with your instance. You can use this instance as is or modify it to suit your specific needs.

Class attributes

When an attribute is typed as a class and a specific class, then this is reuse of that specific class. In Figure 3.12, the Table class has a Table Top attribute typed as a Rectangle. The model of the Table is, therefore, reusing the Rectangle class.

In this example we use a second class to represent the Table. The Table has an attribute that represents the Table's top. This Table Top attribute is typed as a class with class Rectangle. This is yet another way to reuse classes.

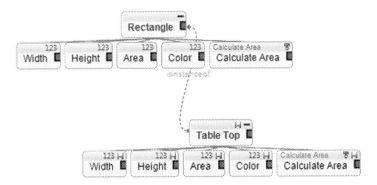

FIGURE 3.11 The Table Top Class Is an Instance of the Rectangle Class

The Rectangle class has been reused to represent a Table Top.

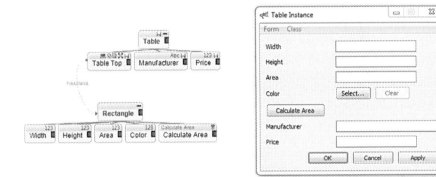

FIGURE 3.12 Reuse of the Rectangle Class

The Table Top attribute's display setting is set to "Expand" and therefore displays in the Table's form.

AREAS OF SUPPORT

The libraries of models for reuse within the DRC (Fig. 3.13) are focused on three areas: (a) Modeling Structures: Tools and Assists that will help you create the structural and functional components of a model, that is, the classes and processes; (b) Computer Technology: Assists that help you create interfaces to real world devices like screens, hard drives, networks, printers, etc; and (c) Subjects. The Subjects area is focused on providing applications and resources that help apply the principles and knowledge of various disciplines such as, math, analytics, and data visualization. Each of these areas of library support is described below.

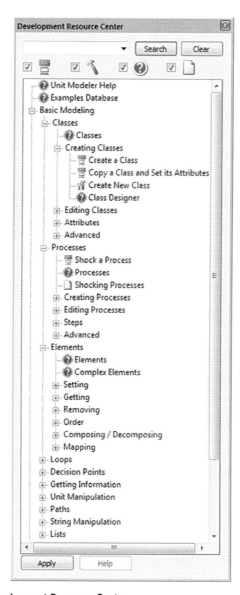

FIGURE 3.13 The Development Resource Center

The tree is opened to assists and tools for creating Unit Model structures.

MODELING STRUCTURES

The domain libraries include utilities and assists that will do just about anything you will need when working with Unit Model structures: classes, attributes, processes, lists, and so on.

Assists are utilities that will add steps in a process. A tool is something that immediately shocks a process to do something. It will often ask the user to select something or to enter some information.

Even though processes can take on an infinite number of shapes and purposes, there is a common set of categories of tasks that you will perform. These are all addressed in the topics below.

Classes

Most of the time you design a class, you will use a tool called Class Editor, which is described in Part 4, section Working With Classes. You may also use functionality directly in the whiteboard. Sometimes, however, you may want to build a class from within a process. In this case, you will need to add steps with operations that create the class, add attributes to the class, set the attribute types, and perform other like actions. The assists in this part of the library will help you do any of these tasks.

Processes

Just as with classes, you will most often create processes using a tool, called Process Designer, and by right-click menus on the step units themselves. The library section devoted to processes includes tools that help you do this. These will mostly be useful to people new to the modeler who are just learning. There is also sometimes a need to create processes on the fly while the application is operating. There are assists that will help you create processes that will actually create new processes.

Another very useful tool is the Create a Launch Process tool. A launch process is a process that will create a new instance of some class and then show the form for that class. Launch processes are useful while you are developing, so that you can see the classes you are designing in their form. They are also useful for application models to actually show the application to the user. Launch processes are often made to be directives so that as soon as a domain is loaded, the launch process will be shocked and the form which makes up the application will be shown to the user.

Elements

Working with elements is one of the most common tasks in modeling processes. When you work with elements you will want to set the elements of a unit, find out what elements exist in a unit, remove elements from a unit, and reorder elements from a unit. The assists in this area will guide you to adding this functionality to the processes of your model.

Loops

Loops are a common part of a process. The assists in the section will guide you to adding loops into your process. There are different types of loops which you may need to implement. The most common loop is where you want to access each element of a unit and then do something with that element. Another type of loop is where you want to carry out some task a set number of times. The assist Loop Over a List With a Counter will add the steps necessary to do this. Other loops will iterate over a variable from some lower value to some upper value.

Decision points

Within your processes you will often have to make some determination about a particular piece of information within your model. Depending upon the value, you may do different things. The steps that make this determination are referred to as *decision points*. There are many different types decisions that can be made and they look at different types of information. The categories of decisions covered within the library are those are concerned with numerical values, classes, lists, units and their elements, paths, and processes. There are too many assists to cover them all here.

Getting information

The assists in this category allow you to find out information that will be useful in your model. You can find out, for example, the user ID of the person logged in and the application name.

Unit manipulation

Anything you can do to a unit in the whiteboard you can also do via a process. You can, for example, create units, set their operators, set or get their comments, copy units, and delete units. Assists in this category guide toward completing these tasks.

Lists

Lists are one of the most common structures in computing. There are many things you will want to do with lists. This section has assists for these operations. Some of the operations include creating, appending, sorting, merging, and finding the intersection and union of lists. You might also want the length of a list, that is, the number of elements it contains. You might also want to know the index of a unit in a list, that is, where does it appear in the list. These are just a few examples of types of operations that you can and will want to perform on lists.

COMPUTER TECHNOLOGY

This category of library domains is concerned with encapsulating the infrastructure to control the computer. This includes technologies such as user interfaces, visualizations and graphs, database interaction, and web services.

Forms/graphical user interfaces

A form is a graphical user interface (GUI) device that displays information to the computer screen and allows users to view, interact with, and provide information to the computer. Forms are also referred to as windows, and simple ones are sometimes referred to as dialogs or dialog boxes. They generally have a header that allows you to move the form and minimize and maximize it. Forms can also have menus and toolbars. The content of the form is made up of items called *controls*. There are many different types of controls, including text, edit, dropdown, grid, and button.

All units can be displayed in a form and each has a unique default display, depending upon how the unit is defined. Forms are automatically created for you by the Unit Modeler engine. This is an important feature of the Modeler that can save you a great deal of time and frustration. The engine does this by understanding your model and creating the appropriate controls and laying them out within the form.

Even though this process is automatic, there is a great deal of customization that you can do. You can define units to tailor the exact way you want your forms to appear and function. Custom forms are useful when complex layouts, responses, and interactions are required. GUIs are traditionally one of the more difficult areas of standard programming. Models have been created of form architectures that encapsulate the tasks and make it very easy to quickly create custom forms with complex behaviors.

Customization can occur in two ways: simple configuration, which is discussed in the Working With Attributes section of Part 4, and full-blown custom forms, which is discussed in the Custom Forms section of Part 4..

Showing forms

You can show the form for any class (or any unit) by right clicking on the unit and selecting **Show form...** (Fig. 3.14). This option shocks the Show Object Form process.

In Figure 3.14, the default form for the Rectangle class is shown to the right. When the Calculate Area button is clicked, the Calculate Area process will be shocked and the Rectangle class will be sent as the argument.

You can also have a form shown from within a process as in Figure 3.15. This process will show the form of the Rectangle. The Show Object Form step can be added by clicking on the down arrow and selecting **Add a show form step**. This is a shortcut to a commonly used assist in the DRC. The DRC is another way of accessing this process.

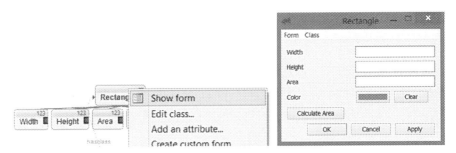

FIGURE 3.14 Right-Click on a Class to Show Its Form

FIGURE 3.15 A Quick Way to Add a Step to a Process That Will Show the Form for a Unit

Printing

All forms can be printed. The option to print is accessed under the **Form** menu on a form. When **Print** is selected from this menu, a "Print Preview" window appears. Within this window you can choose certain controls to be included or excluded from the printout. Check boxes appear on the right side of the print preview window for this purpose. This is helpful when controls are very large (such as grid controls) and they are not desired on the printout. You can also select which pages you want to have printed.

Visualizations

Overview

The visualization system model is designed to enable presentation of information in a 2D or 3D graphical display (Fig. 3.16). The top-level class of the visualization system is the Graph class. Graphs are used for creating 2D graphs, charts, and other visualizations. A graph represents the control that holds and displays everything, all the objects that we want to display.

Similarly to how forms are modeled, Graphs have an Objects attribute that keeps a list of the display objects that are shown in the visualization.

The Graph class defines all of the information about a particular visualization. Within this graph can be axes, titles, legends, and data objects.

The Graph and Charts library provides a wide array of plot types as well as set of primitive shapes that can be put together to create unlimited number of custom graphs and visualizations.

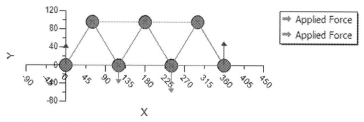

FIGURE 3.16 A Visualization of a Bridge

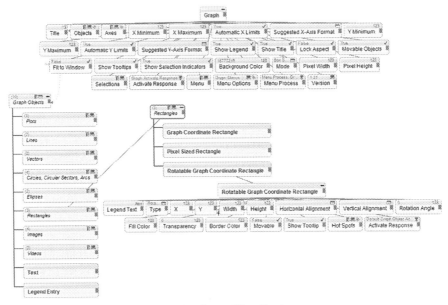

FIGURE 3.17 The Graph Class Is Used to Create Visualizations

It's Objects attribute holds all of the display objects that appear in the visualization. Shown also is one variety of controls that displays a rectangle.

Animations can be made by changing one of an objects values. This can be immediately reflected in the graph window. Continue to change the value and you have an animation.

The graph class

The Graph class models the visualization window (Fig. 3.17). The Graph class has several attributes that control the appearance and function of the window. This attribute contains all of the objects on a graph. Graph objects include plots such as bar charts, histograms, and scatterplots, and simple objects such as vectors, lines, and images.

To create a visualization all you need to do is (Fig. 3.18):

1. CreateInstance (Graph)
2. CreateInstance (Rectangle)
3. Set width, height, and position (Rectangle)
4. Append (Graph.Objects, Rectangle)
5. ShowGraph (Graph)

The ShowGraph process automatically sets most of the graph's attributes for you, so you don't need to worry about setting the minimum or maximum values unless you want to override the default behavior to give your graph specific limits.

The graphs are interactive and it is usually possible to go to the underlying attributes of a model by clicking on their representation in a graph.

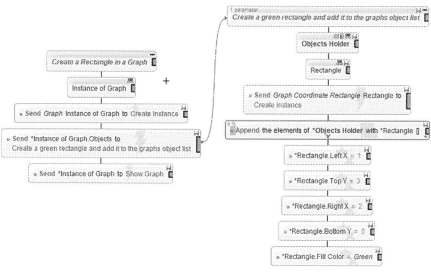

FIGURE 3.18

A process that creates a Graph class instance and adds a rectangle to it. The rectangle's top left and bottom right coordinates are set.

Tools. There are many tools that can be applied to create graphs and they can be found in various places. Of course, the DRC will have a full list. Some also can be found within the Math and Data Analytics Packages. Both packages have toolbar options that enable creating graphs. With these tools you can make graphs from existing data in forms that are already shown. You can also create a blank graph and add visual objects via the graphs menu.

Assists. The assists in the DRC fall within a few categories:

- Creating and showing plots assists guide you through adding steps to a process that show a plot of data that you select.
- Adding additional plots or objects to an existing graph.
- Adjusting some of the graphs properties, such as the axes, legends, and colors.

Custom plots. You are not limited to the graphs created by tools and assists. You can assemble the basic shapes in a wide manner of ways to create virtually any type of plot that you wish (Fig. 3.19). You can even make assists of these new graph types yourself.

Some examples of such graphs included in the libraries are:

- Heat Maps
- Color Coded Scatterplots
- Box and Whisker Charts
- Gantt Charts
- Screenshots

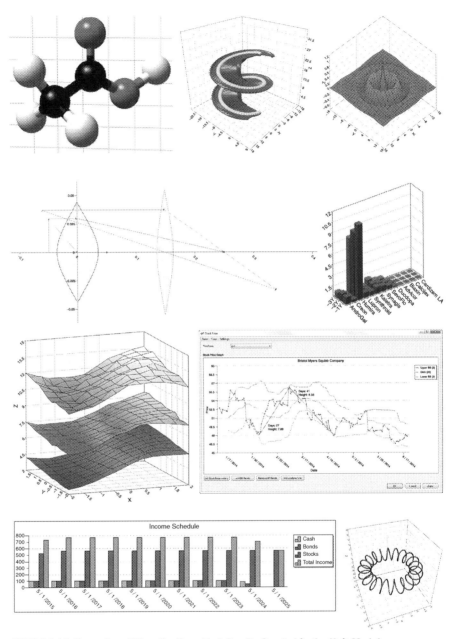

FIGURE 3.19 Examples of Visualizations That Can Be Created in the Unit Modeler

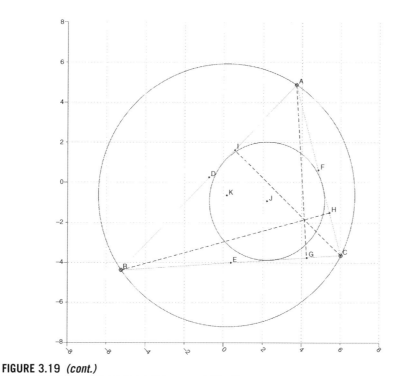

FIGURE 3.19 *(cont.)*

Animation

Animations are created by adding visual objects to a graphical display and then changing some visual aspects of those objects. You could, for example, change the objects' position, size, or color. You could add new objects or remove some.

- Create a New Graph [Graph]
- New Rectangle [Rectangle]
- Show Form
- Loop 1->100

    - Rectangle.x = t

The pseudo steps above would move a rectangle to the right 100 graph units.

Video

Videos are modeled as visualization display objects, just like a rectangle or circle. There are two video display object versions (Fig. 3.20). The second version enables you to specify the size of the video within the visualization window.

To create a video, you need to create a Graph class and add one of the Video classes to its Objects attribute. There is an example for creating a video player in "Part 3: Examples."

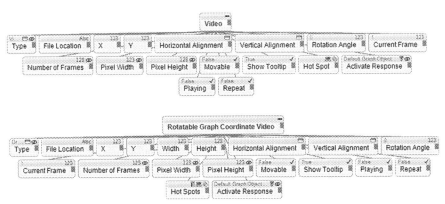

FIGURE 3.20 Videos Are Represented By a Display Object Class

Databases

Databases are important technologies for storing large quantities of data. The most common databases include Microsoft SQL Server, Oracle, MySQL, and Access. The Unit Modeler provides support for all of these products.

The database domains address the requirements of two types of applications (Fig. 3.21). First, given an existing database, we want to be able to query the database, write information to the database, modify the structure of the database, and to generally build a database frontend application.

Second, given an existing model that acts as a database, we want to be able to convert it to storing its data in databases versus data domains. This may be desirable if you need the data in an ODBC (Open Database Connectivity) format or the size of your data will be greater than hundreds of thousands of records.

The Database class is the main class. It holds ODBC information about the database (pictured in Fig. 3.21) and information about the structure of the database.

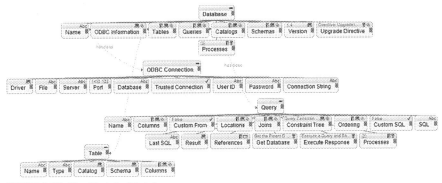

FIGURE 3.21 The Model of Databases

These classes represent the underlying model of the Database tool shown in the "Tour of the Unit Modeler."

It also has an attribute to maintain a list of queries. There is a process that takes the ODBC information, makes a connection with the database, and then scans the database to create a model of all its tables, fields, and other structures.

The Query class encapsulates a portion of the SQL (Structured Query Language) language. The Query class is a tool that understands the structure of the database and uses this information to create an easy-to-use tool for creating a query. There is a visual point-and-click interface to accomplish this. Once having defined the query, the actual SQL statement that will be sent to the database engine will be automatically generated. Thus, the Query class is a way to create queries without having to know SQL. The query tool encapsulates the complexity of SQL so that you do not need to learn the intricacies of the language. SQL is a very robust language. The Query class does not encapsulate all of its capabilities, but will become more capable in time.

There is a tool in the Data Analytics package for creating a new database class instance. You can create ad hoc connections and queries to databases that already exist. You can create the classes that represent the database and the queries to a domain that you are developing. You can then reuse the queries in your application.

The libraries also offer support for creating a database based on an existing model. The build database tool will ask you to select a class and it will then create all of the tables and fields automatically for you. It will also modify your model to keep track of ID fields which are required for databases. Two examples of using working with database are provided in Part 5 Additional Examples.

Web services

Web services is a popular version of a service-based architecture, where distinct software components connect over the Internet in order to perform focused tasks and share data. In fact, web browsers that we use every day can be seen as access points to web services. Every web server is running a software component that when sent properly formatted requests (typically using HTTP [Hypertext Transfer Protocol] as the protocol) sends back HTML (Hypertext Markup Language) responses that can be rendered by the web browser, another isolated software component. The browser is not concerned with and does not know what the server is doing to service the request, and the server is equally isolated from the web browser's use of the data it sends back.

Web servers are equipped to handle bad requests (they respond with particular error codes like "404 Not Found"), and web browsers are similarly prepared to handle situations where the server cannot be reached (bad network connection, the address cannot be reached, etc.).

Theoretically, a web service could respond with any kind of data. Practically, most web services send back XML (eXtensible Markup Language), JSON (JavaScript Object Notation), or HTML data, depending on how they are accessed and what parameters they are sent. Many even allow the requestor to specify the response format they want. Because of its compactness and readability, JSON is quickly becoming the most popular format used.

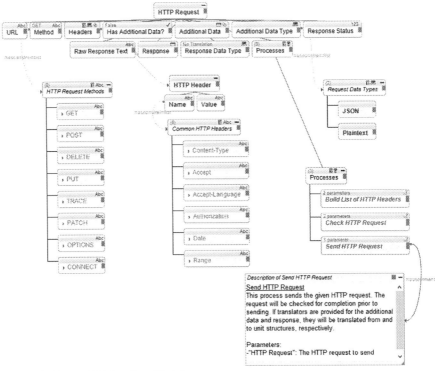

FIGURE 3.22 The Web Services Model

These classes provide for the communication to other websites identified in the URL attribute.

Frequently, websites expose a "Web API" (application programming interface) that developers can use to access, modify, create, and delete information from that server. In many cases, web APIs are free for personal use, but they may require developers to subscribe in order to resell applications that interact with them. Some examples of web APIs include APIs to get the weather in a particular location, or APIs to get information about the current price of a stock.

The Unit Modeler has a domain that encapsulates web interaction. It can execute requests to URLs (Uniform Resource Locaters) and return the response data. Additionally, it can automatically convert JSON data into Information Unit structures and convert Information Unit structures to JSON. The Unit Modeler makes it possible to create web-enabled applications without having to understand how to interpret or create JSON data. Figure 3.22 shows this model.

To use the Web Services model, you need the URL to be sent. After this you create a new HTTP Request instance and set the URL attribute to the URL for the site. Select any other options and then send the HTTP Request instance to the Send HTTP Request process. This process will perform all of the communications with the website and return the results in two response attributes: Raw Response Text and Response. The Raw Response Text is exactly what was sent back by the site, the Response attribute parses the raw data and creates a list of structures to represent the data.

The structure of the response will vary from web query to web query. You will have to run the query at least once to understand what it will be. Each site may structure its data differently. There are two examples of web services in Part 5, Additional examples; they demonstrate getting stock price information and weather data.

Network communication

Sometimes an application running on some computer will have a need to talk to an application on some other computer. For example, client–server applications have a server application that runs on a central server computer and client applications that run on personal computers, wherever they may be. There is also peer-to-peer communications where one application talks to another application but the other application is running on another personal computer.

Network communications is tricky because it is not possible to directly shock a process on the other computer. Or in traditional programming, you cannot directly call another function or directly access a file on the other computer.

Instead, you must communicate in a common language with the other computer that comes in the form of text or binary data. Even lower level than this is that you first have to establish a pipe, or connection, to the other computer so that you can talk. This can involve sockets, encryption, and many other security measures that must be put into place at the lowest level of programming.

The Unit Modeler encapsulates all of this by providing a handful of real operators that concentrate on the necessities you might have when creating a system where computers speak to each other. With these operators you can get a file, shock a process, and get a unit (and its related structural relations). At the lowest level this is what you have to know.

File manipulation

File Input and Output (I/O) is another important area of computer science capability. It enables a developer to write information to a file and to read information from a file. File I/O functions also allow a developer to copy files, create directories, rename files, and do other essential activities related to computer files. The Unit Modeler has a suite of operators (Real- > Files and Folders) that enable developers to interact with the file system.

String manipulation

String Manipulation is the ability to parse, search, and interact with textual information. One of the hottest fields in data research deals with "unstructured data." Although this is a loose term that encompasses many different types of information, unstructured text is certainly one of these areas.

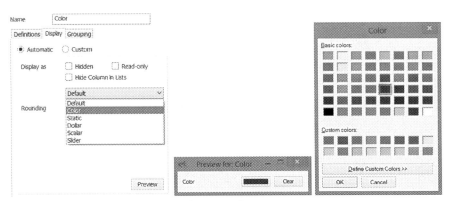

FIGURE 3.23 Displaying a Number Attribute as a Color

The Unit Modeler provides a set of operators that are specifically for string data. These can be found in the Real- > Strings operator menu. Additionally, there is a domain specifically built named String Manipulation. This domain provides many utilities that utilize the operators to perform various tasks. Some examples include splitting strings, finding a term in a string, and replacing characters in a string.

Colors

Setting colors is an important part of computer technology. There is support in the library for working with colors. To use these tools, you must understand how colors are represented within a computer.

In general, computers can represent colors in many ways. One of the most frequent is through its Red, Green, and Blue (RGB) components. RGB values are integers between 0 and 255. For example, a pure red would be represented by an RGB value of (255, 0, 0). The Unit Modeler uses RGB, but creates a single value from the RGB components. There are utilities to convert from color value to RGB and back.

To specify that an attribute represents a color, you should type the attribute as a number. Then modify its display type to color. When this attribute is shown in a form, it will appear as in Figure 3.23. The button will show a color picker dialogue that allows you to select a color visually. The color picker dialogue will fill in the number associated with that color into the attribute.

Dates

Dates are another important concept in information-based applications. There are many utilities to help you work with dates. Just like color values, dates can be represented in various ways. They can be represented, for example, by both strings and numbers.

Strings are probably the way you're used to encountering dates. Examples of strings that represent dates include 12/1/2015, 12-1-2015, or December 1, 2015. For computers to work with dates efficiently, they must represent dates in a standardized format.

In the Unit Modeler, a date is actually stored as a number. This number marks the number of seconds that have passed since 12:00 AM January 1, 1970. Dates before 12:00 AM January 1, 1970 are represented with negative numbers. The date of January 1, 1970 is an arbitrary date referred to as the "epoch" time. It is a commonly used epoch in many computer systems. Dates are stored as numbers so that it is easier to perform calculations between dates, such as how many days there are between two dates or what is the date 20 days after some other date. There are many utilities that help with date calculations (as well as one to get the current date) in the Date domain.

Of course, dates are frequently displayed as strings because they are more understandable to humans. There are also utilities to convert between a date value and a date string and to format dates in a variety of different readable formats.

Rich text format controls

Although plain text is nice because of its simplicity, plain text cannot store information about font styles, sizes, weights, or color. To store and display text that has these characteristics, something called formatted text is used. Formatted text stores information about the formatting of the text alongside the text. As you can imagine, this makes the text itself much more difficult to read unless it is displayed in a Form Control that interprets it and displays it properly.

The Unit Modeler uses a format named Rich Text to encode this information. Attributes typed as rich text are automatically displayed in a Form control that allows users to apply various formatting and styles to that text. The String Manipulation and Utilities domains also include utilities that allow you to create rich text (including links) from plain text.

Encryption

Encryption is a way to encode data such that it cannot be easily read by an unauthorized party. There are two operators in the Unit Modeler which allow you to create applications which implement encryption: EncryptFile and DecryptFile. These operators can be applied to any type of file including Word documents, Excel spreadsheets, and text files. Unit Modeler domain files can also be encrypted with the SaveDomain operator and an optional password parameter. When a file is encrypted a password will be required in order to decrypt that file.

Tools and assists are available for working with the encryption operators. Additionally, the Save button which can be added to any form has encryption capabilities already built into to it.

Scheduled processes/timers

Timers are a commonly used programming feature. Timers allow developers to specify that some action should occur at a later time. The concept of timers in programming translates to scheduled processes in the Unit Modeler. In the Unit Modeler, you can schedule a process to be shocked at a specific time. Additionally, you can specify rescheduling parameters, allowing the process to be run on a recurring basis, such as every minute or every hour.

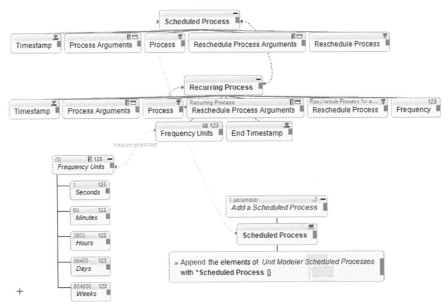

FIGURE 3.24 The Model Used for Creating Scheduled Processes

The library can be found in the DRC under the heading "Process Scheduling." Here you can find assists that allow you to select a process and define when it will be shocked. If a process has a parameter, you will also be prompted to identify that parameter.

Timers can be used for all kinds of purposes. You can use them to update dashboards or update information in an application.

To use scheduled processes, create an instance of the Scheduled Process class or the Recurring Process. Fill in the proper attributes. Then send the class to Add a Scheduled Process (Fig. 3.24).

R language interface

The R Interface domain encapsulates execution of R code for statistics and general mathematical routines. Besides simply providing a tool to execute R code in the Unit Modeler, the R Interface domain encapsulates a subset of the datatypes available in the R language to provide consistent translation between Unit Modeler structures and R code and output. Without a knowledge of the R language, a developer can make use of powerful R routines via the R Interface.

Additionally, the R Interface encapsulates execution of individual R functions and blocks of R code called *scripts*. With the R Function creator, a developer can provide the name of the R function to execute, as well as the types of inputs to be sent, and a process is automatically created that wraps that function call in R. Similarly, entire R scripts can be encapsulated in Unit Modeler processes by providing a template of the R code to be executed and the types of inputs to be substituted into the script. Once a function or script has been encapsulated into a process once, any developer can make use of it by shocking the utility process without having to get into the details of R's syntax or interacting with the R program.

Meta programming

Meta programming refers to programs that can create themselves while they are running. This might happen if a function could modify itself or another function at runtime.

This is readily possible with the Unit Modeler. There are operators that create units and set their operator and their elements. Furthermore, there are operators that can add relationships between units. Thus, if you want to add a new step to a process, all you need to do is to create a new unit, set its operators and elements, and add a > relation to the step you want appended with the this new step.

You could even create a new process entirely and all of the steps within it. This process could then be reused as if it were created and contemplated at design time. The only difference is that a process that calls this process would probably reference the new process via a variable unit that hold that process. So instead of directly shocking the process, you would shock the *[process variable].

MATH

Math is used in almost all information-based applications. From the start, math was a primary area of focus for knowledge-base development, as it would be reusable across a wide range of other areas. We have developed a wide range of tools for including math in your application and math applications for general use.

The Unit Modeler library includes as much math as most applications will ever need. In the event this is not the case, then you can use the model of the R statistics language. You speak to the R engine directly from within the Unit Modeler.

The Unit Modeler has many real operators that perform arithmetic, trigonometry, logarithms, vector and matrix operations, and complex number math (Fig. 3.25).

Expressions and expression editor

An expression is represented in the Unit Modeler by a list of units that correspond to the symbols that would be needed to write that expression out by hand. The units in an expression can be numbers, vectors, matrices, binary operators, special symbols (like parentheses and comma), binary operators, and functions. Hundreds of functions already exist; you also can create your own.

A function is modeled by a process. Processes can be put into mathematical expressions. The domain that evaluates expressions will understand how to process them.

Consequently, an expression can be any combination of the operators presented in the previous section. When one of these operators doesn't quite do the job, then a process can be used as a function in a mathematical expression.

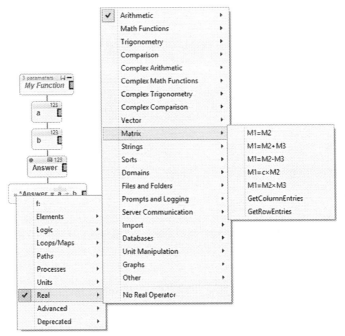

FIGURE 3.25 The Matrix Operators

Expressions can be built using a tool called *Expression Editor*. Expression Editor will help you build and edit expressions in your model (Fig. 3.26). The Expression Editor can be reached from many places and will come up automatically when you need to edit an expression. You can create a new expression with Expression Editor by going to the math toolbar at Expressions > New. Expression Editor has a large array of functions to help add more to your expressions and you can access these in the top menu bar of the editor (Fig. 3.27).

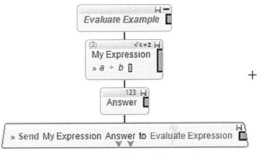

FIGURE 3.26 A Process with a Step Representing an Expression

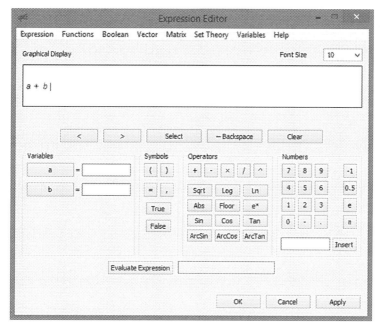

FIGURE 3.27 The Expression in Figure 3.26 Being Edited in Expression Editor

You can right-click on the expression to launch Expression Editor

Example

The example in Figure 3.28 includes a custom function, My Function. A function is just a process. The process's last parameter must be a holder of some variable type so that the Evaluate Expression process can return a value. The beginning parameters will be the functions parameters. Expression Editor understands this convention and presents proper syntax for the function, as is displayed above My Function(a, b).

Vectors

A vector is modeled as a list of numbers (Fig. 3.29).

Matrices

Matrices are modeled as a list of vectors, or a list of list of numbers (Fig. 3.30). Assists to help work with matrices are shown in Figure 3.31.

Symbolic math (algebra and calculus)

There exists a model for performing symbolic math (Fig. 3.32). There are two primary assists:

- Simplify Expression or Equation
- Solve for a Variable in an Equation

Within the Math package there are toolbar options to apply these operations to an expression that you select.

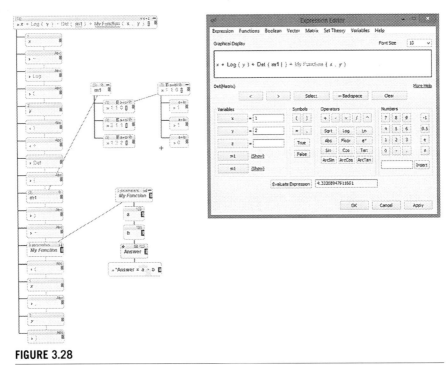

FIGURE 3.28

Expression Editor supports expressions with matrices, processes, logic and many other features. Shown here is an expression with a matrix and user developed process.

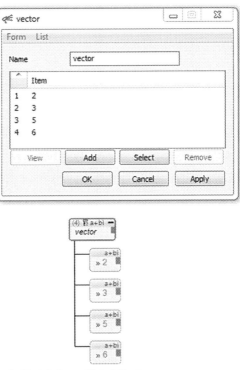

FIGURE 3.29 A Vector Is Modeled as a List of Numbers

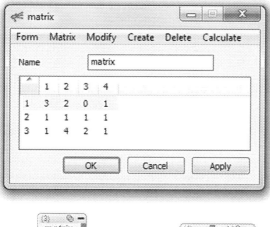

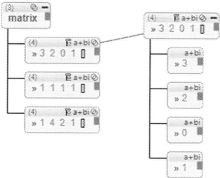

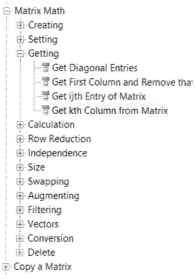

FIGURE 3.30 Matrices Are Modeled as a List of List of Numbers

- Matrix Math
  - Creating
  - Setting
  - Getting
    - Get Diagonal Entries
    - Get First Column and Remove tha┆
    - Get ijth Entry of Matrix
    - Get kth Column from Matrix
  - Calculation
  - Row Reduction
  - Independence
  - Size
  - Swapping
  - Augmenting
  - Filtering
  - Vectors
  - Conversion
  - Delete
- Copy a Matrix

FIGURE 3.31 Matrix Assists in the DRC

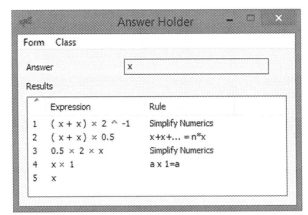

FIGURE 3.32 The Steps Performed in a Symbolic Math Operation

Numerical math

Numerical math models cover root finding, differentiation, integration, ordinary differential equations, and other functions.

Figure 3.33 is the model for Newton's method of root finding.

GRAPHING AND CHARTING

Graphs and charts are created using the Graph class, which was discussed in "Computer Technology" above. The Graph has a list of Display Objects. Display Objects can be plots, histograms, bar charts, and pie charts (Fig. 3.34). These objects are built into the engine. But you can build your own graph because you have control over the creation of individual shapes. Any complex shape can be constructed from the assemblage of the primitive shapes.

DATA ANALYTICS

The Unit Modeler Data Analytics package is a powerful, versatile collection of tools for analyzing data. This analysis includes statistical techniques and discovery techniques for assessing data characteristics and locating patterns within a data set. Data Analytics Runtime is a comprehensive tool in the sense that it can help out at each stage of the process—from data gathering to data preparation to data analysis and display of results. The tool can be used by a novice or an expert. It contains help text aimed at both the beginner and advanced user. It also features a guide that can suggest ways of using the tool on a given data set.

The domains within this area of the library intend to serve two purposes: (a) to provide a library of models to aid in the design of your applications requiring analytics and (b) to provide a comprehensive set of tools to aid people working within this area.

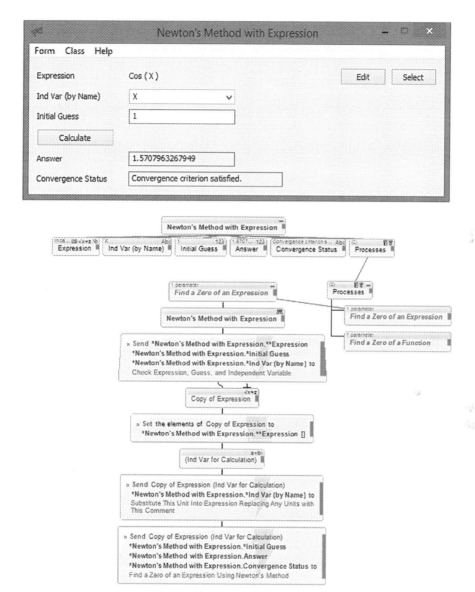

FIGURE 3.33 The Model for Newton's Method

Newton's Method finds the value for an independent variable that results in the expression equaling 0.

Data gathering

To begin your analysis of a data set, you need to get your data into the Unit Modeler. The data gathering portion of the toolbar is dedicated to the task of bringing data into the program (Fig. 3.35). You can import data from a spreadsheet or you can directly

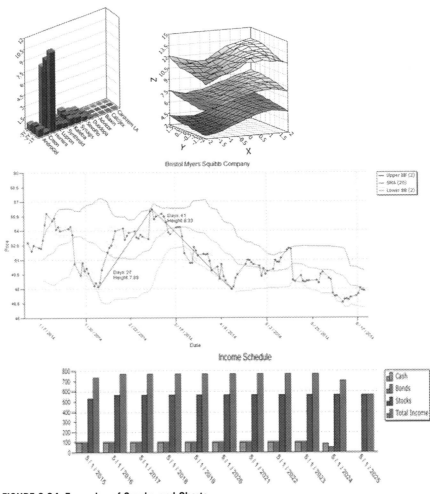

FIGURE 3.34 Examples of Graphs and Charts

FIGURE 3.35 Options for Loading Data to Analyze

connect to a database. The database option brings all of the tools of the Database domain, as discussed in "Computer Technology" above.

Data processing

Before analysis of data can begin, it is a very common task to modify your data set. For example, you may need to add or delete columns, clean certain data entries,

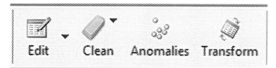

FIGURE 3.36 Options for Manipulating Imported Data

locate outliers (anomalies) in your data set, or restructure your entire data set. The data preparation portion of the toolbar (Fig. 3.36) within the data analytics package is dedicated to these tasks.

Some examples are:

- Editing Data
- Cleansing Data
- Finding Anomalies
- Transformation Data-split, pivot, serialize...
- De-identification and re-identification (Fig. 3.37)

Class converter tool

Class Converter is a tool for converting imported data classes to a specified destination class via attribute conversions that map the original data attributes to destination class attributes.

Merge data tool

Merge Data is a tool for combining two data sets into a single data set. Any two data sets can be combined, as you can specify how attributes (i.e., column headings) of one data set should be mapped to the attributes of the other. Your initial data set can be combined with a second data set by either (a) appending new items to the initial data set or by (b) overwriting data from the additional items onto the initial data set.

Statistics

You can access an entire library of statistic applications by clicking the **Statistics** toolbar button (Fig. 3.38). The first entry in the dropdown, **Statistics tree**, displays a table of contents that you can navigate by traversing the tree of options.

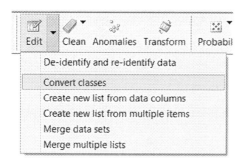

FIGURE 3.37 Options for Editing Data

FIGURE 3.38 The Statistics Toolbar Button

You can navigate the same tree by the other dropdown entries on the **Statistics** button. The statistics applications generally fall into these categories:

- **ANOVA:** The analysis of variance (ANOVA) is a procedure for studying the variation in an observed quantity. This variation is divided into portions that can be attributed to various sources. The goal of ANOVA is to identify important variables that affect the values of an observed quantity.
- **Chi-square:** This section contains some standard statistical tests that make use of a chi-square test statistic. They include a test for goodness of fit and a test for independence.
- **Descriptive statistics:** These applications are concerned with providing a description of your data set by calculating various types of summary statistics. These calculations can range from something as simple as the mean of a list of numbers to a more complicated statistic like the covariance between two columns. Additionally, you can find tools here that allow you to create histograms and bar charts related to the frequency of items in a data list.
- **Normality tests:** These tests provide tools for determining if a given data set representing a sample from a population comes from a population with a normal distribution. The tests include the Jarque-Bera, Anderson-Darling, and Shapiro-Wilk tests.
- **Hypothesis testing:** The idea behind hypothesis testing is to test an assumption made about your data. Such tests usually culminate in the calculation of a p-value. A p-value is a probability that can be helpful in deciding whether to reject or accept your hypothesis.
- **Data manipulation:** This section holds tools for modifying your data. They include more specialized techniques than those that are found in a typical editor.
- **Prediction:** Prediction is the end goal of many statistical studies. Observed data is used to predict outcomes at various states. The outcome may be a continuous variable or a categorical variable. This section includes receiver operating characteristic (ROC) Curve Analysis and Curve Fitting.
- **Regression:** Regression is an important statistical technique that attempts to fit an equation or model to observed data in the best manner possible. Regression is a technique used to make predictions about an unknown outcome variable based on observed values of certain independent variables.
- **Survival analysis:** Survival analysis studies the distribution of survival times. More generally, it is concerned with random variables that measure the time until a certain event occurs. For example, when the event under consideration is death, such a random variable is actually giving survival time, but the event can be any other well-defined event of interest. Survival analysis leads to estimates of survival probabilities, as well as conclusions about what factors affect survival.
- **Multi-trial:** Some tools allow you to select an attribute or set of attributes from your data set. At times, you may be interested in using the tool to try various

configurations of attributes so you can determine the best or most interesting combination. The **Multi-trial** submenu provides access to set of tools that have been created for this purpose.

- **Big data:** In some cases, the amount of information in your data set may be larger than what your computer can hold in memory. If this is the case, you will need to use a big data tool to complete your analysis. The only big data tool currently included calculates basic descriptive statistics of a data set.

Data mining

The **Discovery** toolbar button (Fig. 3.39) provides access to an entire library of data mining applications. These applications can help you identify trends and patterns in your data set. Clicking the **Discovery** button opens a dropdown with many options.

- The Association Rules tool helps you discover relationships between sets of variables. You can use the tool for both discovering predictive rules and as a general data exploration tool to identify data subsets of interest and perform statistical calculations on them.
- You can use the Decision Trees tool to learn sequences of decision boundaries, called decision trees, from data that predict classifications of interest. You can use the resulting decision tree to classify new data.
- You can use the k-Means Clustering tool to identify groups of similar data items, which may indicate patterns in a data set. The clustering tool provides a variety of methods of defining similarity between data items.
- The Naive Bayes tool is a probabilistic classification tool based on applying Bayes' theorem. The model assumes independence among the predicting variables, hence the naive moniker, but it is nonetheless a powerful technique. You can use the resulting classifier to classify new data.

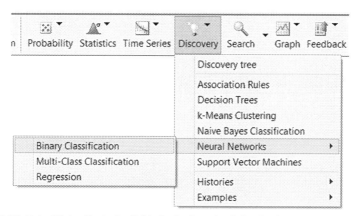

FIGURE 3.39 Data Mining Tools Available in the Data Analytics Package

- The Neural Networks tools can be used to train a machine learning model to learn a function. The function can be a classification function or a mathematical function between numbers. You can make predictions about new data using the trained model.
- You can use the Support Vector Machines (SVMs) tool to train a model to predict a binary classification, such as yes or no, based on variables in your data set. SVMs are a very flexible classifier that can learn a variety of classification functions, through the use of different kernels.
- The Histories submenu gives you access to all of the previous sessions of the tools that you have launched since the Unit Modeler was started. This allows you a quick way to get back to prior work.
- Lastly, the examples submenu provides one example problem for each of the Discovery tools.

Time series

The **Time Series** toolbar button (Fig. 3.40) provides tools for working with time series. A time series is a collection of observations made over time. These observations have a natural order, as each value observed has an associated "time." For the most part, the tools in the **Time Series** toolbar assume that a time series is represented by a column in a data set. It also assumes that the column represents values observed at equally spaced intervals of time. The following tools are available for working with time series:

- **Time series generator:** This tool allows you to create randomly generated time series that can be used in other models or simulations. The starting point is a purely random time series consisting of independent observations from a random variable of your choosing. You can also generate series using moving averages, autocorrelation techniques, or random walks.
- **Linear filters:** A linear filter is a method for transforming one time series into another. A linear filter can be viewed as a sequence of sliding weights that get matched up with points in your original time series to yield new points in the transformed series. A major application of linear filters is smoothing data, but differencing and summing transformations can also be represented as linear filters. The Linear Filters tool allows you to apply various types of filters to your data set to construct new time series columns.
- **Periodogram:** Periodic time series can be decomposed as a sum of sine and cosine waves of various frequencies. Such a decomposition is called a *Fourier series*. The periodogram displays a graph of the intensities of various frequencies that occur in the Fourier decomposition of a time series.

Time Series

FIGURE 3.40 The Time Series Toolbar Button

- **Autocorrelation:** This tool examines the autocorrelation of a time series. Autocorrelation refers to correlation between a given time series and a shift of that same time series by a given lag time. Autocorrelation relates to the question of whether successive terms in a time series are independent or whether current values of the time series generally influence nearby values.
- **Holt-Winters forecasting:** This tool provides a commonly used method for predicting, or forecasting, future values of a given time series. The Holt-Winters method is applicable to time series that show a general linear trend with seasonal variation. A typical application is forecasting the sales of a given product.
- **Durbin-Watson test:** This tool tests the first-order autocorrelation in a time series of residuals. Recognizing nonindependent residuals is important because the assumption of independent errors is an essential prerequisite to many other statistical tests. Sometimes adjustments can be made to correct for nonindependent errors. The Durbin-Watson test helps with the detection of nonindependent errors in a time series regression.
- **Fast Fourier transform:** This tool provides a method for computing the Fourier transform of a data set using a Cooley-Tukey algorithm. The tool shows a graph of the modulus of each term of the transformed series.

Spreadsheets

Spreadsheets are a very common and useful way to present data. A spreadsheet consists of rows and column. Usually the columns have labels and represent a certain type of data, for example, number, text, and date. Each row represents a new set of data. The individual elements are called cells. Cells can be assigned an equation which sets its value equal to some function of the other cells.

A spreadsheet is modeled as a list of class instances. The most common class used to model a spreadsheet is the data class (Fig. 3.41).

In addition to a list of Items, the Data class adds a description attribute, a base class, File Location and a set of processes to perform common functions.

This class is reused often. The Import tool will load information from a spreadsheet and create a Data class. All of the statistics and other analytic tools use the Data class to represent the data they work on.

The Base Class is the base class for each of the items in the list. It is convenient to have this class held in a specific attribute.

Because a spreadsheet is modeled as lists of classes, all of the assists for lists also apply to a spreadsheet model.

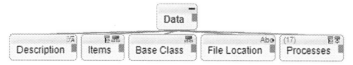

FIGURE 3.41 The Data Class Used for Importing Data

PUBLIC CONTRIBUTION

KeLabs, the developer of the Unit Modeler technology, is a supporter of the goal of the Subject Library and will facilitate it any way it can.

How do I make my domains public? You can make your domains available to others by creating a workspace for your domains. You have all of the configuration options that are allowed by Unit Modeler Workspaces. One configuration should meet your needs. If you want to require a fee for your workspace, then you can setup the workspace membership accordingly.

We cannot all be completely altruistic and provide everything for free to a public sphere of content. Sometimes we all must charge for the use of our wares. The public sphere does include fee-based content. Workspaces supports the distribution of models both for free and for pay. Those who contribute to both will be recognized for their contributions, which will promote their commercial products.

The Unit Modeler Development environment

4

The Unit Modeler Development environment (Fig. 4.1) is an application within which you build models with the Information Unit model language. The Development package provides all the tools to create models. Interestingly, these tools are themselves models and are built upon the Unit Model language.

The development environment is a highly visual and interactive software development toolkit with a "point-and-click" and guided user experience to enable a much broader range of users to develop information-based software applications, with or without programming experience. The learning curve is very low, and its "one-stop shop" Development Resource Center is complemented by online tutorials, example problems and a robust help system that explains every click. A component-based architecture and library of reusable components enables rapid development.

TOOLBAR

The toolbar is the bar containing icons under the application menu. The content of the application menu is controlled by the toolbar attribute of the Unit Modeler ISDE (Intelligent Software Development Environment) Class.

When logging into the Unit Modeler ISDE, a domain named Development Menus sets up the development menu structure. The development toolbar is broken into categories:

Page Navigation

⇐ ▾ ⇒ ▾ Navigate forward and backward through Pages shown on the whiteboard

Creating Structures

Create a new domain

Create a new class

Create a new process

Create a new object

Create a new unit

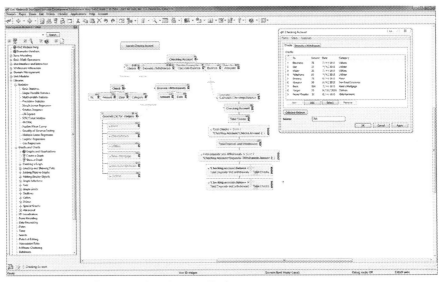

FIGURE 4.1 The Unit Modeler Development Environment

The Checkbook Application model is shown in the Whiteboard with the Development Resource Center docked on the left.

Editing Units and Structures

✂ Cut selected units

📋 Copy selected units

📋 Paste units to the Whiteboard

✕ Delete selected units

↩ Undo last action

↪ Redo the last undo

☑ Clear selected units

⬛ Encapsulate selected steps

Tools and Utilities

🏠 Opens the Development Resource Center

🔍 Opens up the searching tool

📃 Show a form control to Whiteboard

Enterprise Tools

📝 Open the message center

📋 Submit defects and features

Other

 Open the help system

Subitems: View help, Examples database

 Change the current library

APPLICATION MENU

The application menu is the menu at the top of the Unit Modeler ISDE window. When logging into the Unit Modeler ISDE, a domain named Development Menus sets up the development menu structure. The exact contents of the menu will vary depending upon various factors, however, the following items are currently presented to all users.

- **Domain:** contains items that allow you to log in or out of a server, load and save domains, open up commonly used dialogs, or exit the program.
- **Pages:** displays all the available pages of the domains that are loaded.
- **Zoom:** allows you to control the zoom level of the Whiteboard.
- **Edit:** includes cut, copy, paste, delete.
- **Utilities:** access to commonly used tools and preference settings.
- **Libraries:** access the libraries that have been developed such as statistics and discovery.
- **Applications:** access the enterprise applications. These will only be operational for enterprise installations with private servers.
- **Help:** access the help system and examples database.

WHITEBOARD

The main application window is the workbench area for creating models. Because it acts as an electronic whiteboard for the modeling process, it is referred to as the Whiteboard. On the Whiteboard, you can view and edit all of the structures that define a model. You can save pages of the Whiteboard so you may get back to a previous Whiteboard configuration.

WHITEBOARD BASICS

Clearing the whiteboard

You can clear the Whiteboard by right-clicking anywhere on the Whiteboard and selecting **Hide All**. This hides all of the units that are displayed on the Whiteboard (it does not delete them). You can get back to hidden units using the List All dialog.

Moving units

You can move units on the Whiteboard by left-clicking and dragging on their grab bar. Moving units moves the entire structure around the Whiteboard. For example, moving an attribute of a class moves the entire class.

Cursor location

A crosshairs on the Whiteboard indicates the position where the next unit or structure will appear on the Whiteboard. You can change the cursor location by left-clicking on the new location within the Whiteboard.

Zoom in/zoom out

The Whiteboard can be magnified or demagnified. This feature is available through the Zoom menu item in the application menu or by holding shift and using the mouse wheel.

Panning the whiteboard

The Whiteboard is not limited to the viewable portion of the screen. It extends indefinitely in all directions. There are four ways to navigate around the Whiteboard.

- Using the mouse wheel to scroll. Holding control allows you to scroll to the left and right.
- Using the vertical and horizontal scrollbars at the top and bottom of the Whiteboard.
- Dragging unit displays to the edge of the screen. The view of the Whiteboard moves in the direction of the dragged unit.
- Right-clicking on the Whiteboard and switching your cursor to the **Move** tool. Doing so will allow you to left-click and drag the Whiteboard in any direction.

RIGHT-CLICK MENU

The Whiteboard's right-click menu (Fig. 4.2) is accessed by right-clicking anywhere in the Whiteboard.

The first section deals with creating new information units. When the units are created, they go in the working Domain and are displayed at the Whiteboard's insertion point.

Create class... Creates a unit on the whiteboard that represents a class.
Create class in Class Designer... This option is a unit on the whiteboard that represents a class and opens up Class Designer for this unit.
Create process... Opens Process Designer.
Create object... Opens Object Designer.
Create unit... Creates a new information unit.

Paste Pastes the copied units to the Whiteboard.

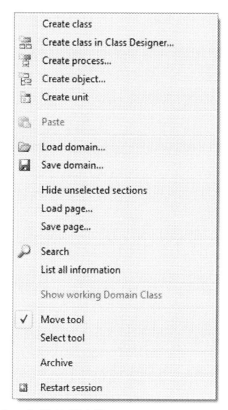

FIGURE 4.2 The Whiteboard's Right-Click Menu

Load domain Shows the file open dialog for selecting a local domain to load.
Save domain Lists the loaded domains and saves the domain selected.

***

Hide unselected selections Hides all information units currently displayed on
the Whiteboard.
Load page... Loads a page. Prompts the user to identify the page (and the
domain of the page) to load
Save page... Saves a page. Prompts the user to identify the page (and the
domain of the page) to save.

***

Search Shows the Unit Search dialog.
List all information Shows the List All dialog.

***

Show working Domain Class Shows the domain class for the domain that is
currently set as the working domain.

***

Move tool If this option is checked, then then clicking and holding down the left mouse button will move the whiteboard. The right button will be used to select items on the Whiteboard.

Select tool If this option is checked, then then clicking and holding down the right mouse button will move the Whiteboard. The left button will be used to select items on the Whiteboard.

Archive Creates a backup copy of all domains in the local domains directory and places them into an archive directory that is automatically created and named with the current date and time.

Restart session Clears all information units from the system. If you are logged in to the server, your default domain is automatically reloaded upon restart.

PAGES

A page is a saved layout of a Whiteboard. You can use pages to take a "snap shot" of your workspace and return to it later. Additionally, you can use these pages to present portions of your work to others, much in the manner of a slide show or presentation tool. In addition to unit displays, a page can contain formatted text, buttons, and graphics. A presentation developed using pages in the Unit Modeler can be very effective, especially when the presentation requires interactive elements and use of Application Models.

Pages can be managed via the Pages attribute of the Domain Class belonging to a domain. Each page in a domain is represented via a Page class instance in the Pages attribute. These Page class instances can be renamed, reordered, and deleted.

Loading a page

Pages can be loaded (Fig. 4.3) using the Application Menu Pages. Navigate to this menu, find the page you wish to load, and select that page. There is also an operator to load a page using a Page class.

Saving

To save a page, right-click on the Whiteboard and select **Save Page...** (Fig. 4.4). The Unit Modeler prompts you select the domain this page belongs to and enter the name of the page. If you have saved this page previously, then you can select the name of the page from the bottom dropdown.

Default pages

Whenever a domain is loaded via the **Load Domain** menu or toolbar option, a default page is loaded. The default page for a domain is stored in the Default Page attribute of the Domain Class belonging to the domain. If no default page is set, loading the domain will not load a page.

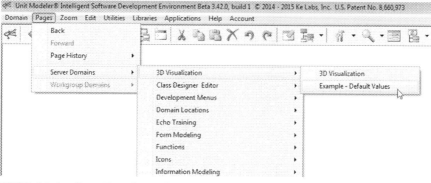

FIGURE 4.3 Loading a Page from a Server Domain

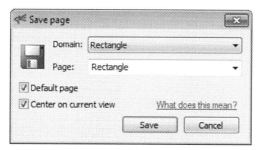

FIGURE 4.4 Right-Click on the Whiteboard to Bring Up the Save Page Form

DISPLAY OF UNITS IN THE WHITEBOARD

Information units are the single data structure in the Unit Modeler ISDE. Even though there is a single definition of a unit, there is more than one way in which the Unit Modeler ISDE displays units. The standard display is the most common and provides a convenient interface for a developer to edit and define a unit. The other modes of display serve other purposes depending upon what the unit represents.

Standard unit display

Units shown to the Whiteboard have various interactive regions that contain and display different types of information (Fig. 4.5). Unit interaction occurs with both the left-clicks and right-clicks of the mouse. Left-clicking a unit allows you to update a unit or grab the unit to be moved. Each unit also has an interactive right-click menu. This menu allows you to show a form, modify the unit's contents, and save the domain the unit belongs to. All units have some right-click options in common; however, there are some options that are specific to certain units. For instance, only in a process can you add a true step.

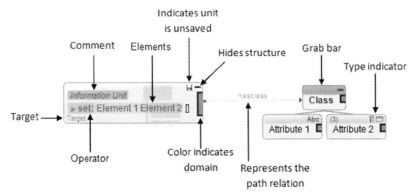

FIGURE 4.5 Diagram Identifying All of the Features of the Unit Display

Grab bar

At the top of many units there is a bar called the *grab bar*. This bar informs you when there are any elements stored within this unit. If there is only one element in the unit, the grab bar displays the name of the element. If the unit contains more than one element, the number of elements is displayed in parentheses. Icons on the right hand side of the grab bar are used to display information about the type of the unit.

Hiding

The Whiteboard may become cluttered with many units and structures as you go about building your model. To free up real estate on the Whiteboard, click the "–" in the upper right-hand corner of a unit. By clicking this "–" you are simply hiding the unit from the Whiteboard, not deleting the unit.

Comment

Every information unit has a section that can be used to insert a comment. Unit comments should be informative to the extent that another user can read a comment on a unit and understand that unit's purpose.

Operator

On the left side of an information unit, there is a symbol >>. By clicking on this symbol, you can change the operator for the unit. Initially when a unit is created, its operator is defaulted to the fact operator. Fact units are meant to contain information, which in the Unit Modeler is either unit(s) or text characters.

Elements

Information units can be used to contain either other information units or a character string. When an information unit contains something, the thing(s) being contained are referred to as elements.

Target

Units can be referenced through a target, which is also referred to as a *target alias*. The target alias of a unit is displayed in the lower left hand corner of the unit and is only shown if one of the following criteria is met:

- The target alias is set to a nonempty string.
- The unit is a copy or create step in a process.
- The unit is an import step that contains less than 4 elements.

Domain indicator

The color of the diamond on the right side of a unit indicates the domain the unit is in. Only local domains have a color associated with them. Server domains are always shown with a gray background.

Save icon

Unsaved units will appear with a save icon on the right side of the grab bar. Clicking this save icon will prompt you to save the domain in which the unit is located.

Tooltips

You can hover the cursor over any part of the Unit Display to get specific help about that component of the unit display. During debugging, you can hover over any element to see what its value is.

Display modes

The lower right-hand corner contains an arrow that allows you to toggle the *display mode* of a unit. There are two display modes:

- **Natural Language**—natural language mode explains the operation of a unit in a sentence.
- **Full Form**—the full form simply shows all the elements of an information unit.

Other unit display modes

Button

Sometimes it is useful to display a process as a button (Fig. 4.6).

Left-clicking on the button immediately runs the process associated with it. You can display a process as a button by right-clicking on a process and selecting **Display as button**. You can move the button around the Whiteboard by left-clicking on it and dragging it to a new location.

Process Displayed as Button

FIGURE 4.6 A Process Can Be Displayed as a Button on the Whiteboard

Clicking on the button will shock the process.

FIGURE 4.7 A Unit Displayed as a Note on the Whiteboard

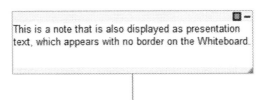

FIGURE 4.8 A Unit Displayed as Both a Note and as Presentation Text on the Whiteboard

FIGURE 4.9 A Unit Displayed as a Bitmap on the Whiteboard

Formatted note

Units that contain RTF text can be displayed as a formatted note (Fig. 4.7). A common use for a formatted note is the note placed on a process.

Presentation text

Presentation text is a method of displaying a formatted comment without displaying the border around the text (Fig. 4.8).

Bitmap

Images can be displayed on the Whiteboard (Fig. 4.9). This is often useful when creating presentations in the Unit Modeler.

Unit right-click menu

The unit context menu (Fig. 4.10) is used to perform various actions on units. This menu is controlled by the unit menu attribute of the Unit Modeler Class.

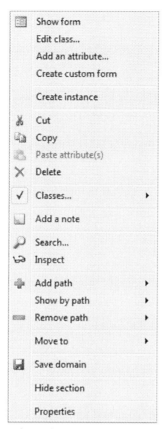

FIGURE 4.10 The Whiteboard's Right-Click Menu

When logging into the Unit Modeler Development Environment, a domain named Development Menus sets up the development menu structure. Unit menus are the most context sensitive of all menus; the menu changes based on the type of unit (class, step, attribute, and so forth). It also changes depending upon whether the domain was loaded from the server or your local drive.

Element context menu

The element context menu (Fig. 4.11) is used to edit the elements of an information unit. It displays in two situations: when a user is editing an existing element and when a user is inserting a new element via the insertion handle.

FIGURE 4.11 A Unit with a List of Numbers

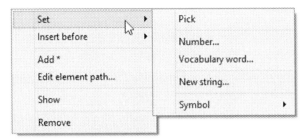

FIGURE 4.12 The Set Menu and Submenu

Existing element context menu

Right-clicking on an existing element displays a context menu that allows you to edit, replace, or insert an element before the element that was clicked on. Figure 4.12 shows the context menu displayed when right-clicking an element.

Right-clicking on the 13 in Figure 4.11 brings up this menu:

- **Set**—The **Set** submenu replaces the element with one of the selected options:
  - **Pick**—Puts the Unit Modeler in selection mode, allowing you to select something from the Whiteboard or from a form.
  - **Number**—Displays a list of System Vocabulary numbers. You can select a number from this list to insert into the element slot.
  - **Vocabulary word...**—Displays a list of all System Vocabulary units. You can select a unit from this list to insert into the element slot.
  - **New string...**—Prompts you to enter in a text string. Once you hit OK in the prompt dialog, a unit containing the string is created (in the same domain as the unit the string unit is inserted into) and inserted into the element slot. The string unit is also placed in the "Strings" attribute of the domain class corresponding to the domain the string unit was created in.
  - **Symbol**—Displays another menu which allows you to select commonly used symbols (found in System Vocabulary).
- **Insert before**—The **Insert before** submenu inserts an element before the element that was clicked on. It contains the same options as the set menu.
- **Add ***—Adds a star in front of the element.
- **Remove ***—Removes a star from the front of an element.
- **Virtual types**—Allows you to change an element to a virtual element (or from a virtual element to a nonvirtual element).
- **Edit element path...**—Shows a dialog that allows you to textually edit the element path of an element.
- **Show**—Shows the base of the element to the Whiteboard. This menu item may sometimes appear as two different menu options: **Show Base** and **Show Destination**. For additional information about these menu items, refer to "Show Base vs. Show Destination" below.
- **Remove**—Remove the specified element from the element list (at the element slot).

FIGURE 4.13 A Unit with a List of Numbers and the Insertion Handle

FIGURE 4.14 The Right-Click Menu That Opens When the [] Character in Figure 4.13 Is Clicked

Insertion handle context menu. Figure 4.13 shows the insertion handle context menu.

Right-clicking on the element insertion handle (the [] at the end of a unit's elements) displays a context menu (Fig. 4.14) that allows you to append to the unit's elements.

This menu, similar to the **Set** submenu of the existing element context menu, contains the following options:

- **Pick**—Puts the Unit Modeler in selection mode, allowing you to select something from the Whiteboard or from a form.
- **Number**—Displays a list of System Vocabulary numbers. You can select a number from this list to insert into the element slot.
- **Vocabulary word...**—Displays a list of all System Vocabulary units. You can select a unit from this list to insert into the element slot.
- **New string...**—Prompts you to enter in a text string. Once you hit OK in the prompt dialog, a unit containing the string is created (in the same domain as the unit the string unit is inserted into) and inserted into the element slot. The string unit is also placed in the "Strings" attribute of the domain class corresponding to the domain the in which the string unit was created.
- **Symbol**—Displays another menu which allows you to select commonly used symbols (found in System Vocabulary).

Show Base vs. Show Destination. Right-clicking on a complex element while in debug mode will often produce two different "Show" options in the element context menu: **Show Base** and **Show Destination** (Fig. 4.15).

Because a complex element *indirectly* refers to another unit (or units), it has two properties:

1. A *base*: This is the unit from which the complex element was initialized. It is always the first unit listed in the complex element path. Thus, the base of the complex element School.*Students.Average GPA would be the School class unit.

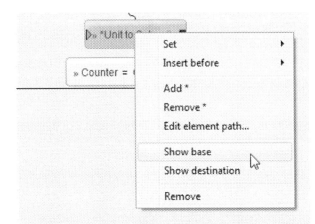

FIGURE 4.15 The Show Base and Show Destination Options Are Useful While Debugging Your Application

2. A *destination*: This is the unit or units which the complex element references. Thus, the destination of the complex element School.*Students.Average GPA would be the GPA attribute units of all of the Student classes in the School (i.e., a list of numeric units).

If we consider the process shown above, showing the base and the destination units could result in the process shown in Figure 4.16.

Warnings on units

A yellow warning (⚠) indicates a potential design flaw in the step's overall structure. For example, in the process shown in Figure 4.17, the remove step displays with a warning because it has both true and false steps stemming from it. Why is this incorrect? Recall that the remove operator removes everything it *can remove* and will

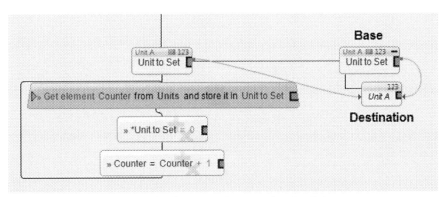

FIGURE 4.16 The Base and Destination Shown for the Unit to Set Unit

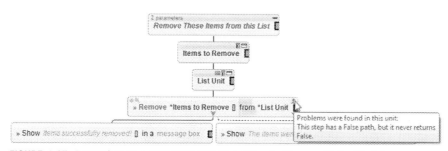

FIGURE 4.17 A Warning on a Step Indicates Something Is Wrong with the Model

never return false, even if the items it is instructed to remove from a list do not appear in the list at all. Thus, the false path from the remove step shown in Figure 4.17 will never be taken.

To understand why a warning appears on a unit, hover over the yellow warning triangle until a small dialog box appears. This dialog box should explain why the warning is present.

Unit shapes

A **rectangular** shape indicates that when shocked, the step can only return true.

A **trapezoidal** (slanted sides) shape indicates that when shocked, the step can return either true or false.

Consider the processes shown in Figure 4.18:

- The gettext step (Show a text entry dialog...) in the process "Is [User Input] Divisible by 5?" is *trapezoidal*. If the user clicks **OK** on the text-getting dialog, the step returns true. If the user clicks **Cancel** or **X**, the step will return false.
- The step in "Is [User Input] Divisible by 5?" that shocks "Is this Number Divisible by 5?" is *trapezoidal*. The process "Is this Number Divisible by 5?" can return either true or false.
- The step in "Is this Number Divisible by 5?" that calculates the quotient and remainder of a division is *rectangular*. This step will always return true, regardless of the numbers it calculates.

Colors

A major benefit of using the Unit Modeler is the way that it visually displays units. The way that a unit and its elements display can tell you a lot of information about the unit. Is the unit a class? Are its elements valid? Is a step structured correctly?

Comment display

The style and color of a unit's comment can be used to visually identify important information about the unit. Figure 4.19 is a key for identifying unit properties via the unit comment's style and color:

FIGURE 4.18 Trapezoidal Shapes Indicate the Step Is a Decision Step and Can Return True or False

Text Color	+	Text Style	=	Unit Property
Black		*Italics*		Independent unit (not part of a process, class, etc.)
				Note: unit might/could be part of a list or an object
Red		***Bold italics***		Process
Blue		(none)		Step in a process
Blue		**Bold**		Parameter in a process
Dark Blue		**Bold**		Class/class instance
Black		(none)		Attribute of a class

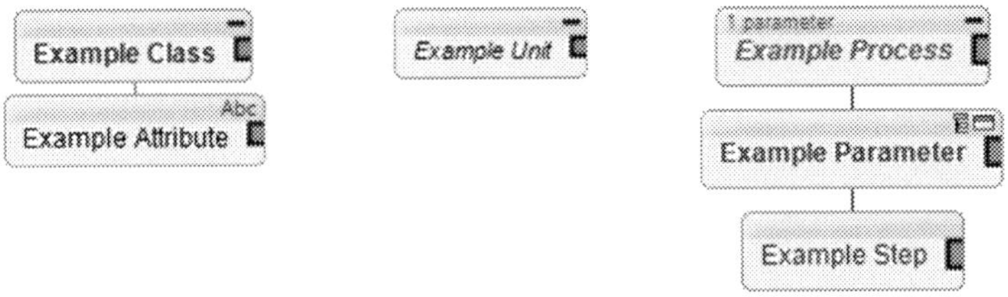

FIGURE 4.19 Color Displays for a Class, Unit, Process, and Steps

Text Color	+	Text Style	=	Element Property
Blue		(none)		Independent unit, step, attribute
				Note: any nonclass, nonprocess unit displays as blue
Red		(none)		Process
Dark blue		(none)		Class/class instance

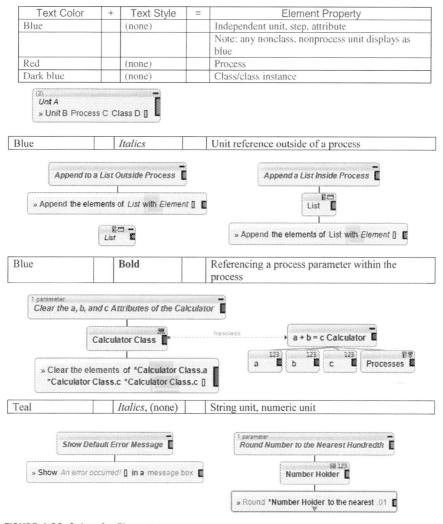

| Blue | | Italics | | Unit reference outside of a process |

| Blue | | **Bold** | | Referencing a process parameter within the process |

| Teal | | Italics, (none) | | String unit, numeric unit |

FIGURE 4.20 Colors for Elements

Element display

The style and color of a unit's elements can be used to visually identify important information about the elements. Figure 4.20 is a key for extracting information via an element's style and color:

Additional element display properties. **Gray, squiggly underlining** indicates an element that the Unit Modeler detects as having a possible mismatch in typing. For example, if we look at the units shown in Figure 4.21, Unit A, which is typed as a number, contains **Unit B, which appears with gray, squiggly underlining. This is because Unit B is typed to hold a unit, the contents of which could be anything. In

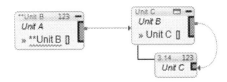

FIGURE 4.21

Grey squiggly lines under an element indicate that there might be an issue with the element, but there is not enough information for the engine to know definitively.

this case, Unit B contains Unit C, which, in turn, contains a number, so the element **Unit B in Unit A is in fact valid. But because the unit held in Unit B can change, and Unit B is not limited to hold only units containing numbers, the Unit Modeler cannot definitively deduce that **Unit B will reference a number. (Note: It also cannot definitively deduce that **Unit B will *not* reference a number.)

Red, squiggly underlining, indicates that the Unit Modeler detects a definite mismatch in typing in the element. For example, if we look at the last step in the process shown in Figure 4.22, *Student is underlined in red because the lowercase operator expects a unit typed to contain text. *Student references the class passed into the Student parameter of the process. If *Student is changed to *Student.Name, the red, squiggly underline will disappear.

Unit color

The background color and shading of a unit tells you various things about the unit (Fig. 4.23):

- If a unit has a **yellow background**, this indicates that unit is in the <> domain. Recall that units in this domain cannot be saved.
- Units with a **gray background** are units in a user-created or domain-created domain. To see the name of the domain a unit is housed in, hover over the unit's grab bar. A small dialog containing the unit's domain should appear.
- If a unit has a **faint green background** (or highlight), this indicates that the unit is currently highlighted by the user's cursor.

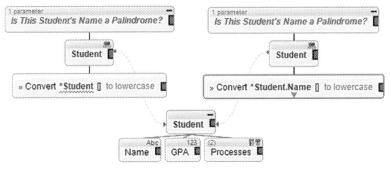

FIGURE 4.22

A red squiggly line under an element indicates that there is an issue with the element. The Convert step expects a text element (*Student.*Name not a class *Student).

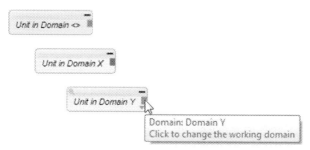

FIGURE 4.23 Background Colors of Unit Displays Indicate Various Information About the Unit

LINES BETWEEN UNITS AND STRUCTURES

Lines between units indicate that there is a relationship between the two units. The Unit Modeler represents relationships though paths.

Relationships can exist between all types of units. Table 4.1 is a sample list of unit pairs and examples of the relations that exist between them.

Except for the solid red line that indicates two units are the same, lines indicate that there is a relationship between two units. Table 4.2 indicates line colors and the relation they represent:

HIGHLIGHTING UNITS ON THE WHITEBOARD

Highlighting units is useful in many circumstances:

- Hiding sections of units
- Moving units on the Whiteboard

Table 4.1 The Example Relations That Can Exist Between Various Types of Units

Unit Pair	Relation
class–class	hascustomform, isinstanceof
class–attribute	hasattribute
attribute–class	hasparentclass
process–step	>
step–step	>, !>
attribute–object	hasconstraintlist

Table 4.2 The Meaning Behind Various Line Colors on the Whiteboard

Line Color	Relation
Solid red	Two units are the same
Solid blue	iselementof
Solid green	hasattribute
Dotted green	isinstanceof
Dotted purple	hasclass
Dotted turquoise	Other paths

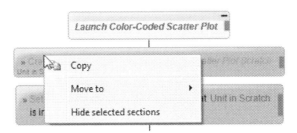

FIGURE 4.24 The Right-Click Menu for Units That Are Highlighted

- Cut/Copy/Paste operations
- Moving selected units to a new domain

You can select units in two ways:

1. You can hold down the Control key and left-click on a unit. You may select as many units as you want.
2. You can right-click on the Whiteboard and drag the mouse cursor. All units within the bounding rectangle of the drag toggle their selection state as you draw and redraw over them. (If the Select Tool is checked within the whiteboard right-click menu, then selecting units will be performed by a left-click and drag.)

Selected units are drawn with a blue background color. When you right-click on any of the highlighted units, a special menu pop ups (Figs. 4.24 and 4.25).

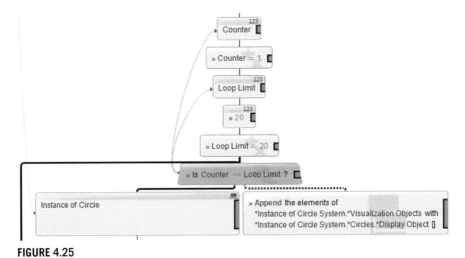

FIGURE 4.25

Selecting a single unit in a process (a step) shows the paths into and out of this unit with bold lines. Additional lines appear that show other units within the process that reference this unit or are referenced by this unit.

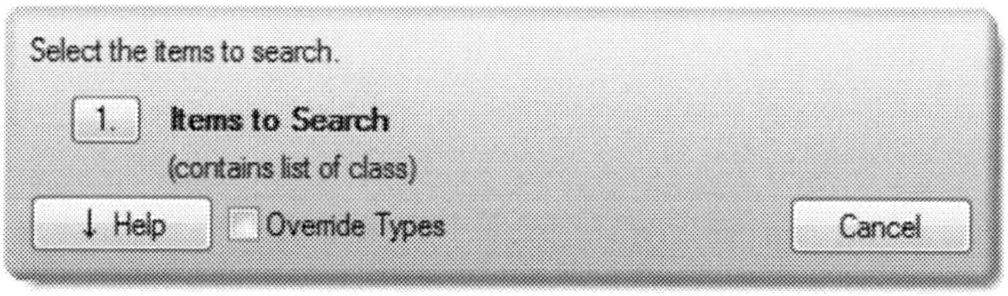

FIGURE 4.26 Form Shown When the Application Is in Selection Mode

The form has a message indicating what to select and other information.

SELECTING UNITS

Selecting items is a common task within all Unit Modeler applications. There are many occasions where you will need to do this while you are developing a model. You might be working in the Whiteboard directly clicking on Unit Displays, or you might be running an assist or a tool from the DRC (Development Resource Center).

Regardless of what the source of the selection prompt is, once you are requested to select a unit, the Modeler will go into selection mode. The Modeler will also provide guidance to you in various ways through its built in Smart Selection technology.

Selection mode

When the Unit Modeler asks you to select something, it enters selection mode. The toolbars gray out and the form below (Fig. 4.26) is shown in the upper left hand corner of the screen.

The program stays in selection mode until you either select or dismiss the selection dialog by clicking **Cancel**. You can select units either from the whiteboard or by selecting a control on a form. Units that make sense for you to select will be highlighted in some way. All others will be grayed out. The Unit Modeler employs a technology called Smart Selection that only allows you to make selections that are appropriate to what you are selecting.

In Figure 4.27, we have an application and a separately imported spreadsheet of data. The Basic Statistics application has a Data List attribute, which is a list of numbers. The Select button allows you to select these numbers. After clicking on this button, the Modeler will go into selection mode. All units that are numbers are highlighted. You can hold the Control key and select as many as you want to be in the list.

It is a unique property of the Unit Modeler that when in selection mode, you can select a unit from the whiteboard, from within a grid, or by clicking on their visual representation in a form.

Columns in the spreadsheet are also highlighted (Fig. 4.28) because they represent a list of numbers. If you select the column header, then all of the cells in that column will be added to the list. When hovering the cursor over a particular cell, it changes to green to indicate that it can be selected. The edit controls within the Basic Statistics form itself are also highlighted as they, too, are numbers that can be selected. When hovering over a column heading, the entire column is highlighted in green. You can hold the Control key to make multiple selections.

FIGURE 4.27 Certain Display Controls Represent Units

For example, the edit control for the sum represents the sum attribute on the Basic Statistics class. If you select this control, you will actually be selecting the unit it represents.

Cylinders	Displacement	Horsepower	Weight	Acceleration
8	307	130	3,504	12
8	350	Select Displacement from all rows		
8	318	150	3,436	11
8	304	150	3,433	12
8	302	140	3,449	10.5
8	429	198	4,341	10
8	454	220	4,354	9
8	440	215	4,312	8.5
8	455	225	4,425	10
8	390	190	3,850	8.5

FIGURE 4.28 Within a Spreadsheet, You May Select Several Items

You can select the entire spreadsheet, a column, a row or a particular cell. The items that are selected are visually identified.

Smart selection

Whenever you are required to select a unit, the Modeler goes into *selection mode*.

If units have been typed properly, the Selection tool provides visual indication of what units may be selected either on the Whiteboard or on a form.

Units whose types conflict with the type of the unit being selected for are grayed out. Units that have the appropriate type remain displayed as usual. Units representing classes that have selectable attributes appear with a blue triangle in their lower left hand corner. When you hover over one of these units, a list of suggested potential selections appear in a new window.

In Figure 4.29, the user wants to fill the last element of the "a = b + c" step in Calculate TV Show Values. This element position is meant to hold a number. The Selection tool knows the user is looking for a number and therefore (a) shows a list of numbers for convenience (dialog box to the right), (b) grays out all units that are not numbers, and (c) places a triangle in the lower left-hand corner of TV Show and TV Episode, which have numeric attributes.

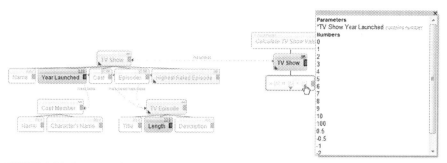

FIGURE 4.29 Example of Smart Selection

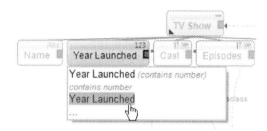

FIGURE 4.30

Options presented by Smart Selection when selecting a number and hovering over a class unit that has number attributes.

There are five units that Smart Selection suggests are reasonable to be selected from the class structure: TV Show, Year Launched, Highest Rated Episode, TV Episode, and Length. When you hover over any selectable unit, a popup window appears with the complex element choices for that unit that make sense given the selection type. Figures 4.30 to 4.34 are the popup windows for each of the five selectable complex elements in this example.

1. Year Launched (Fig. 4.30):
2. TV Show (Fig. 4.31):

FIGURE 4.31

Options presented by Smart Selection when selecting a number and hovering over a class unit that has number attributes.

FIGURE 4.32

Options presented by Smart Selection when selecting a number and hovering over a class attribute whose defining class has number attributes.

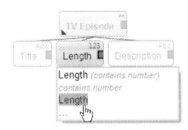

FIGURE 4.33

Options presented by Smart Selection when selecting a number and hovering over a class attribute whose defining class has number attributes.

    a. Select Year Launched "indirectly" from the TV Show class
    b. Select Length "indirectly" from the TV Show class
3. Highest Rated Episode (Fig. 4.32):
4. Length (Fig. 4.33):
5. TV Episode (Fig. 4.34):

All of these selections are technically valid. But because the Calculate TV Show Values passes a TV Show class as its parameter, you most likely want to select a numeric value via the parameter.

FIGURE 4.34

Options presented by smart selection when selecting a number and hovering over a class with a number attribute.

THE DEVELOPMENT RESOURCE CENTER

The DRC is a one-stop shop for finding resources that will aid you in developing models. The DRC (Fig. 4.35) contains assists, tools, help articles and links to pages. The DRC is accessible via the development package toolbar 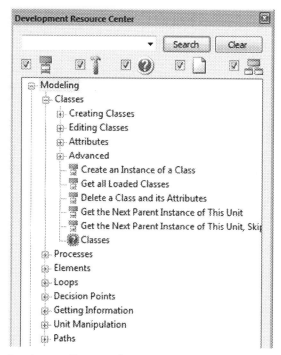.

ASSISTS

Assists are a collection of tools that, when applied, automatically add steps to processes based on user input. There are two reasons why you might want to use assists to do your process modeling:

1. Assists save you a great deal of time because they help you make the right decisions in selecting "input" for each of your process steps. Also, Assists perform many tasks for you, including creating units, adding paths, typing units, and setting operators, elements, and comments.
2. All models built in the Unit Modeler are reusable. A large number of utilities have been developed. Using Assists is the most efficient way to find, learn of, and apply all of the capabilities of these utilities and knowledge. The library of Assists is logically organized enabling easy navigation.

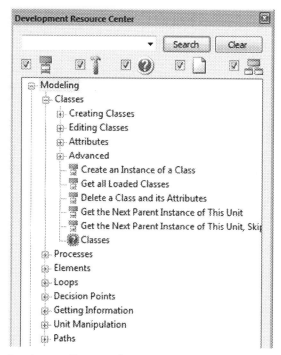

FIGURE 4.35 The Development Resource Center

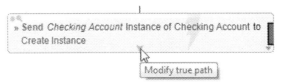

FIGURE 4.36 Click on the Down Arrow to Bring Up a Menu with Options

Assists help you create lists, classes, domains, processes, and other core elements of models. Several library domains have sets of Assists that enable their incorporation into any other model. If you launch the DRC, you'll find hundreds of commonly used assists, along with several assist libraries, which contain assists of various subjects.

Using assists

Assists can be accessed via the toolbar. You can explore the categories of assists in the tree and view help on each item by clicking **Help** at the bottom of the form. To apply an assist, do the following:

1. Left-click on the insertion arrow at the bottom of the step you want to insert steps below (Fig. 4.36). The insertion arrow of a step appears in **orange**. Some steps will have two insertion arrows: a true arrow and a false arrow. If you want to add new steps via the true exit path of a step, select the true arrow (left). If you want to add new steps via the false exit path of a step, select the false arrow (right).
2. Once you left-click on the insertion arrow of your choice, select **Open DRC** (Fig. 4.37). This will perform two tasks for you: (a) set the step and insertion logic (true or false) of the insertion point (where new steps will be added) and (b) launch the DRC tree and set the resource type to assist.

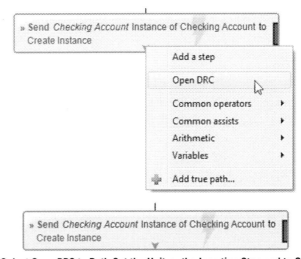

FIGURE 4.37 Select Open DRC to Both Set the Unit as the Insertion Step and to Open Up the DRC

Add step to true path   **Add step to false path**

FIGURE 4.38 Steps That Can Return True or False Have Two Down Arrows

One is for the True step and one is for the False step.

3. Find the assist you need. You can do this by perusing the index of the assist tree or by typing in key words to search on at the top of the assist form.
4. Once you find the assist you want, view the help on it to ensure that you understand what it will do and what step(s) it will/may add.
5. Click apply on the assist and follow the directions.

Insertion point

When a step of a process displays with an **orange border** around it, this indicates that the step is the current *insertion point* (also called the *insertion step*). The insertion point is the step below which new steps get added when an assist is applied.

The insertion step can be selected by hovering over the bottom, middle arrow(s) of a step in a process. You should observe that a faint orange outline will appear around the unit, which indicates that you can set the unit as the new insertion step. Once set, the orange outline appears much thicker, which indicates that the step is now the insertion step.

To set the step as the insertion point, left-click on the arrow with the correct exit logic and select **Open DRC.**

Steps that can return either True or False will have two arrows displayed on the bottom. Steps that can only return True will have just one arrow. When a step displays both arrows, you can select the left arrow to indicate that the next step(s) added by an assist should be connected to the insertion step via a true path. If you select the right arrow, the next step(s) added by an Assist will be connected via a false path.

If the step is a decision point and can return a false value, then it will have two arrows at the bottom of the unit display. Select the left arrow to add a step off the true path and the right arrow to add a step off the false path (Fig. 4.38).

WORKING WITH STRUCTURES

Ultimately, modeling is the act of creating the structures that make up the model. So we will jump right in to seeing how units, classes, objects, and processes are built. You will be introduced to three of the main tools of the Unit Modeler: Class Editor, Process Editor, and Attribute Editor. You will also see how to interact with units in the Whiteboard.

INFORMATION UNITS

The information unit is the fundamental data structure of the Unit Model. All structures are composed of units. Units consist of a comment, elements, operator, and paths.

Setting the comment

To set or edit a unit's comment, hover over the comment text until the *text select cursor* appears. A small dialog should appear that reads *Edit comment*. Left-click to edit the comment. Once you have finished editing, press ENTER or click outside the unit to exit the edit mode.

If a unit has no comment but one or more elements, the field that allows you to click to edit the comment disappears. To reshow this field, change the display mode to expanded. The comment field should immediately reappear.

Comments on units can be changed or retrieved via the setcomment and getcomment operators.

Setting the operator

Left-click the >> symbols on the unit display. A dropdown menu of operators appears (Fig. 4.39).

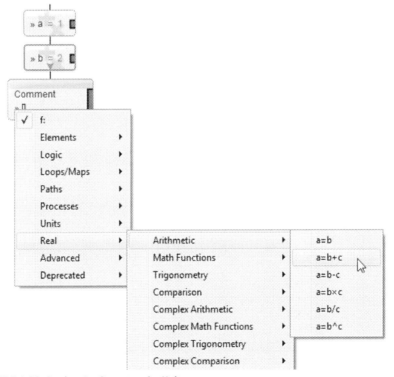

FIGURE 4.39 Setting the Operator of a Unit

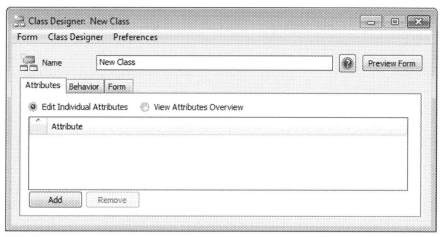

FIGURE 4.40 Class Designer with No Attributes Added

Setting the elements

You can set/pick elements using hot regions. Hot regions appear in the elements list of fact units as "[]" and in nonfact units (units that use operators) as pink text. Clicking on a hot region puts you in selection mode. You can also replace existing elements by left-clicking on the element you wish to replace in the elements list. Clicking on an existing element also puts you in selection mode.

WORKING WITH CLASSES

Described here are the methods for creating new classes and editing their attributes.

Creating a new class

To create a new class, click on the **Create Class** ![icon] toolbar button. A new class unit is created and the Class Designer tool is shown (Fig. 4.40). Alternatively, you can right-click on the whiteboard and select **Create class in Class Designer...** The right-click option **Create Class...** creates the new class unit but does not launch Class Designer.

The name of your class can be changed by editing the name in the **Name** edit box at the top of the form. Notice that as you add attributes and define them, the class on the Whiteboard automatically updates to match what you've selected (Fig. 4.41).

Class Designer

Class Designer is a tool used for defining, designing, and editing classes. To use Class Designer to define a new class, either right-click on the Whiteboard and choose **Create class in Class Designer...** or click the **New Class** (![icon]) button on the toolbar. You can also edit existing classes by right-clicking the class and selecting **Edit class....** Once in Class Designer, you can add new or edit existing attributes using Attribute Designer

There are three tabs within Class Designer: Attributes, Behavior, and Form.

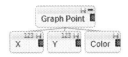

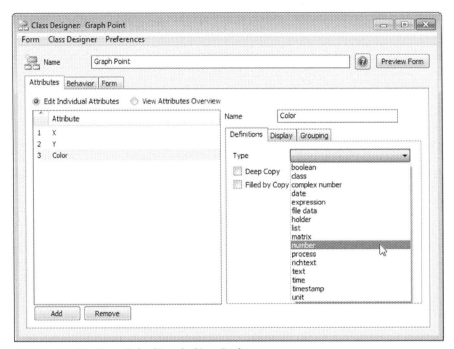

FIGURE 4.41 The Graph Point Class in Class Designer

Attributes tab

Within the Attributes tab (Fig. 4.42) you can add new attributes, edit existing attributes, and remove attributes. When you have selected an attribute, a tool called Attribute Designer will appear on the right side of the Class Designer. Here you can define everything about this attribute. Attribute Designer is described in detail in the next section, "Working with Attributes."

Behavior

Within this tab (Fig. 4.43) you define certain properties of the class.

Whenever you select an attribute from the attributes list, controls will appear that allow you to design the definition and display aspects of the attribute.

Form

The Forms tab (Fig. 4.44) contains a tool for designing forms called *Form Designer*. A description of this tool, as well as a discussion about customizing forms in general, is included in the Appendix.

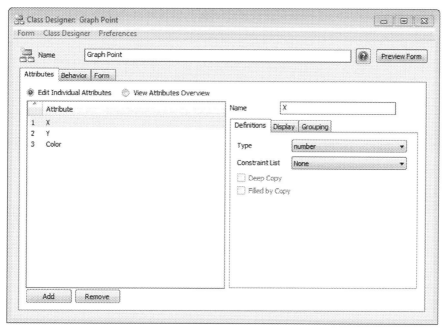

FIGURE 4.42 The Attributes Tab of Class Designer

You can add new attributes by clicking **Add** beneath the attributes list box.

Automatically updating instances

Editing a base class does not automatically update instances of that class. When the Class or Attribute Designer tool detects this, it displays an option to update any instances to match the changes made via the tool. The warning is only displayed if there are loaded instances of the class in a domain that can be saved.

Warnings

Class Designer may display different warnings, depending upon the class you are editing.

Updating instances warning. Editing a base class does not automatically update instances of that class. When Class or Attribute Designer detects this, it displays a

FIGURE 4.43 The Behavior Tab of Class Designer

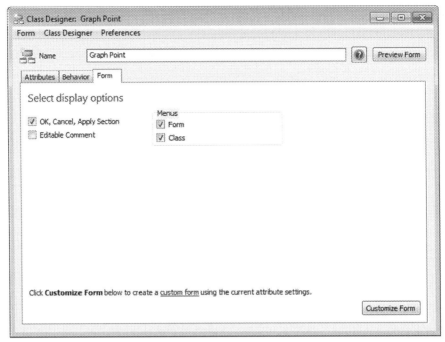

FIGURE 4.44 The Forms Tab of Class Designer

warning about using Class Updater to update those instances. The warning is only displayed if there are loaded instances of the class in a domain that can be saved.

Editing instance warning. If you are editing a class instance rather than a base class, a warning is displayed on the Attribute or Class Designer form. This warning indicates that you may want to edit the base class rather than the instance. Although you most likely want to edit the base class, there are situations where you may want to edit an instance. A common example is adding attributes to make a derived class.

Creating an instance of a base class
An instance can be created in several ways:

- On the Whiteboard, right-click on a class and select **Create instance**. This will immediately create a new instance in the working domain and place it at the crosshair on the Whiteboard.
- Using the copy operator on a class will create a new instance of that class. The instance can be referenced via the step's target alias.
- If a unit is typed as a list of classes and the form is shown, clicking the **Add** button on the form will create a new instance and show the form for said instance.

Class updater

Class updater is a tool used for updating class instances after you edit their base class. Changes to the base class are not automatically reflected in the instances; you must select the changes you want to apply. To access Class Updater, click on the **Class Updater** button on the toolbar ( ).

If the instances are loaded (and not housed in a scratch domain), Class Designer should offer you the option to automatically update these class instances. Otherwise, you can use Class Updater to update your instances.

WORKING WITH ATTRIBUTES

You can work with attributes from both the Whiteboard and from within Attribute Designer.

Attribute designer

Attribute Designer is a subcomponent of Class Designer that allows you to:

1. Define the types of an attribute
2. Define the specific and general display options using display as options to define the appearance of an attribute in the class's form
3. Define how the attribute behaves upon a deep copy
4. Define constraint lists

Definitions

You can access attribute designer (Fig. 4.45) directly by right-clicking on an attribute and selecting **Edit Attribute...**, or from within Class Designer, as shown in Figure 4.44.

FIGURE 4.45 Attribute Designer

Fill by form. When an attribute is typed as a class and the specific class is also defined, then you can check the Fill By Form Check box. Checking the Check box tells Form Modeling to create an instance of this class and place it in the attributes elements when a form is shown on this class.

Deep copy. Attribute designer allows you to specify what attributes are deep copy attributes. The deep copy behavior plays an important role when creates new instances of classes.

Configuring an attribute's display

The Display tab (Fig. 4.46) within Attribute Designer provides several options for configuring how the attribute will be displayed in a form. The specific options vary depending upon how the attribute is defined, for example, what type it has and does it have a constraint list. Display options don't fundamentally change the information in an attribute; they just change how it is displayed in a form.

There are a few options that are general to almost all attribute definitions.

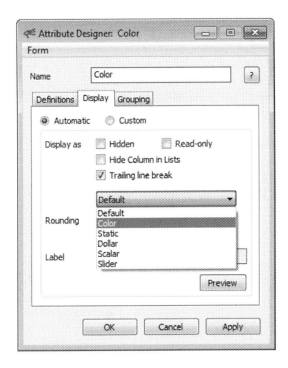

FIGURE 4.46

The Display tab of Attribute Designer allows you to configure how the attribute will be displayed in a form.

In Fig. 4.46, the Color attribute is typed as a number. Shown above are some of the options for how to display a number attribute. The configuration selected (Color) shows the Color attribute as in Figure 4.47.

FIGURE 4.47

Selecting the Color display option for a number shows the attribute as in this screenshot. You can click on the orange button to bring up a color picker form.

Hidden. Hidden attributes are not shown in a form at all. If a list control contains instances of this class, Hidden hides that attribute's column as well.

Read-only. Read-only attributes are shown in a form, but they are not modifiable. The exact effect of Read-only depends on the controls used for that attribute, but it always prevents the user from editing that attribute's value.

Hide column in lists. If the class is used to define a list attribute of a parent class, then the parent form will display a list control. If you do not want this attribute to display as a column in this list control, then you can check this box.

Multiple selection. This option will only appear for list attributes. It defines whether the list control for the attribute will allow a user to select multiple items or just one.

Attributes that are typed as a list of classes have several very powerful display configuration options. For example, consider the model below of a store with inventory items. The Inventory attribute is a list of classes. The specific class is an Item that has a Name, Price, and Description. There are several ways that this attribute can be displayed. Figures 4.50–4.52 show the Default, Expand, and Expand in Tabs.

If these configurations still do not meet your requirements, then you can switch to customizing an attributes display or a classes display. In this case, you are going beyond configuring the attribute display, but you are selecting actual form controls that will be used to represent the attribute.

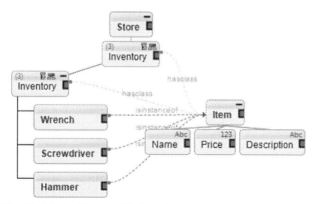

FIGURE 4.48 The Model of a Store and Its Inventory

The Inventory attribute is a list of classes with defining class Item. Figures 4.49 to 4.52 show the various ways in which these can be displayed.

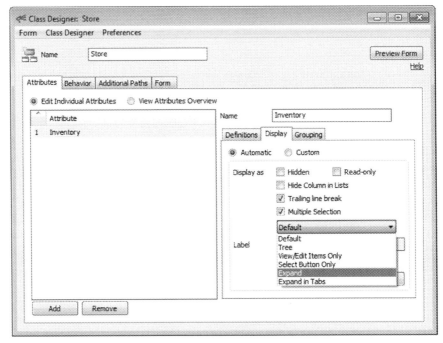

FIGURE 4.49

There are several options on how to display a list of class attribute.

The display of the color attribute above is actually the sum of three individual display controls: a text control and two button controls. These controls were chosen by the Form Modeling domain automatically.

You do have the ability, however, to define what controls are used to represent an attribute. If you click on the "Custom" radio button in the Display tab of Attribute Editor (Fig. 4.53) you will see a list of the default controls. You can add more or

FIGURE 4.50 Default Display of a List of Classes

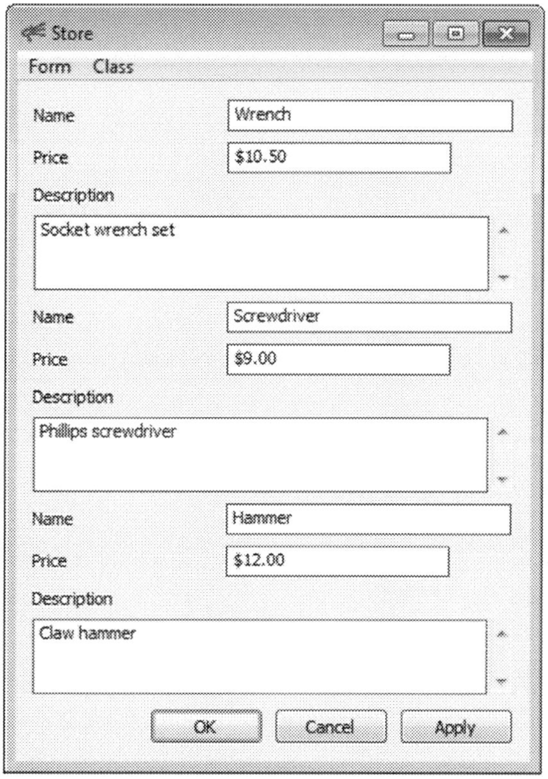

FIGURE 4.51 Expanded Display of a List of Classes

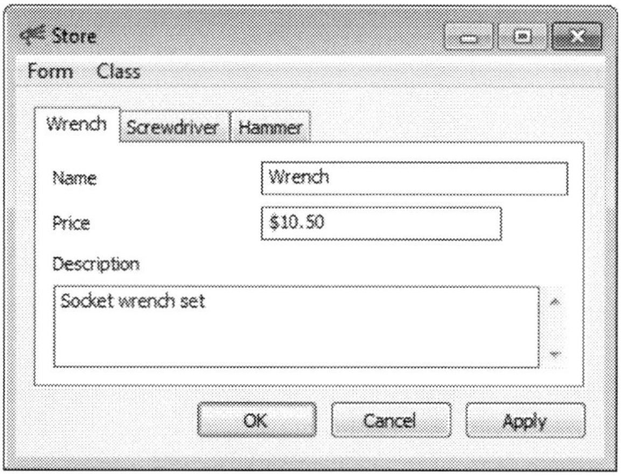

FIGURE 4.52 Expand in Tabs Display of Classes

FIGURE 4.53

Selecting the Custom option for displaying an attribute provides the most control over how the attribute will displayed. You can completely specify the controls that will be used to represent the attribute.

remove any of these controls. For example, let's say we wanted to add a help button next to the other buttons. We can do this in just a few steps that are described in Figures 4.54–4.57.

Grouping

The Tab field puts attributes in tabs. The tab control is inserted at the location of the first tabbed attribute.

Group. The Group field puts attributes in groups. Each group is inserted at the location of the first attribute in that group.

Cut, copy, paste

Within the Whiteboard attributes can be selected by right-clicking the mouse and dragging over the attributes. You can then right-click on the highlighted attributes and select Copy. Then right-click on another class and select Paste Attributes. The copied attributes will be pasted on the new class. All of the definitions and display properties will be copied as well.

WORKING WITH PATHS

Paths are often added for you when you create various Unit Modeler structures. However, you occasionally have to define your own paths. To add a path from a unit, right-click on the unit that should serve as the source of the path and select **Add path....**

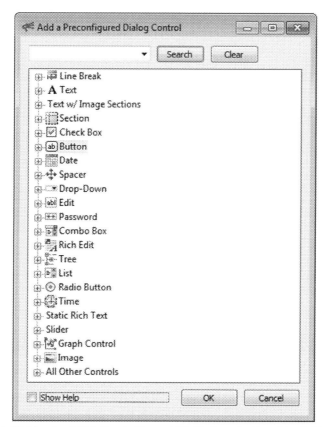

FIGURE 4.54 Clicking the Add Button in Figure 4.53 Displays the List of Available Controls

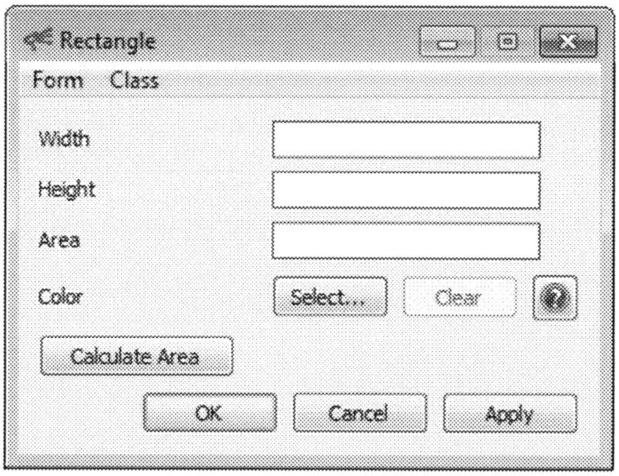

FIGURE 4.55 The Customized Attribute of Figure 4.53 Displayed in a Form

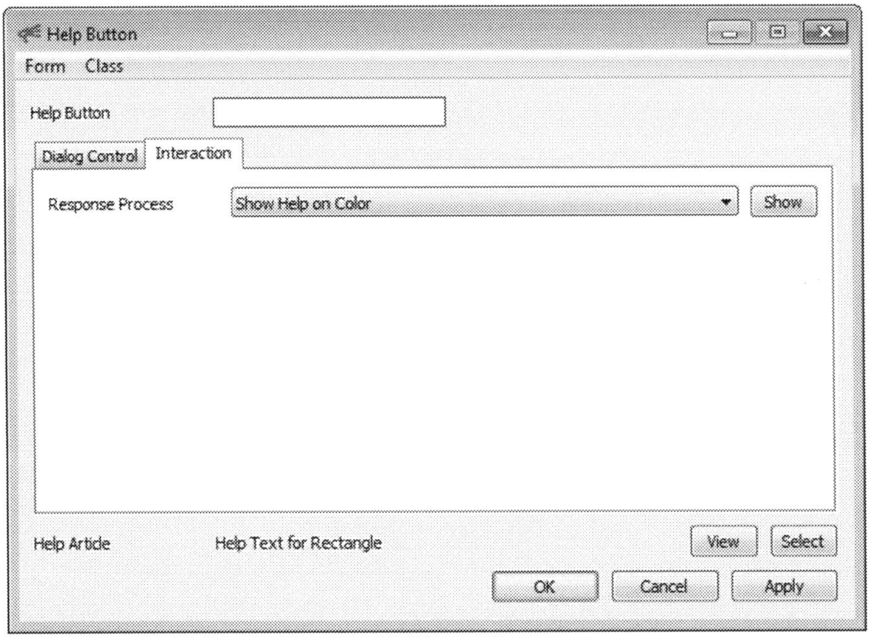

FIGURE 4.56

Choosing a Help Button shows a form allowing to specify what happens when the button is clicked.

Select or enter the relation of the path. Once the relation has been defined, you will be prompted to select the destination of the path. Click on the unit that should serve as the destination unit.

You may also want to examine existing paths to know about their sources or destinations. To view the existing paths from a unit (in other words, the paths for which the unit serves as the source), right-click on the unit and click on **Show by path**. This should show the list of paths from the unit. However, not all paths are necessarily present in this list. Class units, for instance, have many paths directed toward their attributes. These paths are not shown, because this list can become quite lengthy. To view the full list of paths from a unit, right-click on the unit and select

FIGURE 4.57 The Process Representing the Help Button's Response Process

This process will be shocked when the help button is clicked by a user.

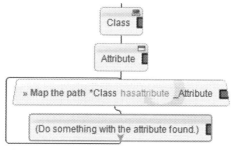

FIGURE 4.58 Example of a Mappath Operator

This step wants to find an attribute of *Class

Edit.... On the right side of the edit dialog, there is a full list of paths for which the unit serves as a source.

Creating paths

To add a path from a unit, right-click on the unit that should serve as the source of the path and select **Add path....** Select or enter the relation of the path. Once the relation has been defined, you will be prompted to select the destination of the path. Click on the unit that should serve as the destination unit.

Paths can also be created via the pathadd operator.

Mapping paths

The mappaths operator can be used to map a path. Mapping a path will find "missing information" of a path.

Path mapping uses virtual atoms. Recall that virtual atoms appear as dark purple with a single underscore in front of the name of the holder unit (_virtual atom). Virtual atoms tell the mappath operator that they are looking for exactly one element to fit into a spot.

Let's look at a few example mappath steps:

Example #1

The mappaths step in Figure 4.58 will find every destination of the hasattribute path where the given Class is the source. The first time the mappaths step is shocked, it will find the first attribute that is a destination of the hasattribute path and place it in the Attribute step. The next time the mappaths step is shocked (since it is looped back to), it will find the next (different) attribute. It will continue to find attributes until there are no more. Once there are no more attributes to find, the mappaths step will return False.

Example #2

The mappaths step in Figure 4.59 is being used to find the relation between two units, should a path exist. If no path exists with Unit 1 as the source and Unit 2 as the destination, the mappaths step will return False. Otherwise, the relation (as text) will be stored in the Relation step of the process and the mappaths step will return True.

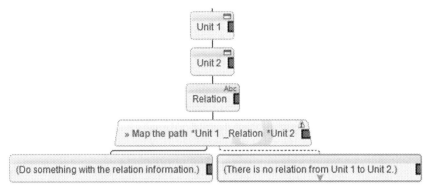

FIGURE 4.59 Another Example of a Mappath Step

Here the step wants to find the relation between *Unit 1 and *Unit 2

Because there can be several relations between units, you can loop back around to the mappaths step to find all relations. Because there is no loop on the mappaths step in the example, a small warning is placed on the step. If we were using this process to verify that any path exists between the two units, we would not need to loop back to the mappaths step, so we can ignore this warning.

Recursion

Element paths in complex elements recursively find all possible destinations of the specified paths.

For example, consider a class structure that models a bakery. The top-level class, which is called Bakery, has a list attribute that is designed to contain a list of Recipe classes. Each Recipe class also has a list attribute, which is designed to hold a list of Ingredient classes.

If we had the complex element Bakery.*Recipes.*Ingredients, what would this be referencing? Let's find the answer by breaking down the complex element into individual steps:

1. Bakery references the Bakery class.
2. .Recipes references the attribute path from the Bakery class to its Recipes attribute, which contains a list of Recipe classes.
3. The star in .*Recipes lets us know that we're referencing all of the Recipe classes inside of the Recipes attribute.
4. .Ingredients references the attribute path from a Recipe class to its Ingredients attribute, which contains a list of Ingredient classes. Because we have multiple Recipe classes, we follow the attribute path on each class to each attribute. We now have a list of Ingredients attributes.
5. The star in .*Ingredients lets us know that we're referencing all of the Ingredient classes inside of each Ingredients attribute. Each Ingredients attribute can contain any number of Ingredient classes. Now we have several lists of Ingredients classes. We're done breaking down our complex element, so the end result is the combined lists of Ingredient classes.

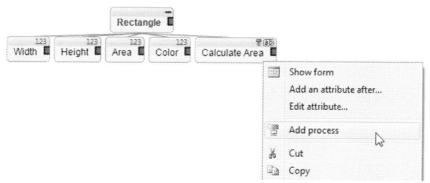

FIGURE 4.60 Right-click on a Process Attribute to Add an Action Process

WORKING WITH PROCESSES

Processes are a series of information units connected with > and !> paths that perform a task or complete a logical operation. The > (true) and !> (false) paths indicate the shock flow after an information unit's operation is completed. Each individual information unit in a process is referred to as a step in that process.

Creating

To begin creating a new process, click on the **Create Process** (▤) toolbar button. This launches the Process Designer tool, which allows you to create and define the process unit, parameters, and note of a new process.

Adding a process to a process attribute

Classes can have attributes that are typed as a process. These attributes will need to have a process created for them. There is a simple and easy way to do this: just right-click on the attribute and select **Add Process**. The stub process in Figure 4.61 will be created and the process will be added as an element of the attribute.

After clicking on **Add Process** (Fig. 4.60) you will be asked to enter a name for the process.

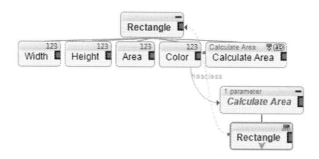

FIGURE 4.61

Selecting **Add process** will create the process with a parameter representing the class and will add the new process as an element of the process attribute.

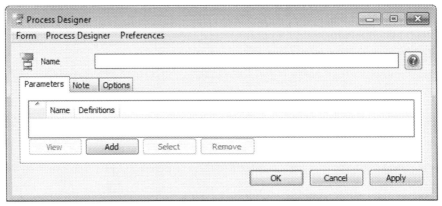

FIGURE 4.62 Process Designer

The **Add Process** selection is actually an assist that has been made conveniently available via a right-click option. You will notice that the assist created the process with a single parameter. It has typed this parameter as a Rectangle class. It has also added this process as a parameter of the Calculate Area attribute.

Process Designer

Process Designer (Fig. 4.62) is a tool for defining the parameters, comment, and note of a process.

Adding a parameter will launch a tool that works similarly to Attribute Designer. It allows you to add type information to the parameter.

Naming your process. At the top of the form, there is a place to enter or edit the name of the process. This name can be anything, but it cannot be left blank.

Process parameters tab. Midway down the form, there is a list box for process parameters in the **Parameters** tab. Each parameter has a name and a list of definitions associated with it. The name of a parameter will be the text that appears as the comment on the parameter step. The definitions help other users determine what the parameter will hold.

Process note tab. If the **Note** tab next to the **Parameters** tab is clicked, then the tab control changes to view the note or note options for the process. If a process has no note, then the tab control will contain a text label that reads "Note: (none)," and a button beside it will allow a user to create a new note. If the process has a note, then the tab control will contain a richedit, which shows the text content of the note. The text of the note may be edited or deleted from the Process Editor form.

Finishing up. Upon clicking the **OK** button on the Process Editor form, a new process will be created (if the Process Editor is being used to create new process) or the existing process will be modified. Any new parameters will be created and any existing parameters will be renamed. All parameters will be moved to the top of the process, in order, with their definitions set properly. If the name of a process is changed and the process has a note associated with it, then that note's comment along with the underlined title of the process within the note will be modified to match the new name. Any user-entered changes to the note will also be applied.

Steps

Steps form the body of a process. There are several different kinds of steps, including:

- The **process unit** (also called the "process header"): This is the top-level process step. This unit is the argument for a shock step that wants to shock the given process. (In Figure 4.63 below, this is the "Find a Unit in a List with Matching Comment" step.)
- The **parameters**: These steps are elements of the process unit. When the process is shocked, arguments are used to fill these parameter steps. (In the Figure 4.63, the "Text to Match" step is a parameter.)
- **Fact steps**: These steps are used to hold information. They perform no operation when shocked. (In the Figure 4.63, the "Unit" step is a fact step.)
- **Operation steps**: These steps perform some kind of operation when shocked. (In the Figure 4.63, the loop step is an operation step.)

Adding true and false steps

To add a true or false step below an existing step in a process, left-click on the true or false insertion arrow (the true insertion arrow is highlighted in the Figure 4.64 below) and select **Add true step** or **Add false step**.

If a step can only return True, only the true insertion arrow will appear.

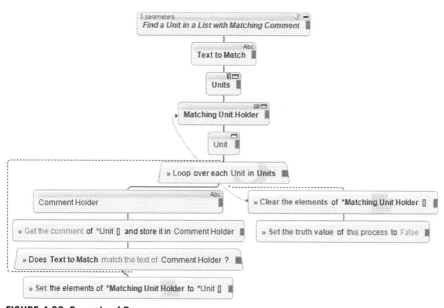

FIGURE 4.63 Example of Process

FIGURE 4.64 Left-click the Unit's Down Arrow to Add New Steps

If there are two areas, the left arrow will add true steps and the right arrow will add false steps

Copying and pasting steps

To copy steps in a process, select the steps to be copied, then right-click on any of the selected steps and select **Copy** (Fig. 4.65). If the selected steps cannot be copied as a whole, the **Copy** option will be disabled.

To paste the copied steps, right-click on the step to add the copied steps and select either **Paste true** or **Paste false**. **Paste true** will paste the copied steps from the selected step's true exit path; **Paste false** will paste the copied steps from the selected step's false exit path.

Variables designer

In many processes, you need to have a place to temporarily hold information while the process is running. Variable steps serve this purpose. Variable steps should always have their operator set to f: (fact) and they should be typed just like attributes

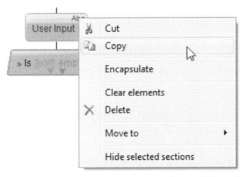

FIGURE 4.65 Highlighted Steps in a Process Can Be Copied and Then Pasted Elsewhere

FIGURE 4.66 Variable Designer Is Much Like Attribute Designer but Does Not Have a Display or Group Tab

are typed. If you use assists, many of them automatically type your variable steps for you. Another option for typing variable steps is through the use of variable designer.

Variable Designer (Fig. 4.66) works similarly to the way Attribute Designer works. You will see the same kind of definition options that you see in Attribute Designer, minus the display options. You can access the Variable Designer by right-clicking on a variable step and selecting **Edit variable definitions…**.

Encapsulating processes

The term *encapsulation* refers to the process of taking something complex and making it simple. It is a core concept to the Unit Modeler and is what enables the environment to become more intelligent. In essence encapsulation makes tasks simpler by hiding the details that are not relevant to a specific task and only exposing those details that are relevant. Encapsulation can be applied to all aspects and structures of the Unit Model.

Encapsulating steps in a process will create a new process for the selected steps and add a step in the original process that shocks the encapsulated process. All you need to do to encapsulate steps in a process is to select the steps and then right-click on any of the selected steps and select **Encapsulate**. Alternatively, you can also click on the Encapsulate toolbar button in the main menu ( ).

The encapsulate tool will appear with default parameters already created for the new process. You will be asked to type in a name for the new process. You can alter the parameters in various ways. For a complete discussion of the use of this tool, click on **Help** in the tools menu.

Directives

Sometimes you want a process to be shocked immediately upon loading the domain. To do this, you must mark the process as a directive in Process Designer.

WORKING WITH DOMAINS

The term *domain* has multiple meanings. The first and most common definition is as a reference to some area of knowledge, such as math, science, law, and so forth. The other definition, as used in the context of the Unit Modeler Development Environment, refers to the file created when a model is saved. All of the units, structures, and paths of a model are saved in domain files. Just as a text editor saves.txt files, the Unit Modeler saves domain files. Domain files have the extension .kb. The kb stands for *knowledge base* and is still used for historical reasons.

Domain management is an important component of the Unit Modeler. All new units you create are placed in a domain called the working domain. The working domain is set programatically using the SetWorkingDomain operator. When a unit is saved, it is saved to the domain file it is part of.

Every domain file has a Domain class. The Domain class indexes many of the domain's key units. Certain attributes of the Domain class control how the domain will operate: its directives, data versus standard, and so on.

Creating new domains

New domains can be created by navigating to the **Domains** in the application menu and selecting **New…**. You can type in the name for the new domain in the prompt that appears.

You can also click on the **Create domain** (▦) toolbar button.

Local versus server domains

Domain files can reside in several places. Many domains reside on the KeLabs public server. The domains that you create reside somewhere on your local drive or network. The domains found on the server are called *server domains* and the domains that you create on your local drive or network are called *local domains*.

Loading domains

A certain set of initial domains are loaded when you successfully login. The exact set of domains will depend upon your personal preferences. After login, domains are only loaded into memory when they are actually referenced by an already loaded domain. This is referred to as dynamic loading.

Some domains, those that you commonly use, may be saved on your local hard drive. This is referred to as being cached. The benefit of cached domains is that they come from your local drive instead of from a server. This provides somewhat better performance.

Noncached domains will come from a server. Domains may come from a multitude of servers. In fact, domains can be loaded theoretically from an unlimited number of servers, which may be hosted by a variety of institutions or individuals.

Loading domain is automatic. The client software knows how to find a unit on whichever server it may reside. Performing this task does require that a server be registered with the KeLabs server registry.

Manually loading local domains

A local domain can be manually loaded by right-clicking on the whiteboard and selecting "Load Domain".

Automatic loading of domains. Looks in the local default directory first, then workspaces and then the server.

Saving domains

There are several ways to save the work you have put into a domain.

The easiest way to save a domain is to right-click on any unit from the domain you want to save and select **Save Domain**.

In many forms there is a **Class** menu item that has a **Save Domain** option. This saves the domain of the class corresponding to the form.

You can also right-click anywhere in the Whiteboard and select **Save Domain**... to save a specific domain from a list.

When a unit is changed, a blue save icon will appear in the upper right corner. You can click on this icon to save the domain.

Moving units from one domain to another

It is possible to move units out of one domain and into another. This is accomplished by right-clicking on a unit (or set of selected units) and selecting **Move to**.

Before you move structure(s) from domain to domain, be sure to check the deep copy tags on all of your attributes and units. The move operation moves the contents of units that are identified for deep copy.

Using the **Move to** function will not only move the selected structure(s) but will move all dependent structures as well.

If you move unit(s) between domains, you should be prompted upon save to save both the destination and source domains. If this prompt did not exist and you were to only save the destination domain, then you would get a duplicate alias error message when loading both of the domains again. This is because the same units would exist in two domains.

Viewing units in a domain

Use the List All dialog to view the classes, processes, objects, class instances, and so forth in a particular domain.

Working domain

Whenever units are created, there must be a domain for the new units to exist in. The domain where units go when they are created is called the *working domain*. The working domain can be set by clicking on the status bar of the program and selecting from the list of domains. Additionally, processes can set the working domain using the SetWorkingDomain operator.

GENERAL FUNCTIONS

Typing units

The types supported by the Unit Modeler are described under the Types article. There are two ways to set the types of units.

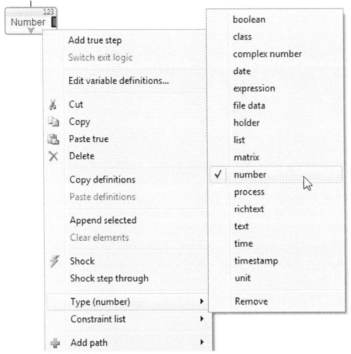

FIGURE 4.67 Units Can Be Typed By Right-Clicking on the Unit and Selecting Type in the Menu

The first method is via the **Type** menu item in a unit's right-click menu (Fig. 4.67). Depending upon the type selected, other menu items appear below it. The menu will indicate the selections that have previously been made.

The other method for defining a unit's type is via a form-based type editor. This editor is also accessed via a unit's right-click menu. The type editor has a slightly different name dependent upon whether you are clicking on an attribute, parameter or step. The form-based type editor is also integrated into other form-based editors, such as Class Designer and Process Designer.

Cut, copy, and paste

You can cut, copy, and paste many different sets of units in the Unit Modeler. Some of these sets of units have already been described elsewhere. The Modeler allows for the selection of individual units, sets of units, and the *head unit* of certain structures (in particular, the Class unit and the Process unit).

Cut, copy, and paste are available via the application menu, toolbar, and various right-click menus.

To cut or copy units, first select the units by left-clicking and drag the mouse until the units are enclosed in the selection rectangle. Then right-click on one of the selected units and click **Cut** or **Copy**.

Cut

The Unit Modeler's cut functionality has many uses. You can cut steps from a process, cut attributes from a class, or simply cut a freestanding unit. The units that are cut can then be pasted elsewhere.

Cut can be accessed by right-clicking a unit, or box-selecting a group and choosing **Cut** (✂) from the toolbar, or by box-selecting a group and right-clicking on the selection.

Cut units are moved to a special location as a group and can only be pasted once. Since the units are moved, this means that references to cut units are not removed. This functionality works in a similar manner to the UnloadUnits operator, except there is special built-in functionality to undo the cut action. Cut and delete work in the same way, except that cut units can be pasted.

Using the Cut function will not only cut the selected structure(s) but will cut all dependent structures as well.

Cutting steps from a process. The most common usage for cut is to cut steps from a process and place them in another process or in a different place in the same process. The steps that are cut must be contiguous and in a form that can be pasted. This means the steps being cut must have one entrance, so that when the steps are pasted to a unit the entrance can be properly linked. The cut steps are removed from the process and the process is stitched back together.

Note that if a cut includes a process step, then the entire process is treated as being cut. The same is true if a cut includes a class step, the entire class is treated as being cut.

Cutting attributes from a class. Attributes can be cut from a class and pasted onto another class, and only onto another class. The pasted attributes retain their name and typing. If they are pasted onto a class with an attribute of the same name, then the cut processes prompt you to enter a new name for the attribute.

Cutting freestanding units. Freestanding units on the Whiteboard can be cut as well. These units remain on the Whiteboard after being cut, but they have been moved to a different domain. The units can then be pasted into another domain or as steps onto a process.

Undoing cut. The last delete action can be undone by going to **Edit** in the application menu and choosing **Undo last cut** or by clicking the undo button (↶) in the toolbar. If you have since issued a cut, copy, or delete action, you must move through the undo history until you get to action you'd like to undo.

Copy

The Unit Modeler's Copy functionality has many uses. You can copy steps from a process, copy attributes from a class or even copy a unit's definitions. The information that is copied can then be Pasted.

Copy can be accessed by right-clicking a unit, box-selecting a group and choosing **Copy** (⧉) from the toolbar, or by box-selecting a group and right-clicking on the selection. This is distinct from the **Copy** option that appears on some forms.

Copied units are replicated in another domain as a group. The copied information can be pasted as many times as you would like.

Using the Copy function will not only copy the selected structure(s), but will copy all dependent structures as well.

Copying steps from a process. The most common usage for copy is to copy steps from a process and place them in another process or in a different place in the same process. The steps that are copied must be contiguous and in a form that can be pasted. This means the steps being copied must have one entrance, so that when the steps are pasted to a unit the entrance can be properly linked.

Note that if a copy includes a process step then the entire process is treated as being copied.

Copying attributes from a class. Attributes can be copied from a class and pasted onto another class, and only onto another class. The copied attributes retain their name and typing. If they are pasted onto a class with an attribute of the same name, then the copying processes prompt you to enter a new name for the attribute.

Copying freestanding units. Freestanding units on the Whiteboard can be copied as well. The units can then be pasted into another domain or as steps onto a process.

Copying definitions. The definitions on a unit, such as type, class, constraint list, and so forth, can be copied from a unit and pasted onto other units. This can be a quick way to replicate a complex definition set across multiple units.

Paste

The Unit Modeler's Paste functionality has many uses. You can paste steps into a process, paste attributes onto a class, or simply paste to the Whiteboard.

Paste can be accessed by right-clicking a unit, right-clicking the Whiteboard and selecting **Paste**, or by choosing **Paste** (▨) from the toolbar. The **Paste** on the toolbar is equivalent to right-clicking on the Whiteboard.

You can paste units that have been cut or copied. Pasting units that have been cut *moves* them from the clipboard and those units cannot be pasted again. Pasting units that have been copied *copies* the units in the clipboard and this type of paste can be executed multiple times.

Pasting steps into a process. The most common usage for Paste is to paste steps into a process. Right-clicking allows you to **Paste true** or **Paste false**. These options paste the units after the selected unit and connect the pasted units by a true path or false path depending on the selected option.

The pasted units are inserted into the process and process are stitched together to incorporate the new steps. Pasted steps are always placed in the same domain as the process they are pasted into.

Pasting attributes onto a class. Attributes can be cut or copied from a class can be pasted onto another class, and only onto another class. The pasted attributes retain their name and typing. If they are pasted onto a class with an attribute of the same name, then the pasting processes prompt you to enter a new name for the attribute.

Pasting to the whiteboard. Units can be pasted to the Whiteboard as a freestanding structure. These units are placed in the working domain.

Pasting definitions. The definitions on a unit, such as type, class, constraint list, and so forth, can be copied from a unit and pasted onto other units. This can be a quick way to replicate a complex definition set across multiple units.

Undoing paste. The last paste action can be undone by going to **Edit** in the application menu and choosing **Undo last paste** or by clicking the undo button ( ) in the toolbar. If you have since issued a cut, copy, or delete action, you must move through the undo history until you get to action you'd like to undo.

Delete

The Unit Modeler's Delete functionality allows you to remove units from a domain. Unit deleted in this way are moved to a special location as a group. This functionality works in a similar manner to the UnloadUnits operator, except there is special built in functionality to undo the delete action. Since the units are moved, this means that references to the deleted units are not removed. Note that this type of delete is in contrast to the deleteunits operator, which does remove all references to the deleted units. Delete and cut work in the same way, except that cut units can be pasted.

Delete can be accessed by right-clicking a unit, or box-selecting a group and choosing **Delete** ( ) from the toolbar, or by box-selecting a group and right-clicking on the selection.

Using the Delete function will not only delete the selected structure(s) but will delete all dependent structures as well.

Deleting steps from a process. The most common usage for delete is to delete steps from a process. The steps that are deleted need not be contiguous. However, the process must be able to be stitched back together before the deletions are allowed to proceed.

Deleting attributes from a class. Attributes can deleted from a class. This deletes all relations between the class and the deleted attribute.

Deleting free-standing units. Freestanding units on the Whiteboard can be deleted as well. Any deletion that includes a process step or a class step results in the entire process or class being deleted.

Undoing delete. The last delete action can be undone by going to **Edit** in the application menu and choosing **Undo last delete** or by clicking the undo button ( ) in the toolbar. If you have since issued a cut, copy, or delete action, you must move through the undo history until you get to action you'd like to undo.

Dependent structures

When a process is moved from one domain to another, its note is also moved with it. But why? This occurs because the note "belongs" to the process. Structures that belong to other structures can be described as *dependent structures*. These structures are carried along with the structure they belong to when the structure they belong to is cut, copied, pasted, moved, or unloaded.

What are the various types of dependent structures in the Unit Modeler? The list of structure types is confined to:

- **Notes:** A note is created from a unit to describe the contents or purpose of the unit. Thus the note is a dependent structure to this unit.
- **Custom forms:** A custom form is created from a particular class or structure. Thus the custom form is a dependent structure to that class or structure.

- **Custom attribute sections:** A custom attribute section is created from an attribute. Thus the attribute section is a dependent structure to the parent class to which the attribute belongs.
- **Class Designer–created units:** Class Designer creates "in tab" and "in group" destinations for attributes in order to signal to Form Modeling in what tab or group an attribute should appear. These destination units are dependent structures to the class corresponding to the attributes from which they were created.

Searching units

There are two tools that provide the ability to search for units. The first tool is built on the engine and looks through all units loaded at the current time. The first search tool is useful for developers when creating and defining domains. The other tool, accessed through the search toolbar icon 🔍, is a search model built to walk down the structures and paths of any other particular model. This tool looks at the contents of units and is constrained itself to units within the structures that are defined by the user. Generally, the second search tool is useful for the end user of models built by developers.

DEBUGGING

The Unit Modeler provides a powerful set of tools for debugging your model. You can enter *Debug Mode* (also referred to as *step through mode*) in two ways:

1. Right-click on a process or step in a process and select **Shock step through** (Fig. 4.68).
2. Click on **Debug mode** (Fig. 4.69) in the status bar at the bottom of the Unit Modeler toggles Debug Mode.

   When Debug Mode is on, the program automatically stops on steps that are shown on the Whiteboard. Note that the program always stops on steps that have a break point set, whether they are shown to the whiteboard or not.
   When Debug Mode is on and execution stops on a unit, the following will occur:

- The Whiteboard background fades to yellow.
- The debug toolbar appears below the application toolbar.
- The *current step* (the step that will be shocked next) is highlighted in green.

THE DEBUG TOOLBAR

Under the application toolbar is the Debug Toolbar (Fig. 4.70). On the left of the Debug Toolbar are buttons that allow you to step through the process, run the process, or stop the process. On the right side is the stack of all processes and subprocesses that are currently being shocked. You can click on any of these labels to go to that process. The hour glass will center the Whiteboard on the current step.

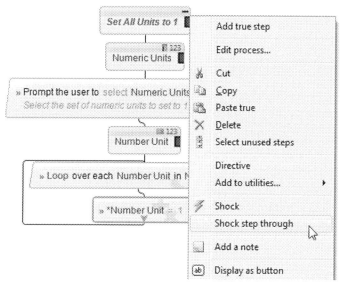

FIGURE 4.68 Right-Click on a Process Unit and Select Shock Step Through to Enter Debug Mode

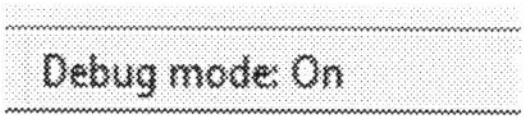

Debug mode: On

FIGURE 4.69

You can turn on Debug Mode by clicking of the portion of the status bar at the bottom of the Whiteboard labeled Debug Mode.

- **Step**—shock the current step
- **Run**—turn off Debug Mode and continue shocking
- **Stop**—stop all shocks
- **Show Runtime Information**—shows a runtime information dialog with information about the current step
- **Move to current step**—repositions to the Whiteboard to center on the current step

The *shock stack* is seen to the right of debug controls. It shows the process originally shocked and all subprocesses that are in the middle of being shocked. The domain that each process is in is displayed underneath the name of the process. The shock stack is interactive. You can click on any process and it will be shown to the Whiteboard. The step being executed in that process will be highlighted.

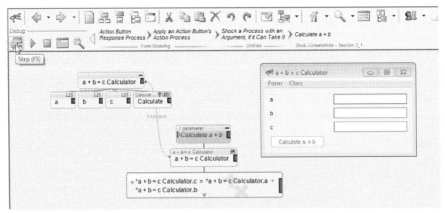

FIGURE 4.70 The Application in Debug Mode

The green unit is the current step.

RUNTIME INFORMATION

Runtime information refers to the basic information about a unit at any given point in the shock process. Runtime information can be accessed in one of two ways:

To view run time information about the current shock step, click on the **Run Time Info** toolbar button ( ) that appears during Debug Mode. In the debugging example shown in Figure 4.71, the first dialog is an example of runtime dialog of this type. The dialog shows information about the current shock step (highlighted in green), which includes the step's operator, truth value, and elements.

To view the information about a particular unit or step regardless of the current shock step, right-click on the unit and navigate to **Run time info....** In the debugging example shown in Figure 4.71, the second dialog is an example of runtime dialog of this type. The dialog shows information about the loop step above the current shock step, which includes the step's loop counter, truth value, and elements.

BREAKPOINTS

Breakpoints can be used to stop a shock at a specific step. To set a breakpoint on a step, hover over the upper-left corner of the step until a small, gray circle appears underneath your cursor (it will be subtly highlighted in green). A small dialog should appear that reads *Toggle breakpoint*. Click the gray circle to enable the breakpoint. You know your breakpoint has been successfully set if the gray circle turns red (Fig. 4.72).

In the example shown in Figure 4.72, a loop step is set to be a breakpoint. This means each time the loop step is about to be shocked, the Unit Modeler will stop (and enter debugging mode, if it is not already). The user now has the choice as to whether he wants to *step, run,* or *stop shocking.*

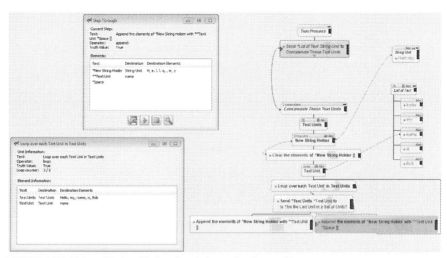

FIGURE 4.71 Debug Mode with Runtime Information Forms Shown

FIGURE 4.72 Breakpoints Can Be Set By Clicking the Circle in the Upper Left Hand Corner of a Step Unit

If a step is set as a breakpoint, but is not shown to the Whiteboard, the program will still halt when the breakpoint is reached. A dialog will appear asking the user to decide whether to continue, stop, or debug at the given breakpoint.

WATCHPOINTS

Watchpoints can be used to stop a shock whenever the contents of a "watched" unit are changed. To set a watchpoint on a step, hover over the upper-left corner of the step (Fig. 4.73) until a small, gray magnifying glass appears underneath your cursor (it will be subtly highlighted in green). A small dialog should appear which reads *Toggle watchpoint*. Click the gray magnifying glass to enable the watchpoint. You know your watchpoint has been successfully set if the magnifying class appears in color.

In Figure 4.73, the "GPA" attribute of the "Student: Bob Smith" class has been set as a watchpoint. This means that each time a step that will modify the contents of "Credit Hours" is about to be shocked, the Unit Modeler will stop (and enter debugging mode, if it is not already) and show a dialog indicating that a watchpoint has been triggered. The user now has the choice as to whether he wants to *step*, *run*,

FIGURE 4.73

Watchpoints can be set by clicking on the magnifying glass icon in the upper left hand corner of a step unit.

or *stop shocking* (see the main debugging article for more information about these terms) starting at this step.

TERMINATING INFINITE LOOPS (CTRL + BACKSPACE)

What is an infinite loop? An *infinite loop* is a sequence of steps that loops endlessly, either because the loop has no terminating condition, has one that can never be met, or has one that causes the loop to start over.

For instance, consider the process depicted in Figure 4.74: Set These Units' Elements to Zero. If the List of Units Parameter has at least one unit passed to it, this process will be caught in an infinite loop. But why? Track the Counter variable through the process. It gets set to 1, then gets used to get an indexed element of List of Units. But it never gets incremented so that the loop will loop over each of the units in the List of Units. Instead, it will continually get the first element of the list.

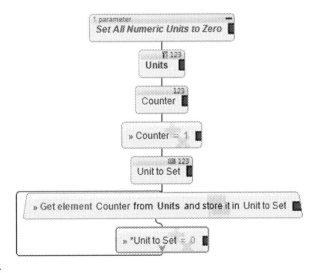

FIGURE 4.74

This process will enter an infinite loop, because a step to increment the counter is missing. You can stop this process by pressing the keys Ctrl and Backspace at the same time.

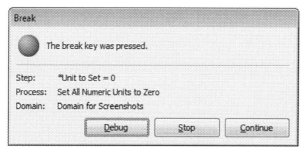

FIGURE 4.75 The Form Shown After Pressing Ctrl + Backspace

If you suspect that your process is caught in an infinite loop, you can press and hold the keys **Ctrl** and **Backspace**. This should break your infinite loop. This will bring up a message box that allows you to debug your process, stop your process, or "undo" the break by continuing to shock your process (Fig. 4.75).

SPECIAL UNITS

There are special kinds of units that can be used to perform special tasks, define other units, or that display differently on the Whiteboard.

NOTES

A note is a unit connected to another unit by the relation "hascomment" ([unit][has-comment][note unit]). A note is used to store help text regarding the unit it is connected to.

Notes are rich text units which are displayed in a special way on the Whiteboard. To display a rich text unit as a note, right-click on the unit, navigate to **Display as**, and select **Note**. The unit should display like the note in Figure 4.76.

The most common type of unit for which notes get created is the process. If a process doesn't have a note associated with it, right-click on the process head and select **Add a note**. You'll notice that a note template has been applied for the process's note. The top section of the process's note is used to describe the functionality of the process. The bottom section is used to describe the process's parameters. Below is a note for a process "Calculate the Average of this List of Numbers."

FIGURE 4.76 A Rich Text Unit Displayed as a Note on the Whiteboard

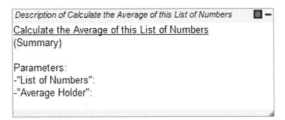

FIGURE 4.77 Adding a Note to a Process Displays This Template Note

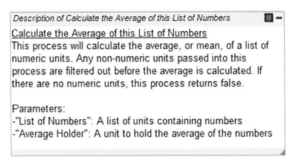

FIGURE 4.78 The Note After Filling Information into the Template Note

FIGURE 4.79 The Process Unit Shows a Yellow ? Icon Indicating It Has a Note

Clicking on this icon will display the note onto the Whiteboard.

Figure 4.77 is the note just after it was added (the automatic template was applied). Figure 4.78 is the note after it was filled in by the process creator.

Once a note has been added for a unit, that note can be accessed by clicking the "?" on the upper-right corner of the unit (Fig. 4.79). Only units with notes will have the "?" displayed.

Notes on processes can also be edited via Process Designer.

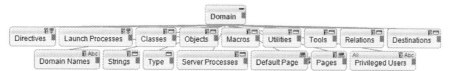

FIGURE 4.80 Every Domain Has a Domain Class That Defines Several Properties of the Domain

DOMAIN CLASS

Every domain created in the Unit Modeler has a Domain class. This class is designed to hold the top-level information that a new user exploring the domain would want to know (Fig. 4.80).

The Domain class is always named after the domain that it corresponds to. Thus, the Domain class for a domain named "Business Manager" would be titled "Business Manager."

Each of the attributes on the Domain class serves a specific purpose. These attributes are discussed below.

Directives

This attribute holds a list of directive processes. Recall that a directive process is a process that gets automatically shocked when the domain it is in gets loaded into the Unit Modeler.

Launch processes

This attribute holds a list of launch processes. Recall that a launch process launches some tool or user interface.

Classes

This attribute holds a list of top-level or important classes in the domain. When the **List all...** class selection tool is used in Attribute Designer, these classes appear in the list of classes to choose from for a specific domain. When developing a domain, classes can be quickly added to the Domain class by right-clicking on the class unit and navigating to the **Add to classes...** menu.

Objects

This attribute holds a list of important objects in the domain.

Assists

This attribute holds a list of any Assists created from or for the specific domain.

Utilities

This attribute holds a list or tree structure of utility processes created for the domain. Recall that utility processes are noninteractive processes pertaining to the domain they are housed in. Utility processes are processes that are useful externally in more than one instance ("nonspecific"). When developing a domain, utility processes can be quickly added to the Domain class by right-clicking on the process unit and navigating to the **Add to utilities…** menu.

Tools

This attribute holds a list or tree structure of tool processes. Recall that tool processes are processes that are interactive with the user in some way. Tool processes typically perform some kind of task or provide some type of assistance to a user. Tool processes usually do not have any parameters; users can just shock them and go.

Relations

The attribute holds a list of custom relation units created specifically for the domain.

Destinations

This attribute holds a list of custom destination units created specifically for the domain.

Domain names

This attribute holds a list of domain name units, which are used in CreateDomain steps within the domain. For instance, a domain called "Business Manager" might have a domain name unit containing the domain name "Business Manager Scratch." Whenever the Business Manager domain creates new scratch data, it will first use a CreateDomain step with the "Business Manager Scratch" unit as an argument (this puts the new data units in a scratch domain with the name "Business Manager Scratch").

Strings

This attribute holds a list of text units that are used within the domain. Whenever you right-click on an element insertion handle and select **New string…**, the new text unit that gets created is automatically put in the Strings attribute of the Domain class corresponding to the unit whose elements are being modified.

Type

This attribute is either set to Data, Model, or Scratch. It tells the Unit Modeler what kind of domain the domain is.

Server processes

This attribute is only used in server domains. It contains a list of processes that can be shocked from the client.

OTHER TOOLS
CLASS UPDATER

In some cases, you will have a model that has a base class and multiple instances of this base class. After having already created these instances, you may make a change to the base class. The Class Update tool can be used to update all of the instances this base class.

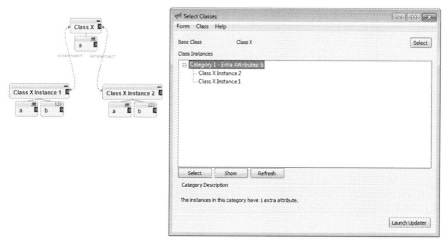

FIGURE 4.81 The Class Updater Tool Will First Find All Instances of a Base Class That Has Been Modified

Click on the ▦ button in the development toolbar to access Class Updater. The form shown in Figure 4.81 will appear. Now click on the **Select** button to identify the base class that you have modified. After doing this, a form will appear that finds all of the instances of the base class. Click on the **Launch Updater** button to show the actual Class Update tool (Fig. 4.82). You will now see all of the exact modifications that have been made and you will have the option to apply them to the instances.

FIND REFERENCES

It has been discussed that any domain may reference units (Processes, Classes, etc.) in another domain. It is often helpful to know exactly what these references are. The Find References tool will do this for you. In Figure 4.83 the tool has been run on the Bank Model domain described at the beginning of this book. You can easily see that the Bank Model referenced units in five other domains and you can see the exact place they were referenced.

CLEAN

Let's say you create a unit in a domain, but then never use it. Or perhaps you do use it, but then you decide not to use it and remove it from all places where it is referenced. You may also create an instance of a class to test it, but do not first change the domain. In all of these cases, your domain will have units that are not used by the model. Cleaning a domain means getting rid of these types of units. The Clean tool (Fig. 4.84) will find all of these units. It does so, by looping over all units in the domain and looking to see if they have any connections to other units in the domain; if they do not, then they are considered orphaned and of no use. These units will appear in the tool after clicking on Find Units.

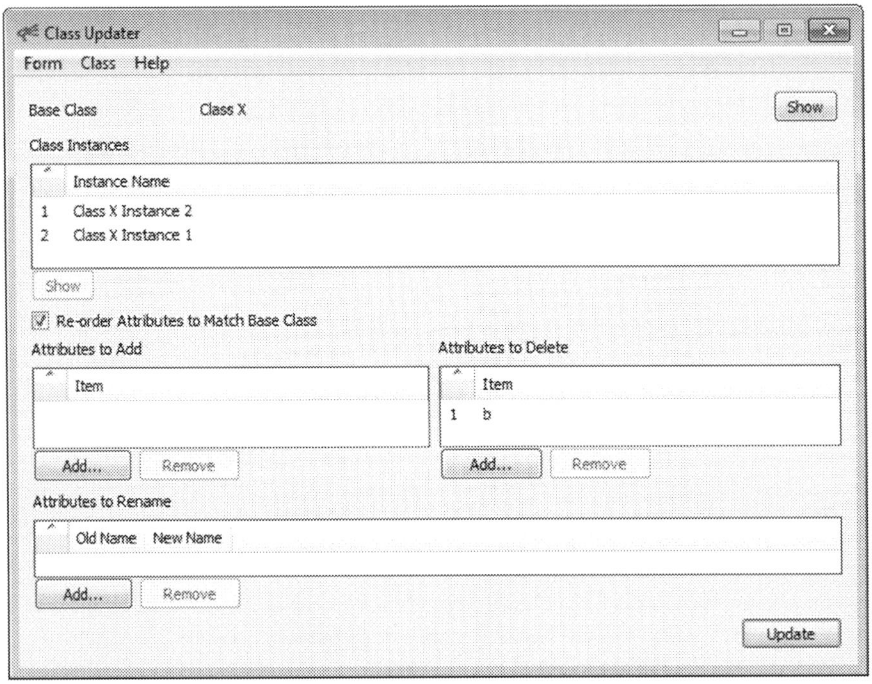

FIGURE 4.82

Clicking on Launch Updater in Figure 4.81 shows the Class Updater form which identifies the changes that it will make. Clicking **Update** makes the changes.

You should exercise some caution when using this tool, as some orphaned units may still be of use, even though they are not yet connected to anything. For this reason, and others, the Clean tool will create a recovery domain, so that such units can be retrieved if they are inadvertently removed from the original domain.

SEARCH

The Unit Search tool (Fig. 4.85) is a tool that allows that user to search for units with specified characteristics. There are five different types of unit searches: comment search, element search, element text search, path search, and element path search.

The Comments tab allows the user to search for units based on their comments. The Elements tab allows the user to search for units that contain the specified units as elements. The Paths and Element Paths allow for searches of paths and complex elements.

INSPECT TOOL

Within the General Modeling Process discussion it was noted that the functional model should be designed in such a way that as many processes as possible should

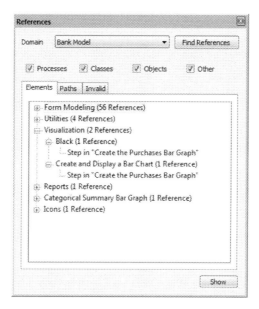

FIGURE 4.83

The Find References tool shows all of the domains that are referenced by the selected domain.

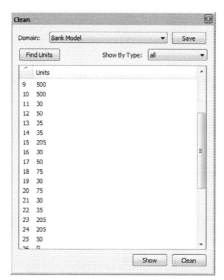

FIGURE 4.84 The Clean Tool Will Find and Delete Units That Are Not Being Used in the Domain

Usually these "orphaned units" are created while testing a model without setting the active domain to a scratch or empty domain.

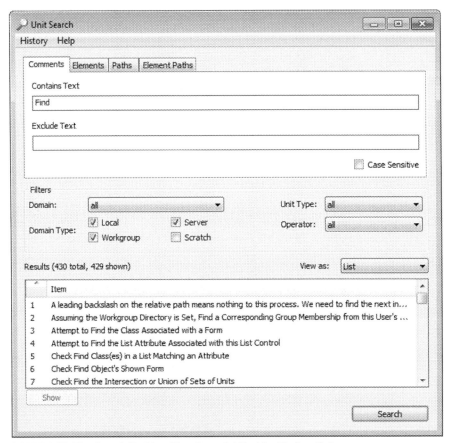

FIGURE 4.85 The Search Tool Is a Very Powerful Tool for Finding Units

be placed in the process attributes of a class. It was further noted that this makes a class and the model wherein it resides easier to understand. Nevertheless, it was also noted that this was not always possible and that form processes and watch processes would also be necessary from time to time. The Inspect tool (Fig. 4.86) is very useful in these situations as it will identify all processes (and other information) that are associated with a class, whether these processes are in an attribute, the form or watches.

WHITEBOARD PATHS PREFERENCES

The lines drawn on the Whiteboard indicate relationships between units. Actually, not all of the relationships are always shown. This is done to reduce clutter. In other situations, there may be some relationships that want to be shown, but are not. The Shown Whiteboard Paths Preferences (Fig. 4.87) tool allows you to customize the paths that are shown in the Whiteboard.

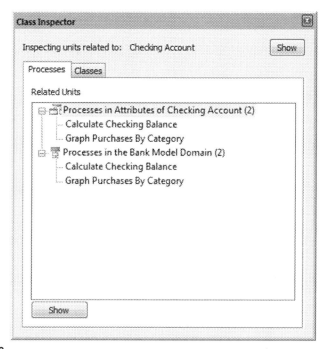

FIGURE 4.86

The Inspect tool will provide immediate insight into the design of a class and its custom form.

EXPLORING AN EXISTING MODEL

It is an important requirement of the Unit Modeler Technology that it be easy and straight-forward to understand any existing model. There are some techniques that can help you accomplish this (Fig. 4.88):

1. View the pages for the domain. A polished domain will have pages that help explain what it is about and how it was constructed.
2. Look for comments on various structures that explain what they are for.
3. Look at the domain class. This holds the classes and processes that are important for a domain. It is always a good starting point.
4. If there is a form shown from the model, there are tools for showing the underlying class of the form and then drilling down to explore its properties and processes. This technique is demonstrated in Figure 4.88.

DISTRIBUTION OF APPLICATIONS

Developers who create applications within the Unit Modeler have multiple options for distributing their creation.

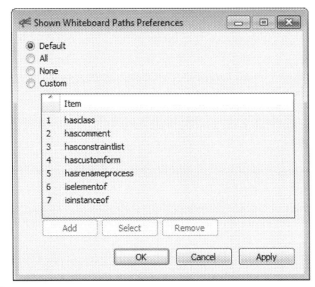

FIGURE 4.87

The Shown Whiteboard Paths Preferences form allows you to define what paths will be shown in the Whiteboard.

1. You can simply send it to the people who you want to use it. You can send it via the Unit Modeler messaging system or via email. If you send it as an attachment in a UM message, then the domain will automatically load. If you send it via standard email, the recipient can save it to their local drive and then load the domain from within the either the UM standard or Professional versions.
2. You can create a workspace and place your domains there. Members of the workspace can then load the domain upon joining the group. Workspaces can be public, private or semiprivate. Membership can either be free or require subscription.
3. You can submit your domain to KeLabs for inclusion in its public libraries.

POLISHING YOUR MODEL

After you have created your model and tested it, you should take steps to polish the model before considering it finished. There are a number of items to address.

CREATE A HOME PAGE

Any saved domain can have any number of pages associated with it. A default page is shown to the whiteboard whenever the domain is loaded by a user through the Load Domain menu. The other pages of the domain will be listed under the Pages menu item.

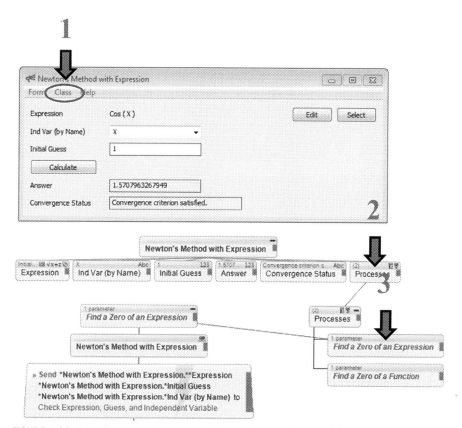

FIGURE 4.88 Techniques for Exploring the Design of an Existing Model

(1) Show the class upon which the form is based to the Whiteboard. (2) Show the list of processes associated with the class. (3) Click on the process that you want to see. (4) You can click on the header area of any unit that shocks a process to see the process that it shocks.

The home page (Fig. 4.89) should present the models that the domain contains, in a well-organized manner, such that anybody could come in and understand it right away. The classes of the domain should all be listed in the Domain Class's Class attribute. Utilities should also be listed with the Domain class.

Items of special importance and interest can be shown. If there is a top-level class within the domain, this class should be shown on the home page. The class should have a comment associated with it that explains what the class encapsulates and this comment should probably be displayed as well. You can save multiple pages and these can have hyperlinks between them.

From the items shown on the home page one should readily be able to drill down and find any component of the model that want to see. If somebody is handing a domain to me for review or for reuse, then I will go to the home page to get me started.

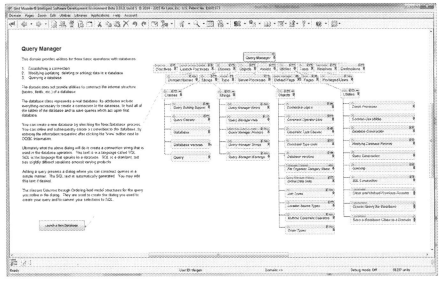

FIGURE 4.89

A well-designed home page will enable any user to quickly understand the contents of the model and drill down to any area of interest.

NAME YOUR UNITS PROPERLY

The comment on a unit is intended to provide humans a good understanding of what that unit represents. If the comment, however, does not do a good job of this, then it can be confusing to understand a model by someone else, or even yourself when you want to look at it later. Go through the classes and process of your model, to ensure that they are good indicators of a unit's purpose.

ADD NOTES TO CLASSES AND PROCESSES

You can add a note to classes and process, or any unit for that matter by right-clicking on the unit and selecting **Add a Note**. It is a good convention to add a note that explains what that process or class does. Sometimes this is obvious from the class's comment and design, but sometimes a few words of description can help understand the class very quickly.

ENCAPSULATE PROCESSES

Encapsulate process steps. Encapsulate all of the processes that would benefit from it. Encapsulating processes is important for understanding your model for identifying reusable components. If a process looks complicated or if it is very wide or very long, then it could probably stand to be encapsulated. If the process does some function within its body that is general in nature and might be done again, then this portion of the process should be encapsulated. Encapsulation takes a little extra time, but it saves a lot of time in the long run.

SETUP THE DOMAIN CLASS

The domain class, among other purposes, has attributes to identify important classes and utility attributes. Look at the domain class to make sure that these attributes are populated with the important classes and processes of your domain. The contents of these Domain class attributes are what show up in the DRC.

ADD ERROR CHECKING

This is a task that is often overlooked when developing a domain, but is an extremely important task for creating professional quality products. There are many places that error checking is relevant. For example, if you are prompting a user to enter a number, you should check to make sure that their input truly is a number before using this input.

CUSTOMIZE YOUR FORMS

Customizing forms should generally be one of the last tasks in building your model. This is just in case you modify the structure of your classes. However, after your classes are of a solid design, then the way they are displayed should be made to fit their purpose exactly. The default form display, may be functional, but often will have more than is necessary. A very common form customization is to remove certain buttons from the display of a list attribute.

THE SIMPLE SOLUTION

In all projects undertaken within the Unit Model, there are simple solutions and all others. Out of the many solutions that could successfully solve a problem, the simple solution is the one of least complexity. In fact, there is a quantitative measure of a domains complexity called the entropy factor and a tool for calculating it.

It is important that the design of a model, its classes and their attributes, be a good representation of the situation. Following the steps in the General Modeling Process will help ensure a model is a simple solution. If it is, then the myriad resources that act on classes and their attributes can be used. Forms can be shown automatically. A great deal of infrastructure comes for free.

CLEAN THE DOMAIN

The Clean Domain tool was created so users can find all of the orphaned units residing in their models. It is important to run this utility from time to time so that your domain does not get loaded with unused units.

To run this utility, navigate to the **Domain** application menu and click on the **Clean...** menu item. A dialog box with the title "Clean-Up" appears. This dialog helps you find all of the orphaned units residing in any locally loaded domain. Select the domain that you are working in and click on **Find Orphaned Units**. Once the units have appeared, you can show them to the Whiteboard to determine if they should be deleted. If a unit is not referenced by another unit, this utility considers it to be orphaned. Be careful that you do not delete some of your main classes or objects that are never referenced.

CUSTOM FORMS

The Modeler allows you to go far beyond just customizing the way individual attributes are displayed. You can customize nearly every aspect of the form including its menu, toolbar, content layout and dynamic processes. You can also make forms dynamic where they will change appearance while the application is actually running. To take advantage of this ability, it is helpful to have an understanding of the way forms are modeled. And to understand this model, it is helpful to have some background understanding of how forms work in general.

FORMS BACKGROUND

To understand the model created for building custom forms, it is beneficial to have a basic understanding of how graphical user interface (GUI)-based forms work and operate.

Forms serve several purposes: they display information, allow for a user to enter information and they allow a user to initiate some activity. Forms usually have a menu, a toolbar and will always have some content. This content consists of items called controls in programming and display objects in modeling. There are various types of display objects/controls such as edit boxes, rich edit text fields, buttons, list boxes, grids, and so forth. These controls display information and provide a way for a user to enter data and initiate some activity.

Controls can be grouped and arranged in many different useful layouts. There are several special controls, such as group controls and tab controls, that provide organizational structure. All of these controls have a list of other controls that are contained within the group or tab. Groups and tabs can be nested, meaning that a group can contain multiple other groups. This can theoretically go on indefinitely.

Forms are often dynamic. A dynamic form may change its appearance at any time, depending upon various factors that exist in the application. The Unit Modeler's model of forms supports dynamic forms. Dynamic forms are useful in many places, for example, when you want a control to be disabled until some information has been entered.

Another example of dynamic forms is when the contents of the form itself changes. This may happen depending upon some option that a user selects, for example, more detail, less detail, or a watch may be triggered by a unit undergoing some change. In either case, changing the form is easily achieved by altering the elements of the Form's Object attribute.

The life cycle of a form starts when it is first shown, it is then viewed and interacted with by a user, and, finally, it is closed. At each of these steps the form might want to do something special. For example, when a form is shown, it might want to first retrieve some information from a database to populate the form. When a form is closed, you might want to ask the user if they really do want to close the form. Forms have processes that will be shocked when the form opens and when the forms close. With these processes, a developer can control what happens at these points in the forms life cycle.

Forms have an additional mechanism for shocking processes: watches. Watches are something that identifies some variables that when anything about them changes, a response process will be shocked. This is an important way in which forms can be made dynamic and change as information changes.

THE FORM CLASS AND FORM DESIGNER

The model of forms begins with the Form class (Fig. 4.90). The Form class is the highest level class defining a custom form and includes attributes that govern the appearance and function of a form. The showform real operator takes a form class instance and displays it to the screen.

The model of a form views the form as a collection of display objects. Display objects are all of the individual items that appear in the form, and include things such as text, edit boxes, lists, buttons, and so forth.

Sections, groups and tabs are also display object types. These controls allow for complex organization of controls in a form. Sections can even include other sections. Groups of controls can be shown in separate tab controls.

The Form class has several attributes, which can be grouped into several categories:

- Layout attributes, which specify the top-level layout of the form itself
- Menus and Toolbars
- Objects that specify the content of the form (the dialogue controls)
- Response attributes, which specify response processes for specific user actions
- Functional attributes, which specify functionality used internally by the form

FIGURE 4.90 The Form Class Completely Determines How a Form Is Displayed By the Engine

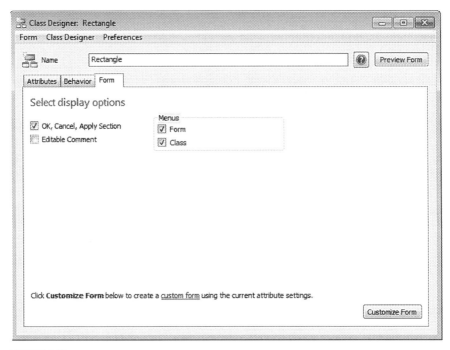

FIGURE 4.91

The Forms tab in Class Designer allows you to customize certain aspects of a class's form. If these are not sufficient you can create a custom form for the class by clicking the Customize Form button.

Like all classes, you can also add additional attributes to your custom form to keep track of additional information as needed.

When you show a class that does not have a custom form, a Form instance is created for you with all of the appropriate display objects and is then sent to the engine. When you add a custom form to a class, you are creating a Form instance and attaching it to the class via a "hascustomform" relation. When showing a form for a class, the Show Object Form process will look for the hascustomform path. If it finds one, then it will use the custom form provided.

Form Designer is a tool to configure the custom form for a class. It is accessible from within Class Designer by clicking on the Form tab (Fig. 4.91). This is pictured below. Initially you are presented with a few configurable items. If these do provide the detail you need, then you can click on the Customize Form button to create a Form class instance specific to this class. The Form instance is referred to as the class's custom form.

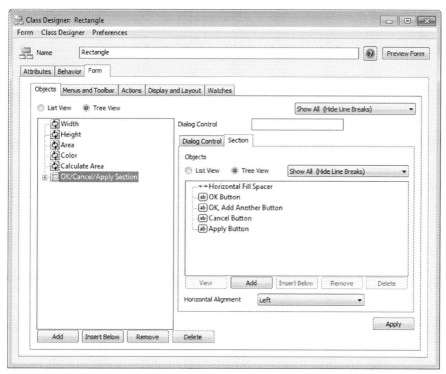

FIGURE 4.92 After Clicking the Customize Form Button Form Designer Will Appear in the Forms Tab

After clicking the Customize Form button, the Form tab will dynamically change and appear as pictured in Figure 4.92. A Form class will also be created and will have a 'hascutomform' path added to the class being designed (Fig. 4.93).

The tabs within the Form Editor allow you to directly edit the Display Objects, the Menus and Toolbar, the Actions, that is, the initialization, close, and store processes, and watches for the Form. Each tab is briefly described below.

Objects tab

The Objects tab allows you to directly edit the contents of the Form's Objects attribute. The Objects attribute of the Form class is a list of all the Display Objects in the form. The Unit Modeler supports over 20 categories of display objects and is able to build robust, beautiful forms. When the engine shows the form, it will loop over these display objects and place them on the screen one by one. Controls can be added or removed from this attribute while the form is open, which changes the form's layout. This is the basis of creating dynamic forms.

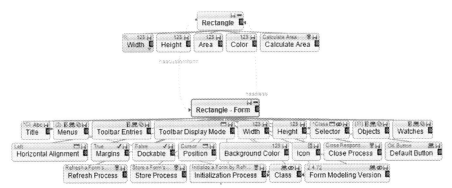

FIGURE 4.93 A Form Class Instance Is Created and Attached to the Class Via a "hascustomform" Path

There are many different types of form controls. The form control used depends on the type of information the computer needs to convey or receive from the user. Examples of some of the more common controls are as follows:

- Text:

Text control

Text controls are used for displaying static text to the user. These are sometimes referred to as "static text" controls since users cannot change the text.
- Edit:

Edit control

An edit is a control that allows the user to edit the text inside the control. These are sometimes referred to as "Text Boxes" because of the box drawn around the text inside the control.
- Check box:

Check box

Check boxes allow the user to make a binary selection (yes/no) about an option. Clicking the Check box toggles the state of the Check box between its checked and unchecked state. Sometimes, Check boxes are displayed in tristate mode, meaning the Check box has an indeterminant state in addition to a checked and unchecked state.
- Dropdown:

Pick a state ▼

Dropdowns allow the user to select an option from a list. Dropdowns are used when the options in a list are mutually exclusive, meaning only one option may be selected at a time. Clicking a dropdown reveals all of the options in the list.
- Radio buttons:

Never   Sometimes   Always

Radio buttons are displayed in a group with multiple options. Within a group of radio buttons, only one can be selected at a time. This means that selecting one radio button will unselect any other radio button already selected in that group. Radio buttons, like drop downs, are used for selecting an item in a list when only one item may be selected. Radio buttons are sometimes used instead of dropdowns when the number of choices is small.

- Lists:

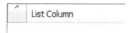

List controls are used to display many items that have common attributes. List controls allow users to sort, reorder, add, and remove items from a list. Many lists also include inline editing functionality that allows users to modify list items directly from the list control.

Menus and toolbar tab

Within the Menus and Toolbar tab (Fig. 4.94) a developer can completely define the contents of a form's menus and toolbar. The Form class's Menus attribute is a list of menu items. It defines the menus shown at the top of the form. Menus can contain any number or combination of menu items, submenus, and separators.

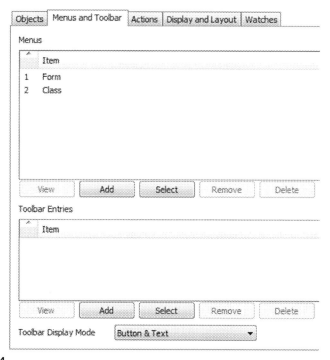

FIGURE 4.94

The Menus and Toolbar tab of Form Designer allows you to specify custom menus and toolbars for the class.

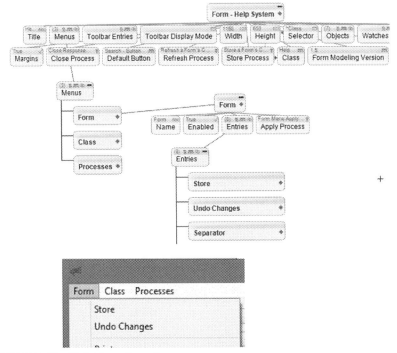

FIGURE 4.95 The Model for a Menu Item

Shown are the Form and Class menu items, which are added by default when a custom form is created.

The Toolbar Entries attribute on the Form class defines the toolbar shown at the top of the form. The toolbar on a form can contain any number or combination of buttons, dropdown menus, and menu items. Each menu item or button will shock a process whose parameter is the Form class to which the item belongs. The models for a menu item and toolbar button are shown in Figures 4.95 and 4.96 respectively.

Actions tab

The Actions Tab (Fig. 4.97) contains option to control certain functional aspects of the form. All of the processes listed have defaults, but you can also specify your own.

Default button

The Default Button attribute controls the default button in the form. Pressing the Enter key activates this button. This is the form's OK button by default, but for some forms it might be an action button.

Close process

The Close Process is shocked whenever the user attempts to close the form, such as by selecting the "X" in the upper-right corner, closing the form from its taskbar

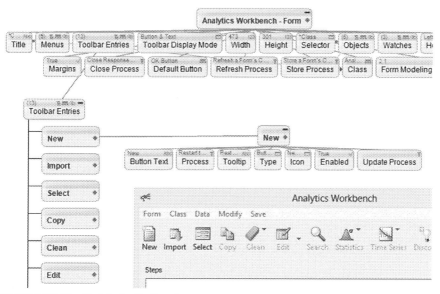

FIGURE 4.96 The Model of a Toolbar Item

Shown is the toolbar for the Analytics Workbench application described in Part 1 of this book.

button, or by pressing Alt + F4. The Close Process is responsible for closing the form and taking any other actions that should occur when the form is closed.

Refresh process

The Form's Refresh Process is responsible for taking data from the class and updating the form's controls. Normally, it does this by sending the form to "Refresh Controls and Child Controls," which shocks each control's Refresh Process. The Refresh Process can also take other actions, such as refreshing the class from the server if necessary. A forms refresh process is shocked when the form is shown or when it is triggered by some control that causes it to be shocked.

Store process

The Form's Store Process is responsible for storing data from the form's controls into the class. If you use a custom Store Process, you should shock the default Store Process to do this. The default Store Process also shocks the class's Rename Process if it has one.

Initialization process

The initialization process is shocked when the form is first shown.

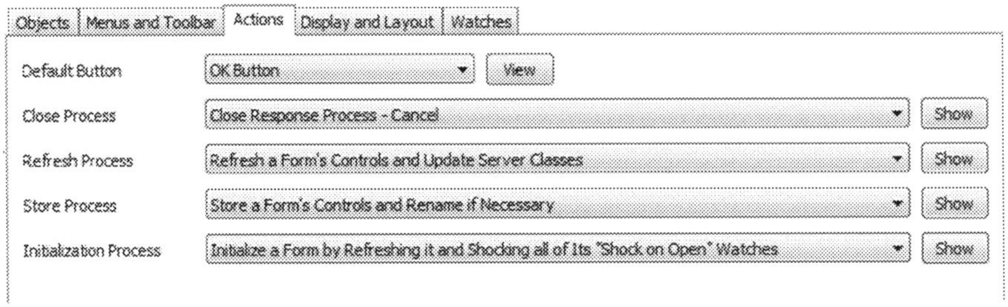

FIGURE 4.97 The Actions Tab of Form Designer

Default processes are created, however, you can also create your own to further customize the forms functional properties.

Display and layout tab

The Display and Layout tab (Fig. 4.98) allow you to specify a number of properties about how the form will appear when displayed.

A form's controls are laid out left-to-right. When a Line Break occurs, the next control is placed at the beginning of the next line.

A control's size is configured with its Width and Height attributes. These attributes can be a number, which indicates a fixed size, or they can use special values for resizable controls. Width and Height also support some special values:

- "Minimized," which minimizes the form
- "Maximized," which maximizes the form

If a whole row of controls does not fill the width of the form, it is left aligned, right aligned, or centered according to the form's Horizontal Alignment attribute.

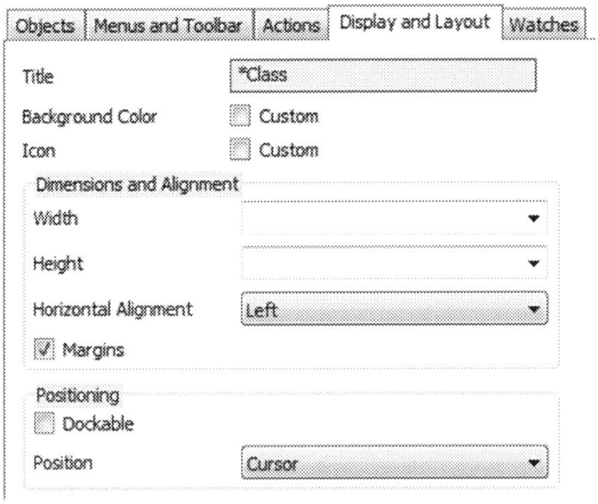

FIGURE 4.98 The Display and Layout Tab of Form Designer

FIGURE 4.99 The Model of a Form Watch

Watches

Watches shock a process whenever certain units are modified. Watches are very use-ful for a number of purposes including dynamic forms. Watches are defined using a Watch class (Fig. 4.99).

The Watch class has four attributes, each of which performs a special function:

1. The Units to Watch attribute can contain references to any number of units. If this attribute contains an element such as *List, then it will also watch all of the elements of the List. For example, Watch can watch an attribute of the form's class by using "*Class.Attribute," or it could watch the "Selections" attribute of a list control in that form. Any change in any of the units identified by that element triggers the Watch Process. There is no limit to how many items can be watched.

2. The Watch process can be any process of your choosing (or creating!). It can take any number of parameters and perform any task.

3. The Modified Units attribute of a Watch class is filled by the engine. Whenever a unit in the Units to Watch is changed and the Watch Process is shocked, the engine will fill the Modified Units attribute with the set of unit(s) from the Units to Watch that have changed in some manner.

4. The Modified Units *can* be passed as an argument to the Watch Process, but it is not mandatory.

Additional examples

5

The example models that follow will build applications that demonstrate the use of many of the important concepts and techniques of modeling. They will also address the reuse of many components of the domain library.

Each example will begin with a description of the application that will be built. It will then go through the steps of the General Modeling Process in order to develop a design for the classes and the processes necessary to build the application. Each example application can be created from scratch in less than 15 minutes.

All of the examples can be found in the Elsevier Examples workspace within the Unit Modeler software that you can download. Because of this, only the high level points will be made here.

A + B = C

We begin with a simple example of a working application domain. We have seen the a + b = c Calculator a couple of times already. This time, we will walk step-by-step through the model's construction. Subsequent examples will not include step-by-step instructions.

DESCRIPTION

We wish to create an application that will allow a user to enter two numbers and find their sum (Fig. 5.1).

GENERAL MODELING PROCESS

Our first step is to identify the main components of the application. We have the application itself, the two input numbers, and the third number representing the sum of the first two numbers. We additionally have a button that will shock a process to add the first two numbers and set the value of the third number to the result.

The application is modeled as a class. We will call this class the "a + b = c Calculator." The numbers are attributes of this class and each are of type number. The fourth attribute, entitled Calculate has a type process. We therefore have the class structure shown in Figure 5.2.

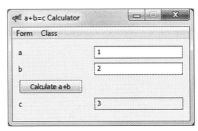

FIGURE 5.1 a + b = c Calculator Example

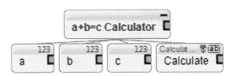

FIGURE 5.2 The "a + b = c Calculator" Class

By default, the process attribute will be shown as a button. When the button is clicked, the process that is the element of the Calculate attribute will be shocked with the class itself as a parameter.

PROCESSES

There is one process that is required for this application. This process is an element of the calculate attribute. This process can be added by right-clicking on the attribute on the Whiteboard and then selecting **Add Process**, as shown in Figure 5.3.

The process and its parameter will be created automatically for you and shown to the Whiteboard. The parameter will be given the name of the class. The parameter will

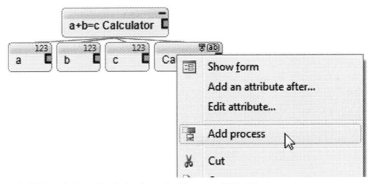

FIGURE 5.3 Right-click on the Calculator Attribute to Add a Process.

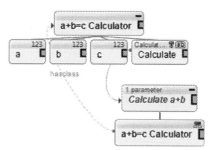

FIGURE 5.4 After Clicking "Add Process"

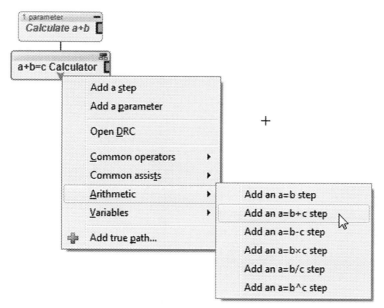

FIGURE 5.5 Add an a=b+c Step

also be automatically typed as a class with a specific class of the "a + b = c Calculator." You can see this by the path hasclass between the parameter and the class (Fig. 5.4).

The final step is to add the step that does the calculation. There are a few ways to do this. One way is to right-click on the parameter unit and select **Add true step**. Then click on the operator >> symbol and navigate to the a = b + c operator.

Alternatively, you can use one of the short cuts provided for common operators, as shown in Figures 5.5 and 5.6.

Now click on the [a] (Fig. 5.6) and hover over the parameter step right above it. After clicking, the Unit Modeler will go into selection mode as shown in Figure 5.7.

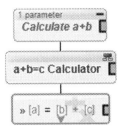

FIGURE 5.6 The Process After Selecting "Add an a = b + c Step"

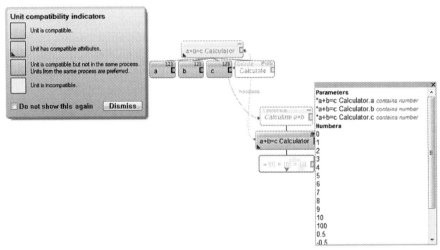

FIGURE 5.7 Select the Very First Option "*a + b = c Calculator.a"

Repeat This for [b] and [c].

Repeat this for [b] and [c]. We are now done. Figure 5.8 shows the complete model.

While we have now completed the example, there are few things to note in Figure 5.8.

1. The white box with gray border is smart selection showing you some options that seem reasonable. You could also make your selection by clicking directly on the units themselves.
2. The star in front of the first three options indicates that you want the contents or element of the parameter. The element of the parameter will be the a = b + c Calculator class.

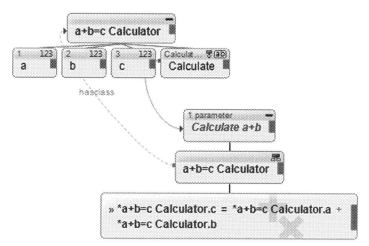

FIGURE 5.8 The Complete Model for the a + b = c Calculator

3. The .a on the options means that you want the a attribute of this class.
4. The parameter is highlighted in blue with an arrow in the bottom left corner. This indicates that this unit has attributes that might be reasonable selections. If you hover over this unit, you will see the following:

```
a+b=c Calculator (contains class, a+b=c Calculator)
contains number
*a+b=c Calculator.a
*a+b=c Calculator.b
*a+b=c Calculator.c
...
```

5. Finally you will notice that the units on the class itself are not grayed, but are highlighted in red. The red means that you can select these units, but that they are probably not the best choice. In this case, this is because you really want to select the * of the parameter, as smart selection is suggesting. The reason for this is that if we make a copy of the calculator class, then this process will still work properly. If you selected the class itself, then after making a copy of the class, the a = b + c step would still reference the original class and would not work properly.
6. Type your units properly and pay attention to what smart selection is telling you. You will be rewarded for it.

LIST ANALYZER
DESCRIPTION

We wish to build a tool that will allow a user to type in a list of numbers and then calculate the mean and standard deviation of the list (Fig. 5.9).

THE GENERAL MODELING PROCESS

We will call the application "List Analyzer." Within this application we have just a few items. We have the application itself, List Analyzer, a list of numbers, and the mean and standard deviation values. We also have a process that calculates the mean and standard deviation. This naturally leads to the model shown in Figure 5.10.

Notice that the first attribute, List, is typed as a list of numbers. So when we show the default form for this class, we get the form shown in Figure 5.9.

We now must finish off the Calculate process. First add the process as we did in the previous example, by right-clicking on the Calculate attribute and selecting **Add process**. Now we add the steps to calculate the mean and the standard deviation. We will use two assists from the DRC (Development Resource Center) to do this (Fig. 5.11).

The first assist is "Calculate Mean." We can find this by typing in "mean" in the search field (Fig. 5.11). After selecting calculate mean, the window on the right will

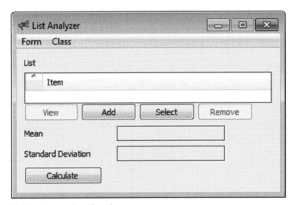

FIGURE 5.9 The List Analyzer Application

FIGURE 5.10 The List Analyzer Model

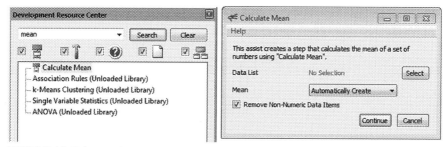

FIGURE 5.11 Using the Calculate Mean Assist

appear. This window is prompting us to identify the list that contains the numbers to calculate the mean and the unit that will hold the answer.

For the data items, we will select the * of the List Analyzer parameter and the * of its List attribute (Fig. 5.12). Smart selection offers this as the first option when we hover over the List Analyzer parameter.

For the Answer Holder, the assist can either create a unit to hold the answer for us, or we choose to **Select…** it ourselves (Fig. 5.13). Because we want the answer to be placed in the Mean attribute, we will select it ourselves.

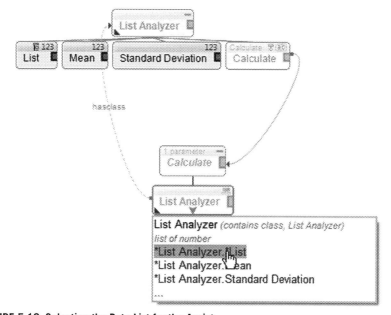

FIGURE 5.12 Selecting the Data List for the Assist

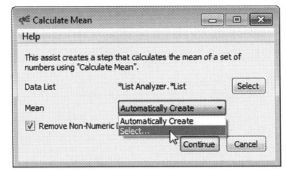

FIGURE 5.13 The Calculate Mean Assist

Selecting the unit that will be used to hold the calculated mean value.

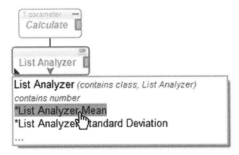

FIGURE 5.14 Hover Over the List Analyzer Parameter and Select the First Option That Smart Selection Provides

Once again smart selection presents the mean attribute to us after hovering over the List Analyzer parameter (Fig. 5.14). You will notice that the parameter itself is grayed, but it still has a blue arrow in the bottom left hand corner. This indicates that you don't want the parameter, but there are options based on this parameter that are valid.

After doing the same for the standard deviation, our model looks like Figure 5.15.

AUDIT MANAGER

In this example we create a tool to track information and activities that people commonly attempt to manage using spreadsheets.

Projects that work with data and that exceed the capabilities of commonly used spreadsheet applications, but that do not warrant a comprehensive software engineering effort, are ideally suited for the Unit Modeler Development Environment.

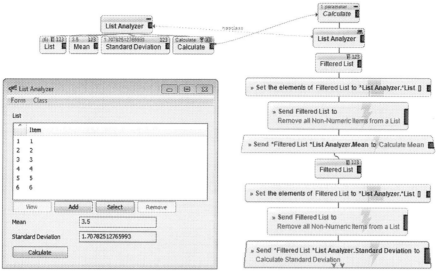

FIGURE 5.15 The Final Model of the List Analyzer with Its Form Shown

Every step in the Calculate process was added by assists.

If you currently use a spreadsheet to store data, ask yourself the following questions:

- Do you have several spreadsheets that contain related information?
- Do changes made in one spreadsheet force you to make changes in others?
- Is the amount of data unmanageable or becoming unmanageable?
- Can you view all relevant data through one screen, or do you have to keep scrolling through the spreadsheet to find information?
- Do you have a difficult time accessing certain information?
- Do you need to maintain records for ongoing use?

If you answered "yes" to even just a few of these questions, then the Unit Modeler Development Environment should be a much more effective alternative.

DESCRIPTION

In this example, we presumably work in an internal quality control department. On a periodic basis this department audits other departments for a variety of quality assurance purposes. The auditing department wants a tool that can track the results of these audits. More specifically, the tool should:

- Document and view internal audit periods and a list of internal audit areas for those periods.

- Document and view all of the details for each separate internal area (i.e., department audited, scheduled audit date, auditor, audit completion date, and a list of the audit findings), together with the ability to view the applicable internal audit report.
- Document and view all of the details for each internal audit finding (i.e., type, title, owner, description [necessary action], status, target date for completion, comments, and completion date).

SOLUTION

The internal audit management tool will consist of the following four interrelated forms (Figs 5.16 to 5.19):

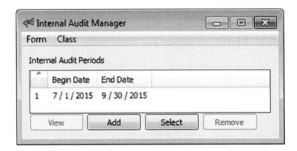

FIGURE 5.16

Form to allow a user to document and view a list of internal audit periods and a list of areas audited for those periods.

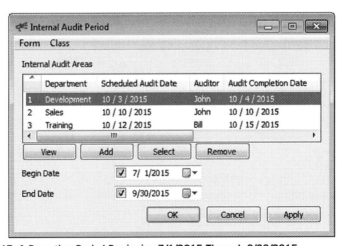

FIGURE 5.17 A Reporting Period Beginning 7/1/2015 Through 9/30/2015

Three departments were audited.

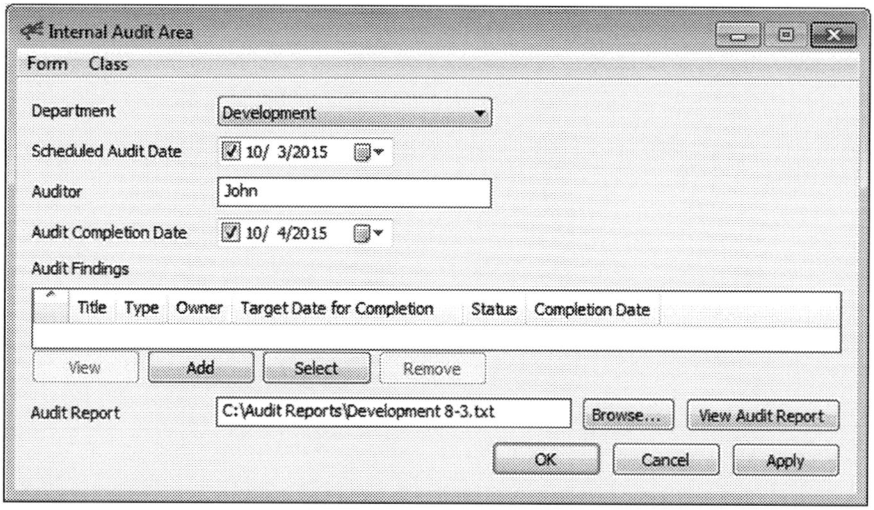

FIGURE 5.18

Form to enter and view details for any given internal audit area, including a list of audit findings and the ability to view the applicable internal audit report.

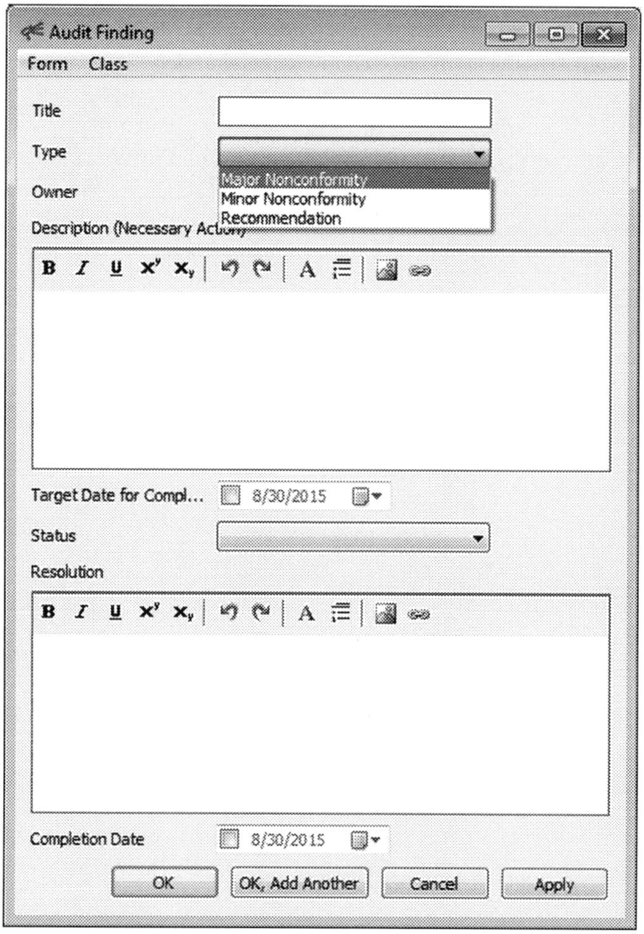

FIGURE 5.19 Form to Enter and View the Details for Any Given Internal Audit Finding

This class form will also track the status and resolution of the finding.

GENERAL MODELING PROCESS

First, we will create the two class structures that will give us a form to document and view the internal audit periods and the areas audited during those periods. The first class (Internal Audit Manager) will have a single attribute:

	Attribute	Type
1.	Internal Audit Periods	List (List of class, with a new class of 'Internal Audit Period')

This gives us the class structure shown in Figure 5.20.
Next, we'll define the new class Internal Audit Period:

	Attribute	Type
1.	Internal Audit Areas	List (List of class, with a new class of "Internal Audit Area")
2.	Beginning Date	Date
3.	End Date	Date

This gives us the class structure shown in Figure 5.21.
Next, we'll define the new class (Internal Audit Area) that will give us the form to document and view the information for each area audited, including a list of audit findings and a button to view the applicable internal audit report. This class will have seven attributes:

	Attribute	Type
1.	Department audited	Unit (Constraint list of designated departments)
2.	Scheduled audit date	Date
3.	Assigned auditor	Text
4.	Audit completion date	Date
5.	Audit findings	List (List of class, with a new class of "Internal Audit Finding")
6.	Audit report	Text (change Display from "Default" to "File")
7.	View audit report	Process (change Display from "Default" to "Action Button")

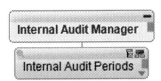

FIGURE 5.20 The Internal Audit Manager Class

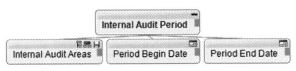

FIGURE 5.21 The Internal Audit Period Class

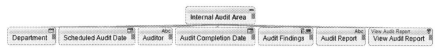

FIGURE 5.22 The Internal Audit Area Class

FIGURE 5.23 The Internal Audit Finding Class

Note: By changing the Display of the attribute type for "Audit Report" from "Default" to "File," we will have the ability to browse our computer and select the file representing the applicable audit report.

This gives us the class structure shown in Figure 5.22.

Lastly, we'll define the new class (Internal Audit Finding), which will give us the form to document and view the details for each internal audit finding. This class will have eight attributes:

	Attribute	Type
1.	Type	List (Constraint list of "Recommendation," "Minor," and "Major")
2.	Title	Text
3.	Description (Necessary Action)	Rich Text
4.	Owner	Text
5.	Status	List (Constraint list of "Open" and "Closed")
6.	Target Completion Date	Date
7.	Comments	Rich Text
8.	Completion Date:	Date

This gives us the class structure shown in Figure 5.23.

PROCESSES

Now that the overall class structure has been defined, we can complete the model by building the View Document process. This process will allow us to view the selected the file representing the applicable internal audit report by clicking the View Audit Report button. Figure 5.24 shows process created to accomplish this task. This is a simple process consisting of a single Assist available in the DRC ("Open a File or domain").

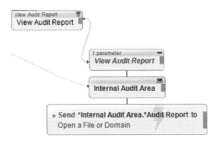

FIGURE 5.24 The Process to Show the Audit Report Document

2D GRAPHING

Graphs are an important feature of the Unit Modeler technology. There is is a comprehensive set of 2D and 3D graphing capabilities. The Graph class represents the model behind all graphs. This example will demonstrate the use of this class and how to use it to display multiple 2D line plots.

DESCRIPTION

In this example, we want to create an application that stores and plots the temperature over two days (Fig. 5.25).

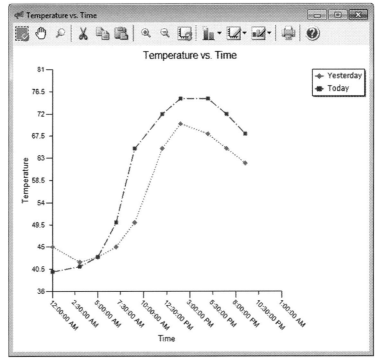

FIGURE 5.25 Graph of Yesterday's and Today's Temperatures

GENERAL MODELING PROCESS

First, we will create the class structure that we will use to store the information. We'll start by defining the class we'll use to store the temperature at any given time. This class will therefore have two attributes:

- Time
- Temperature

In this example, we'll choose to store the temperature in degrees Fahrenheit, so we'll name the temperature attribute "Temperature (°F)" (Fig. 5.26).

Next, we'll define a class that holds the temperatures for the two days. For this example, we'll store the temperatures for yesterday and today. We'll want to store these in two separate lists so we can plot them separately. This means we'll have two attributes: one for yesterday's temperatures and one for today's temperatures. Each of these attributes will store a list of the Temperature at Time classes. Lastly, we'll want to have a process that actually does the graphing. We'll store this in an attribute named Plot. This leads us to the class structure shown in Figure 5.27.

PROCESSES

Now that the class structure is put together, we can focus on building the Plot process. The Visualization domain provides many of the utilities that you'll need to build graphs. If all you're doing is creating a single line or scatterplot, there are prebuilt utility processes that can do this in a single shock step. In this case, we're adding two different plots to a graph, so we'll use other utilities in the Visualization domain to accomplish this task.

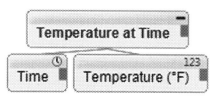

FIGURE 5.26 The Model of a Temperature Point

FIGURE 5.27 The Class Representing the Temperature Plotter Application

There are three main steps to programmatically creating a graph or visualization for display. The DRC provides Assists that help with each of these tasks.

1. Create an instance of the graph class (normally this should go in a scratch domain).
2. Add objects, plots, and axes to the graph.
3. Show the graph.

Figure 5.28 shows all the processes created to accomplish these tasks:

These processes were all created using assists from the DRC as well as the encapsulation tool. Note how each task is encapsulated into separate processes. This is a technique that improves the readability of your processes. Generally, if a process cannot fit on your screen it could probably be encapsulated into smaller processes.

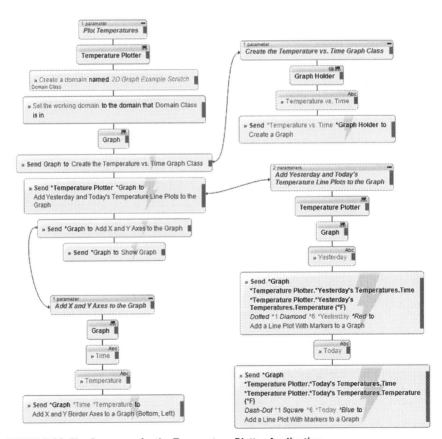

FIGURE 5.28 The Processes for the Temperature Plotter Application

4D SCATTERPLOT

In the previous example we saw how to use the Graph class to create line plots. The Graph class, however, can display more than just line plots, scatter plots and bar graphs. It can also be used to create visualizations containing circles, rectangles, pictures and a variety of other types of display objects.

DESCRIPTION

In this example, we will use the Graph class to visualize a list of circles, with each circle having a position (x, y), a radius, and a color (Fig. 5.29). Since each circle has 4 degrees of freedom, this domain could be reused as a 4D scatter plot.

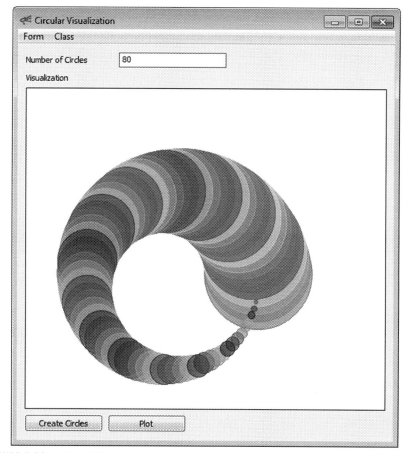

FIGURE 5.29 A Plot of Circles

Each circle has an x and y position, a radius and a color.

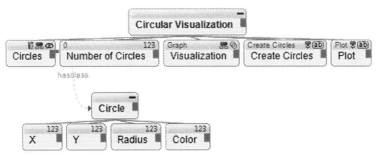

FIGURE 5.30 The Sturctural Model of the Application

Two solutions will be presented to this project. The first will reflect a more traditional approach in that a process will be built that adds circle display objects for each circle within the system. The second approach will employ the use of complex elements to define the application. This approach will require no processes for adding the circles to the graph, and will instead use the infrastructure of the Unit Model to create the visualization automatically. It will also update itself automatically when new circles are added.

Design 1

As stated above, this design will involve two processes: a process to create the circles and a process that adds the circles to the graph. The two classes for this are the top-level application class, Circular Visualization, and a class that holds the information about a circle (Fig. 5.30).

The Circular visualization class includes two process attributes: one to create the circles and one to plot the circles. It also includes an attribute that holds the graph that the circles are displayed on. This attribute is set to Deep Copy so each instance of the Circular Visualization class gets its own graph. In this method, the default graph has one attribute modified to be different than the original graph: it is set to lock the aspect ratio so our circles always look like circles regardless of what size we make the window.

Both of the approaches will reuse the same process to create the circles. This process determines the position and color of each circle based on the number of circles that are defined to be displayed on the graph. The Create Circles process and its subprocesses are shown in Figure 5.31.

Once we've created the circles, we also have to add the circles to the plot. To do this, we'll use a combination of two prebuilt utilities as well as a utility process created specifically for this domain.

The first prebuilt utility we'll use is from the Visualization domain. It contains a utility process for adding a circle to a graph. This process takes almost everything that we've defined on our Circle class: the X and Y positions, the radius, and the color. With this utility process, adding our circle to an existing graph is as easy as including one shock step (Fig. 5.32).

Now, we'll use this process in conjunction with a utility process to apply this to all of our circles (Fig. 5.33).

We've now completed all of the processes for this design.

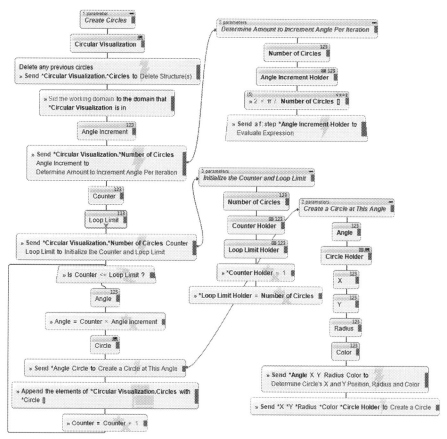

FIGURE 5.31

The Create Circles process creates circle display objects for each Circle added to the Circle Visualization.

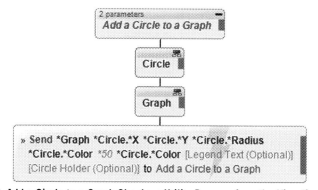

FIGURE 5.32 Add a Circle to a Graph Shocks a Utility Process from the Visualization Domain

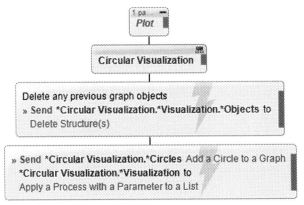

FIGURE 5.33 The Completed Plot Process

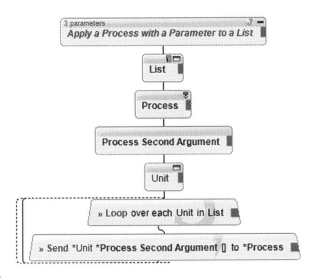

FIGURE 5.34

The Apply a Process with a Parameter to a List process is from the Utilities domain and demonstrates sending a process as a parameter to another process.

Note: The **Apply a Process with a Parameter to a List** process (Fig. 5.34) is one of the resources available in the public libraries. It demonstrates the use of sending a process as a parameter to another process. While this is not unique to the Unit Modeler, it is nothing special in the Modeler, because a process is a unit just like anything else. It can be an efficient technique at times.

Design 2

As with the previous two examples, our top-level class will be a class representing the application itself, which we will call Circle System. In the first example, we made a process that added a circle display object for each of our circles, but here we will demonstrate a powerful feature of the Unit Modeler—complex elements.

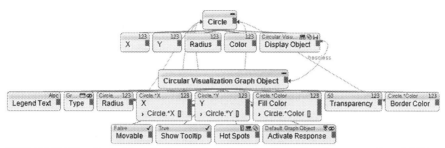

FIGURE 5.35 The Circle Class Revised to Include an Attribute That Represents How It Will Be Visualized

To do this, we will want to reuse the infrastructure of the Visualization domain, which was discussed earlier in "Areas of Support" in Part 3. In that discussion, we learned that any visualization is represented by the Graph class and that everything that appears within the visualization is a visual object that is listed in the Graph's objects attribute. In this model, we will still have our set of circles defined in a similar way as the first design, but we will include an additional attribute to the Circle class: the graph object that will be used to display the circle on the graph. This graph object will have complex elements that refer to attributes on our circle class (Fig. 5.35).

Because the display object is a deep-copy attribute, the references to the Circle's attributes are automatically updated when the circle is copied. With this model, it is no longer necessary to have any additional steps to set the attributes on the Circular Visualization Graph object. Using these references also means that if the circle's attribute values change, the visual display will automatically be updated.

Because we know another property of our graph now, we will set the objects attribute of the graph class with a complex element that references all of our Circle's Display objects (Fig. 5.36).

Using this technique means we do not have to create any processes to add the circles to the graph; as we add new circles, that they will automatically be created and added.

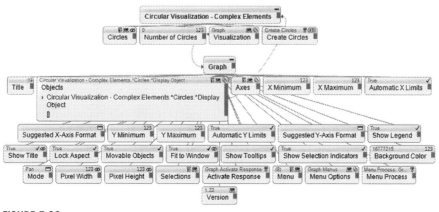

FIGURE 5.36

The Graph instance used to visualize the circles has its objects attribute set to the Display objects of all of the Circle classes.

STUDENT CLASS MODEL

DESCRIPTION

This example creates a model of a student and the courses they are taking (Fig. 5.37). A student can take one or more "Courses" during their time in school. Each time a student takes a course, the course is logged in the student's list of courses (Fig. 5.38). The Course class records the title of the course, the number of credit hours that the course is worth, and the grade the student received after taking this course. Once a student has one or more courses logged, the weighted GPA can be calculated via the process "Calculate Weighted GPA" (Fig. 5.39).

GENERAL MODELING PROCESS

This is a very simple and straight-forward model. There are two classes: the Student and a Course. The student has a name, the list of courses that they are taking, a process attribute to calculate the weighted GPA and the weighted GPA.

The Course class has a title, number of credit hours and the grade that the student received.

The Save button can easily be added by clicking on Add Save Button... within the Form tab of Class Designer. The Save button is an important feature as it allows a user to save their work to their local drive or a Workspace. It also provides an option to add the saved file to their personal File Organizer as shown in Fig. 5.40.

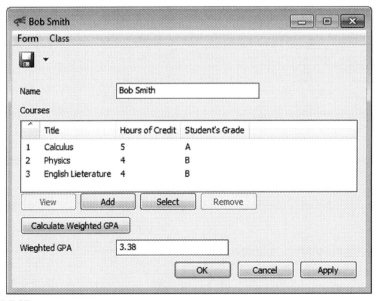

FIGURE 5.37

An application to track the courses a student is taking and to calculate a weighted GPA for the student.

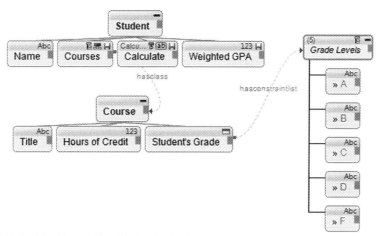

FIGURE 5.38 The Classes That Model the Student and the Courses They Take

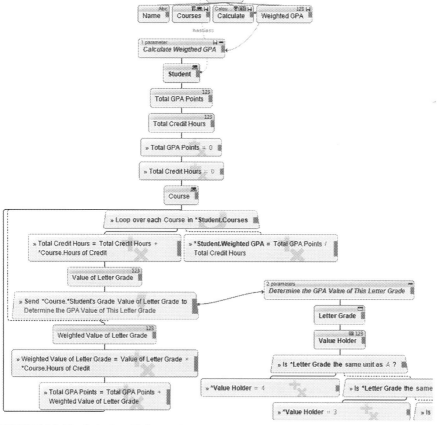

FIGURE 5.39 The Calculate Weighted GPA Process

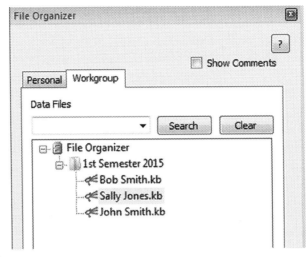

FIGURE 5.40

Clicking the Save button allows the student model to be saved to a Workspace or to a Personal File Organizer. The student information can be recalled by double clicking on the student's name.

SCHEDULED PROCESSES
DESCRIPTION

Frequently, programs or applications want to execute some task on a timed interval. For example, the alarm clock on your phone needs to execute a task that makes your alarm go off at the specified time. Email programs can be setup to check for new messages on a specified interval. The Unit Modeler provides a set of utility processes that enable you to schedule processes to occur at a specified time and on a recurring basis. In this example, we'll create a simple application that schedules a process to run at a specified time.

GENERAL MODELING PROCESS

First, we will create the class structure that we will use to store the information. We'll start with defining the Alarm Clock class. The alarm clock will need to know the time for which the alarm is scheduled, and it will need a process to actually schedule the alarm. Therefore, we'll give the alarm clock two attributes (Fig. 5.41):

1. Time
2. Schedule

Processes–alarm clock

The processes for scheduling the alarm clock are relatively simple. We'll have to build two processes. The first process will schedule the alarm. This will go in the "Schedule" attribute of the Alarm Clock class. The second process is the process that

FIGURE 5.41 Alarm Clock Class

will actually execute when the alarm goes off. This process will be passes as an argument when the first process sets up the scheduled process.

We'll first create the process that runs when the alarm goes off. We could have this process do anything we want. For this example, we'll just have it display a message box (Fig. 5.42).

Process Scheduling domain contains a set of utilities that help with scheduling processes, and the DRC provides access to these. There are many different ways to specify a scheduled process, depending on how far in advance it should run and how frequently it needs to reschedule. In this example, we're going to use one of the simplest utilities, "Schedule a Process to Run Today." We'll need to provide two arguments to this process: the process that should be executed at the specified time, and the time at which the process should run (Fig. 5.43).

We also provided some error checking to this process. If the user doesn't enter a valid time, it will inform the user and the process will not be scheduled.

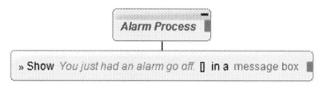

FIGURE 5.42 Process That Will Run When the Alarm Goes Off

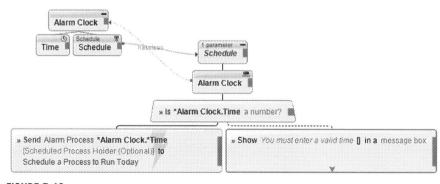

FIGURE 5.43

Process to Schedule the Alarm

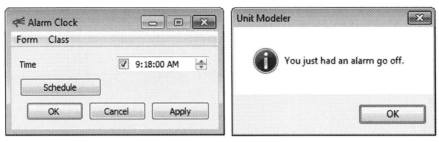

FIGURE 5.44 Alarm Clock Form and Resulting Message Box

Figure 5.44 shows the form for the Alarm Clock as well as the message box that is displayed when the alarm clock goes off.

WEATHER (WEB SERVICE)
DESCRIPTION

In this example, we will build an application to access current and forecasted weather information using Yahoo!'s YQL Platform. The basic API (application programming interface) provides current weather conditions and a five-day forecast, given a Where on Earth (WOE) ID (Fig. 5.45). A WOE ID is a unique geographical identifier for a location that can be determined via a lookup given a location name: http://woeid.rosselliot.co.nz/.

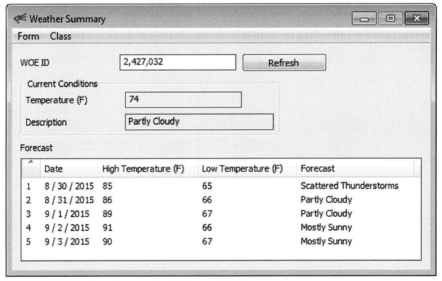

FIGURE 5.45 Weather Summary for Indianapolis, IN

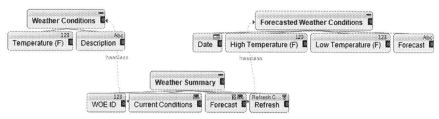

FIGURE 5.46 Classes for the Weather Summary Application

Solution

The primary component is the Weather Summary application itself. The application requires one input, the WOE ID, and has two outputs: the current weather conditions and the forecasted weather conditions. The WOE ID is an integer, so we will represent it using a number attribute. The current conditions is a composite structure containing the current temperature and description of the weather conditions, so it is best represented as a class with two attributes. Similarly, a forecast is made up of a date, high temperature, low temperature, and description of the forecast, so it will be modeled as a class as well. The Weather Summary class will hold a list of Forecasted Weather Conditions classes to show the five-day forecast (Fig. 5.46).

PROCESSES

There is one primary process in this domain: Refresh Current Weather Summary (Fig. 5.47). This process takes a Weather Summary class and fills in its Current Conditions and Forecast information.

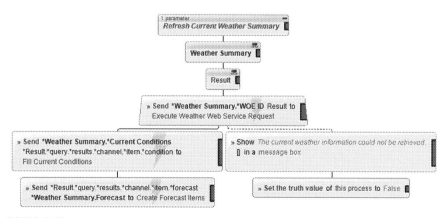

FIGURE 5.47

The Refresh Current Weather Summary process executes the web query and sets the applications information to the results of the query, both the current conditions and the forecast.

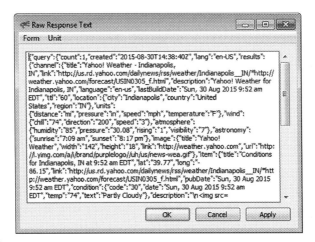

FIGURE 5.48

The information sent back by the weather website in response to our web query.

To get the current weather conditions, we will query Yahoo!'s APIs with a URL like the following:

https://query.yahooapis.com/v1/public/yql?format=json&q=select * from weather.forecast where woeid= 2427032

This URL specifies the query we want to execute as well as the type of the output (JSON [JavaScript Object Notation]).

To execute the request, we first build an instance of the HTTP (Hypertext Transfer Protocol) Request class (from the Web Services domain) and then update its URL and response data type. Setting the response data type allows the Web Services domain to automatically convert the raw response (text) into a Unit Modeler class structure, like Figure 5.48 shows. On the left is a section of the raw response from the web service. Shown on the Whiteboard is the class structure automatically translated from this text (Fig. 5.49).

Putting together such an HTTP Request is very simple (Fig. 5.50). We take the WOE ID and use the Create Instance utility and a pair of set steps to set the necessary attributes. We then use a utility from the Web Services domain to send the HTTP request and check the response status from the server. The server's response status indicates whether the request succeeded or not. We can only interpret the response if the request succeeds, so we pass in the list of Success response statuses to check for. In this case, if the request fails, we set the truth value of this process to False to indicate to processes shocking this one that the process did not successfully complete the intended action.

Lastly, we copy the received data into our Weather Summary class. These steps have been encapsulated for readability and potential reuse. Note that we use the utility Apply a Process with Output to a List to create a list of Forecasted Weather Conditions from our list of results (Fig. 5.51).

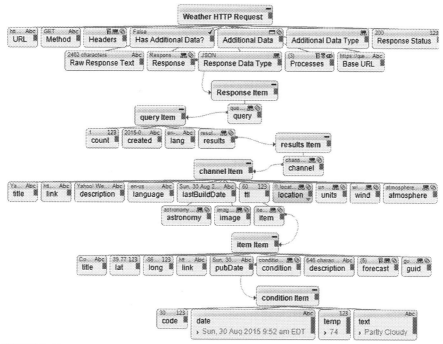

FIGURE 5.49 The text data sent back from the website in Figure 5.48 is parsed automatically and the class structure pictured is created. The condition data is shown.

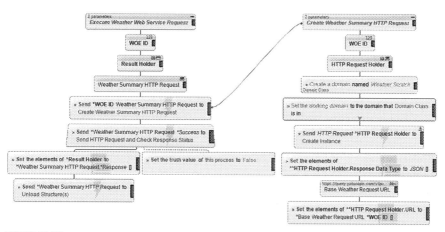

FIGURE 5.50

The **Execute Weather Web Service Request** shocks the **Create Weather Summary HTTP Request** process which in turn creates an instance of the **HTTP Request** class from the Web Services domain. It sets the **Response Data Type** attribute to JSON and then creates the URL for the request.

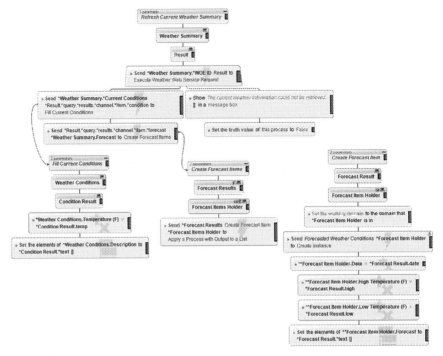

FIGURE 5.51

The rest of the subprocesses which take the results of the HTTP Request and fill in the current conditions and the forecast information. Note the use of the Apply a Process with Output to a List which takes a process as a parameter.

Extend the example

After reading the example on scheduled processes, can you extend this application to automatically refresh every hour?

After reading the example on 2D graphing, can you extend this application to plot the forecasted high and low temperatures?

VIDEO PLAYER
DESCRIPTION

In this example, we will use the capabilities of the Visualization to create a video player (Fig. 5.52). This video player will be capable of playing MPEG and AVI video files and can be extended to display additional annotations over the video. In this example, we will implement the following functional buttons on the video player:

- Play/Pause
- Previous Frame

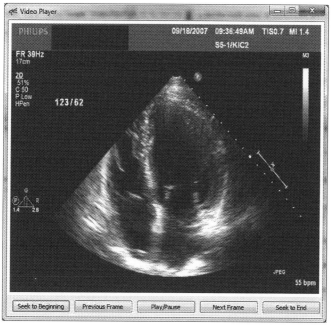

FIGURE 5.52 The Video Player Application

- Next Frame
- Seek to Beginning
- Seek to End

Solution

There is only one class we need to create for this example: Video Player (Fig. 5.53). This class represents the application that will play a video. This application's primary purpose is to hold the graph used for displaying the video. Additionally, this class will have process attributes for the five functions available on the video player.

The Graph attribute was set in Class Designer to be "Filled By Copy" so that a Graph instance is created in the attribute whenever an instance of Video Player is created. It was also set to "Deep Copy" so that the graph is unloaded when the Video Player is unloaded. The Video attribute was set in Class Designer to be "Hidden" because we do not want to show that attribute on the form directly; rather, the video itself will be shown on the graph.

FIGURE 5.53 The Model of the Video Player

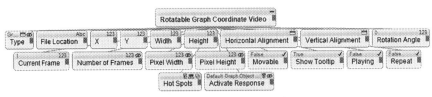

FIGURE 5.54 The Rotatable Graph Coordinate Video Control Class

PROCESSES

To start up the video player, we need to select a file and create the video on the graph. First we use the Prompt the User to Select a File assist to allow the user to pick the video to play. Using that file path, we use the utility Add a Rotatable Graph Coordinate Video to a Graph to add a video with that file path (Fig. 5.54). To make sure the video is centered in the display, we also set the graph's limits to match up with the width and height of the video (10, 10). Lastly, we use the GetDisplayObjectInfo (Get the display information) operator to get information about the video; namely, we need to have the length (number of frames) of the video for the seek functions to work (Fig. 5.55).

Note: This example does not account for differing aspect ratios. The Width and Height are arbitrarily set to 10 and 10. After retrieving the display object info, we could use the pixel width and height to more accurately display the video.

At this point, we can implement the processes for the five process attributes, starting with play/pause.

FIGURE 5.55 The Initialize Video Player Process Asks the User to Select a File to Display

It then creates a video control for this file and adds it to the Video Player's Graph class.

To play or pause the video, we use the Toggle the Playing Status of a Video assist and pass in the video we were handed back during the initialization process (Fig. 5.56).

The remaining four functions will seek a particular frame in the video, so we'll use the Visualization assist "Seek to a Frame in a Video" for each of these. Note that the Current Frame automatically wraps around, so we do not need to do any bounds-checking here. If we reach the end of the video, seeking to the next frame will take us back to the beginning (Fig. 5.57).

The processes for seeking to the beginning and end of the video are also very straightforward (Fig. 5.58). The first frame is frame 1, and the total number of frames were retrieved when the video was initialized (using the GetDisplayObjectInfo operator).

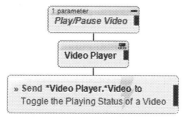

FIGURE 5.56 The Process of Playing and Pausing the Video

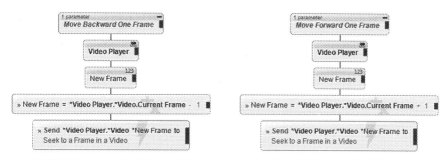

FIGURE 5.57 Processes for Stepping Through the Video Frame by Frame, Both Forward and Backward

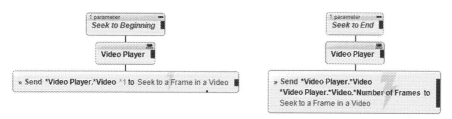

FIGURE 5.58 Processes for Seeking to the Beginning and End Frames of the Video

ESTIMATING THE ACCELERATION OF GRAVITY
DESCRIPTION

The purpose of this example is to show how to incorporate an existing tool into your own application. We will reuse the Curve Fitting tool from the Statistics package (Fig. 5.60 and 5.61) in an application that estimates the acceleration of gravity at the earth's surface. We will also demonstrate how to explore the model which defines this tool. The setup is as follows.

Trial data was created simulating the vertical motion of projectiles with several different sets of initial conditions. This data is plotted in Figure 5.59.

Each trial represents a collection of ordered pairs (t,y), where t gives the time (in seconds) and y gives the height (in meters) of a projectile in freefall motion near the earth's surface. The acceleration of gravity can then be estimated as 2|a|, where $y = a t^2 + b t + c$ is the quadratic curve of best fit through the given ordered pairs.

For the above example, the coefficient a is calculated to be -4.8935 leading to an estimate of 9.787 m/s^2 for the acceleration of gravity. The actual value for the acceleration of gravity, usually denoted by g, is 9.80665 m/s^2.

Using curve fitting

The purpose of this example is to reuse the model behind the Curve Fitting tool in a process. By doing this, we will not have to use the form pictured shown in Fig. 5.61 and 5.63. We could then reuse this process to automatically calculate the acceleration

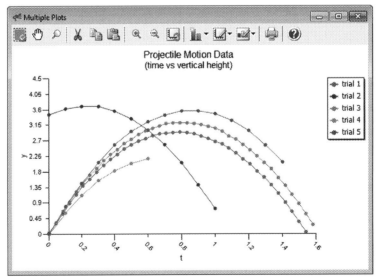

FIGURE 5.59

Simulated data representing the vertical height of projectiles having various initial conditions of velocity, height and angle. The sampling rate of the data also varies.

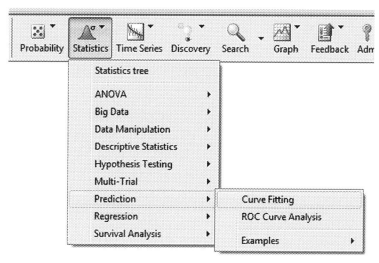

FIGURE 5.60

The Curve Fitting tool is located in the Data Analytics package and can be accessed via its toolbar.

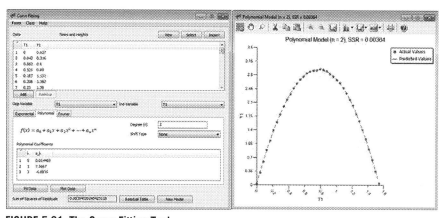

FIGURE 5.61 The Curve Fitting Tool

Data from the first trial has been entered into the tool. The actual data is plotted against the projected data.

for several trials. Here are some general steps for incorporating an existing tool into your own application:

- Create an instance of the tool.
- Plug your data into the tool.
- Run the tool.
- Extract the desired information from the tool.

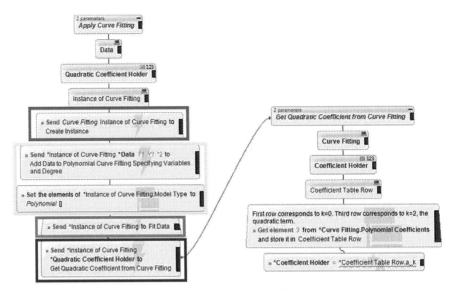

FIGURE 5.62 The Main Process That Reuses the Curve Fitting Tool

Figure 5.62 is a snapshot of the process that carries out these steps for this example of estimating g. Each step corresponds to a colored box.

Steps 1 and 2 above were completed with help from the assists that can be found in the DRC. You may have to load a certain domain to get certain assists to appear in the DRC. In this case, if you want to access the assists related to Curve Fitting, you will want to make sure that the Curve Fitting domain is loaded, which you can do simply by running the tool.

We could also use an assist for adding the step to fit the data; however, we want to demonstrate here how to explore the underlying model of a tool. There are naturally built-in ways to dig in to the contents of any form. In this case, we are interested in what process is run when you click the button "Fit Data." If you right-click on the "Fit Data" button and choose Show Action Process, you can see the process that is called when the button is pressed (Fig. 5.63 and 5.64).

As for step 4, this, again, may require some digging into the structure of the tool you are using. Fortunately, navigating down through a form and into its structures can be done with clicks of the mouse. Clicking on the red circles from top to bottom will cause a picture like the one shown in Figure 5.65 to unfold—in this case leading you to the location of where the quadratic coefficient is stored.

Note: The online example within the Elsevier Book Examples workspace contains much more than has been presented here. Here we have focused on the main process that reuses the Curve Fitting tool (Fig. 5.66). The online example also has an interesting tool to generate simulated data trials and a process to automate the application of the curve fitting process developed above to these trials.

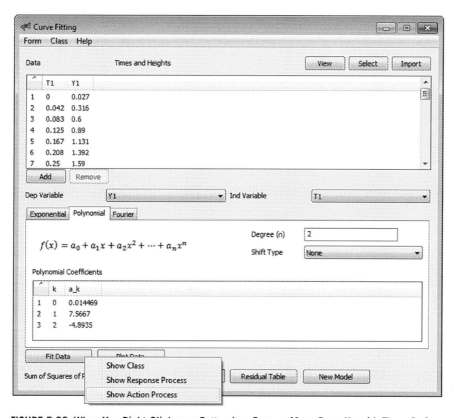

FIGURE 5.63 When You Right-Click on a Button in a Form, a Menu Pops Up with Three Options

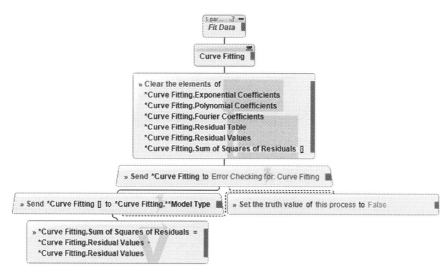

FIGURE 5.64 Fit Data Is the Action Process for the "Fit Data" Button

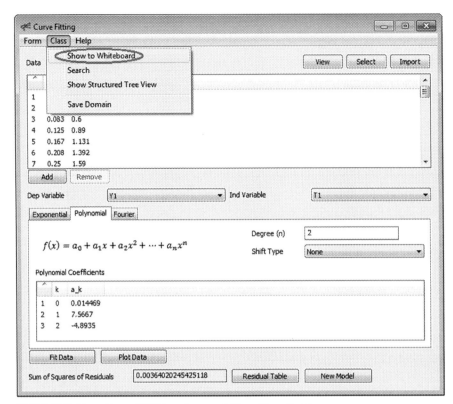

FIGURE 5.65 Many Forms Will Have Form and Class Menu Items

You can use these to show the classes that define the underlying model of the form. Here we will show the Curve Fitting class instance to the whiteboard.

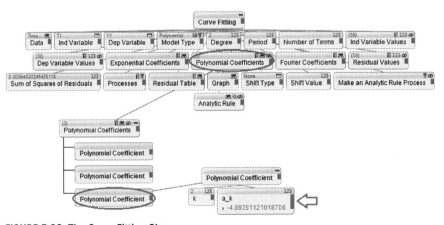

FIGURE 5.66 The Curve Fitting Class

We can now show the contents of its attributes to find out exactly where the information that we need is located within the class.

GRAPH THEORY AND NETWORK CONNECTIVITY
DESCRIPTION

The purpose of this example is to demonstrate the use of matrices in an applied problem involving networks. For those familiar with graph theory, the term *network* can be taken as synonymous with *directed graph*.

Notation

Consider a network consisting of nodes and connections between pairs of nodes. For example, here are some networks:

- An airline's destinations and flights between them.
- A franchise of stores across the country. Two stores are considered connected if supplies can be shipped from one to another in a day or less.
- A computer network. Two computers are connected if information can be passed from one to the other.
- Social circles. Each node is a person. Each person is connected to his or her acquaintances.

A network can be visualized as a collection of points (nodes) in the plane with paths (connections) drawn between them. The *adjacency matrix* for a network with n nodes is the $n \times n$ matrix whose ij-entry is the number of paths from Node i to Node j. Figure 5.67 is a visual representation of a network with eight nodes. Its adjacency matrix and cumulative adjacency matrix are show below.

Matrix algebra is helpful in keeping track of the number of connections between nodes of various lengths. If A is the adjacency matrix and k is a positive integer, then the ij-entry of A^k gives the number of connections from Node i to Node j consisting of exactly k steps.

We introduce one more notation. The *cumulative adjacency matrix* of order k is defined to be the $n \times n$ matrix whose ij-entry gives the number of connections from Node i to Node j consisting of at most k steps. We denote the cumulative adjacency matrix by $C(A, k)$, where A is the regular adjacency matrix specifying the network and k is a positive integer. The above fact about powers of A leads to the following formula:

$$C(A,k) = A + A^2 + L + A^k$$

The cumulative adjacency matrix is useful in answering questions about the connectivity of the network. Our ultimate goal is to build a tool that can display the cumulative adjacency matrix.

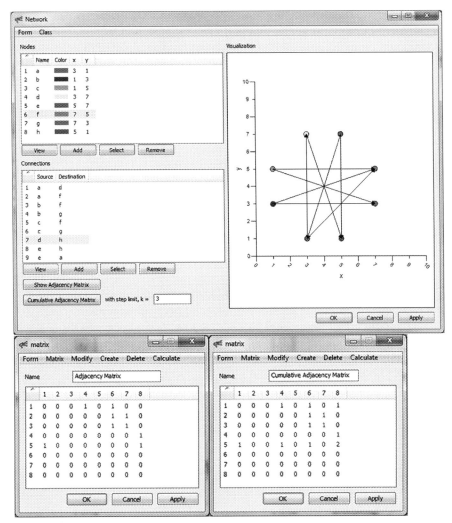

FIGURE 5.67

The Network tool with nodes and connections added as well as the resulting Adjacency Matrix and Cumulative Adjacency Matrix.

Model

The model of our application is composed of a top-level class called Network (Fig. 5.68). The Network class has an attribute representing a list of Nodes and Connections. The Node class has a Name attribute so that it can be uniquely identified. In addition, it has attributes similar to the 4D Scatter Plot example so that we can visualize the nodes.

The Connection class is modeled with an attribute representing the source node and the destination node. It also has a Display object attribute that is typed as a

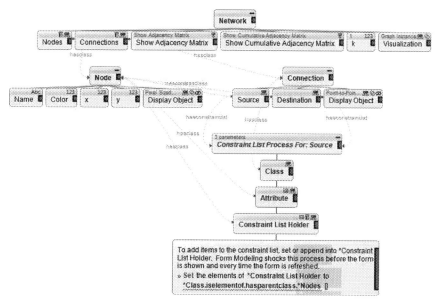

FIGURE 5.68 The Model of the Network Application

Line Segment. The constraint list process for the Source and Destination attributes is the same for both. The constraint list limits are choices to the nodes that have been entered for the Network. The complex element used in this process, *Class. iselmentof.hasparentclass.*Nodes, is used to reference the list of nodes. *Class is the Connection class; *Class.iselementof references the Connections attribute of the Network; *Class.iselementof.hasparentclass references the Network class and *Class. iselementof.hasparentclass.*Nodes references the Nodes that have been entered. When you click on the Add button under the list of connections you see Figure 5.69.

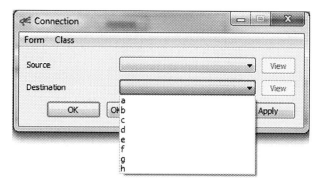

FIGURE 5.69 The Connection Class Form Allows Entering a Connection

The Source and Destination attributes have a constraint process that sets their possible choices to the Nodes that have been entered for the network (Fig. 5.70).

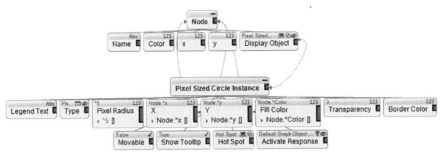

FIGURE 5.70

The Node class uses a technique seen previously to display itself as a circle in the application's visualization.

Just as in the Scatterplot example, the attributes of the Circle display object are set to the appropriate attributes of the Node class. In this example, we have used a Pixel Sized Circle instead of a Graph Coordinate Circle. This was done so that all circles would show up with the same size no matter what the what the size of the visualization is.

Functional design

Matrices play an important role in this domain for modeling a network. The online version of this domain can be explored for more detail about how matrices can be used. We point out some tips here for using matrices:

Typing

A unit should be typed as a matrix when it is expected to contain a single matrix. Note the matrix header itself is not given the type matrix. Instead the matrix header is demarcated by a path "isa matrix." This setup is completely analogous to the way the type class is used. See the two steps circled in red in the process shown in Figure 5.71. The first is typed as a holder of matrix, while the second is typed as a matrix. The first step is a parameter of the process. When this process is called, the user is expected to send a unit that will hold the created matrix. This first step is not to be filled with a matrix itself, which is why there is a holder in the typing. The second step is filled directly with a matrix and hence gets the matrix type.

Assists

The DRC offers many assists related to matrices. Figure 5.71 shows some of the assists associated with creating a matrix of a specific kind. The highlighted steps in the process in Figure 5.71 were created using matrix assists.

Matrix algebra operators

The matrix algebra operators can be found under the real operators. These include the standard algebra operators as well as some operators for extracting a row or column from a matrix.

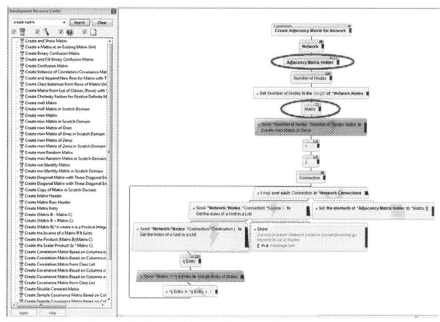

FIGURE 5.71 The Process for Calculating the Adjacency Matrix

Shown on the left is the DRC opened to assists for working with matrices.

Matrix tools

There are several tools for manipulating matrices. First on the matrix form itself, the menus provide many standard matrix techniques including the ability to transpose, row reduce, set the *ij* entries by formula, and calculate terms like rank or determinant. In addition, the math library provides a Matrices button on the toolbar that can be used to create new matrices. This button also lets you add, subtract, and multiply matrices (Fig. 5.72).

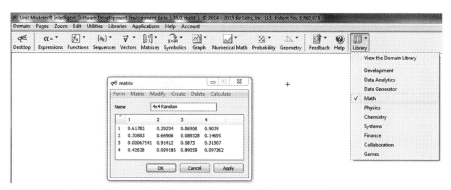

FIGURE 5.72 Matrix Tools Are Available from Within the Math Package

USING AN R SCRIPT
DESCRIPTION

This example demonstrates an interface with an outside software application, R, a computational and graphing package that enjoys immense popularity among statisticians and data analysts worldwide. The ability to access a versatile programming language like R directly from the Unit Modeler development environment enlarges the scope of problems that can be solved by either package on its own.

PROBLEM

Consider the standard normal distribution, having mean 0 and standard deviation 1, whose probability density function is the bell curve shown in Figure 5.73. If you take a random sample from this distribution, you expect to obtain both positive and negative numbers in roughly equal proportions. This problem explores what happens to the mean if you filter the sample to just the positive results. Probability theory can be used to calculate an expected value for the positive results: $\sqrt{2/\pi} \approx 0.798$. What this means is that for large random samples drawn from the standard normal distribution, the mean of the positive results should be close to 0.798.

We will test this calculation by drawing random samples from the standard normal distribution, keeping only the positive observations, and then computing the mean of these positive terms. These computations will all be completed in an R script to demonstrate use of the interface.

RUNNING AN R SCRIPT

Once you have R installed on your computer, the Unit Modeler ISDE (Intelligent Software Development Environment) should be able to access the software automatically.

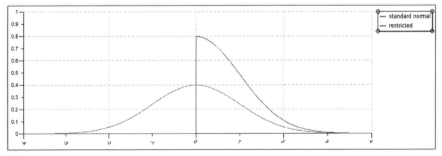

FIGURE 5.73

The standard normal distribution is shown in red, while the normal distribution restricted to positive values is shown in blue.

Here are the lines of R code that can be used to create the random sample and return the average of the positive terms:

```
v <- rnorm(1000)
pos<- v[v>0]
stats <- list(numpos = length(pos), avg = mean(pos), stdev = sd(pos))
stats
```

The first line creates a vector with 1000 components, each of which is a random number drawn from the standard normal distribution. The second line creates a vector consisting of just the positive entries of the random vector. The third line creates a named list which contains the number of positive entries, their mean, and their standard deviation. Finally, the last line prints the results to the screen. You can run this script in the "R Script Runner," which is accessible from the DRC, to get a sense of how it works.

CREATING AN R SCRIPT WRAPPER PROCESS

Once you have written your R script, you can create a wrapper process for running that script with inputs and outputs that are converted to and from Unit Modeler structures automatically. From the DRC, the "Create New R Script" tool enables you to enter the R code, as well as the expected inputs and outputs (Fig. 5.74).

The inputs are substituted into the code in place of their name (e.g., "NTOTAL" in the script above), and the output of the R script is placed in output units corresponding to each of the output types you specify, filled in the same order that they appear in the output of the R script.

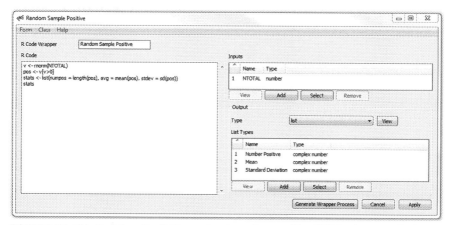

FIGURE 5.74 This Tool from the R Library Creates a Process That Will Implement a Script of R Code

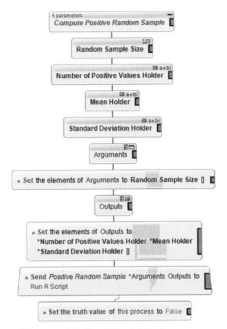

FIGURE 5.75 The Process Generated By the R Script Tool

When finished, click Generate Wrapper Process to build a process that encapsulates the execution of the R script for easy reuse (Fig. 5.75).

Now that we have a process that will talk to the R engine to compute the mean of a standard random sample filtered by positive values, we can easily set up a model for displaying the results of many samples (Fig. 5.76).

If we create an instance of Sample Generator and run the process, we get a result like that shown in Figure 5.77.

Looking at the values in the column "Mean of Positive" we see that the means do indeed cluster around the expected value.

STOCK MANAGER
DESCRIPTION

If you are an entrepreneur and/or small business owner, investor in a small company, or board member, you will have many fiscal decisions to make. One such decision is how much stock you need to sell and at what price. You may also consider offering stock options to your employees. The Stock Manager tool is used to (a) keep track of the stock purchases in a company, (b) calculate information about the company's stock, and (c) enable one to investigate various scenarios for a new offering, stock

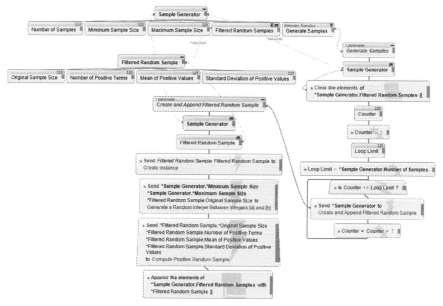

FIGURE 5.76 An Application That Uses the Generated R Wrapper Process

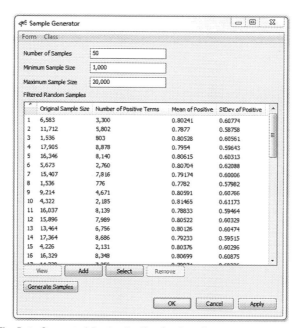

FIGURE 5.77 The Data Generated By the Application Reusing the R Script Process

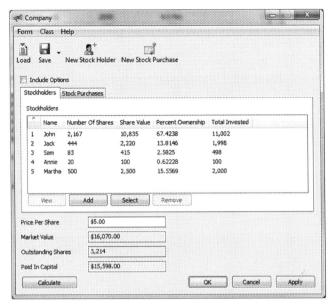

FIGURE 5.78 The Stock Manager Tool Is One of a Suite of Tools for Small Businesses

The Stock Manager tool (Fig. 5.78) tracks information relevant to investment in a company. It allows a user to explore the implications of possible new purchases and price changes, as well track past investments.

options, or buybacks of stock. It will calculate everyone's stock value at a given price, their percent ownership of the company, the value of the company and other information.

The model of this tool is fairly simple and presented in Figure 5.79.

BUILDING A DATABASE FROM A MODEL
DESCRIPTION

In this example, we want to create an application that gets data from and writes data to an external database. This application will be a contact management tool that stores individual contacts and the companies with which they are associated.

GENERAL MODELING PROCESS

First, we will create the class structure that we will convert into the database. Each list of classes in the class structure will represent a table of the database, and each attribute within those lists will represent a column of the tables. Therefore, the top-level class of the model will usually consist of a class with list attributes. For the

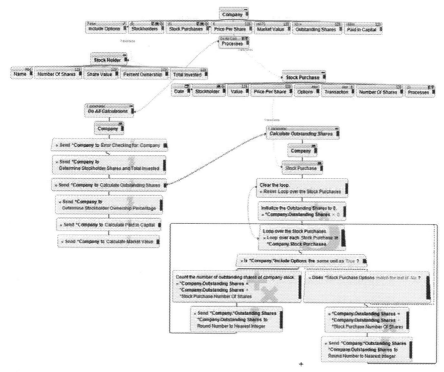

FIGURE 5.79 The Model for the Stock Manager Application

contact management application, the top-level class is Contact Manager as shown in Figure 5.80.

The Contact Manager class has two class list attributes that contain the individual contacts and the companies. Also, the Contact class has an Employer attribute that holds a Company class. This represents the Company with which that Contact is associated.

BUILDING THE DATABASE

Now that the model is complete, we need to prepare the model to specify exactly how the database is to be built. Assists for preparing the model can be found in

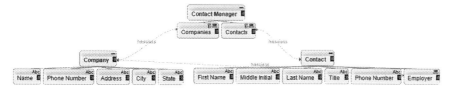

FIGURE 5.80 A Model of a Contact Manager Application

the Development Resource Center in Libraries > Databases > Databases from Unit Modeler Structures.

For this model we want to use the "Add the 'references same table as' Path Between Selected Units" assist in Adding Database Paths. Adding this path between the Employer attribute of the Contact class to the Companies attribute of the Contact Manager class will indicate that the two attributes reference data in the same database table.

To build the database, we will use the "Build a Database from a Model" assist within the DRC. This will show the window in Figure 5.81.

Enter the database driver information and click **Build Database**. Upon completion, the model should look like Figure 5.82.

Your model has now been converted to a database front-end application. Custom forms have been added to the classes that will read and write to the database as required. Now adding data to the database is as simple as adding new classes to the model as these will be automatically added to the database (Fig. 5.83).

Show the form for the Contact Manager class and add classes to the two list controls. When adding new contacts to the list, make sure to select an existing company from the application as the contact's employer. This will create a relationship between the two records in the database. Figures 5.84 and 5.85 are examples of a company and contact to add.

Once the contacts are added, look at the data in the database and see that the items added here were also added to the database. Also, if you restart the session and

FIGURE 5.81 The Build Database Tool

The tool supports Access, MySQL, SQL Server, and Oracle databases. The tool is used to create a database from a model. It will create all of the tables and fields in the database as well as modifying the model to read and write data to these tables.

FIGURE 5.82 The Contact Manager Model After Running the Build Database Tool on It

Note the classes now have ID attributes on them to support the way a database works.

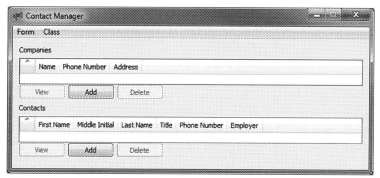

FIGURE 5.83   The Contact Manager Form Can Now Be Used to Enter New Companies and Contacts

The new data will be written to the database.

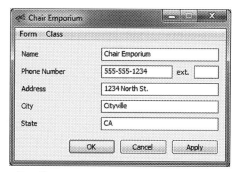

FIGURE 5.84 Entering a New Company

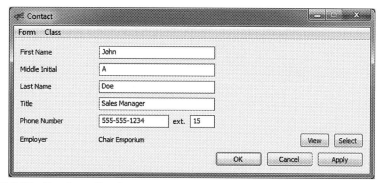

FIGURE 5.85   Entering a New Contact

The employer has a constraint list set to the companies contained in the Contact Manager application.

reopen the Contact Manager form, the items you added before will again show up in the application.

SEARCHING CONTACTS IN A DATABASE
DESCRIPTION

This example builds upon the Contact Manager application created in the "Building a Database from a Model" example. We will improve the application by turning it into a front-end search tool for the contacts database (Fig. 5.86).

GENERAL MODELING PROCESS

Starting with the Contact Manager model, we want to convert it into an application that allows a user to enter parameters used to search the contacts database. To do this we make changes to the top-level class Contact Manager as shown in Figure 5.87.

The Last Name and First Name attributes are the search parameters, the Search Process holds the process used to actually query the database and return the results,

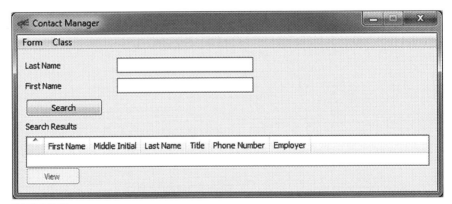

FIGURE 5.86

This example creates a front end to the database of the previous example enabling a user to type in a contact's first and/or last name and search for their contact information.

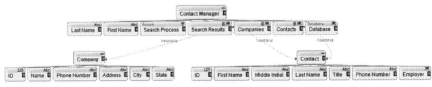

FIGURE 5.87

Last Name, First Name, Search Process, and Search Results attributes are added to the Contact Manager class.

and the Search Results attribute holds the search results. The Companies and Contacts attributes now possess the path "isa-Hidden attribute" so that they are not shown in the Contact Manager window.

PROCESSES

The search process for the Contact Manager search feature contains three stages:

1. Check the parameters of the Contact Manager class.
2. Insert the user-defined parameters into the Query.
3. Execute that Query and return the results.

The first stage checks to make sure that the processes will be able to create a query for the specified parameters. Therefore, it needs to make sure that the parameters are nonempty. If the user doesn't specify either search parameter, the application should show an error (Fig. 5.88).

To query the database with the search parameters, we will first need to create the Query using Query Manager: a simple, point-and-click tool for constructing queries. To do this, show the form for the Contact Manager Database class and click Add under the Queries list (Fig. 5.89). This Query should return all of the columns of the contact table, have two constraints for the Last Name and First Name columns, and have an Order for the Last Name column so that the results are ordered alphabetically by Last Name. With this Query, the search process will set the constraints using the Last Name and First Name search parameters entered by the user.

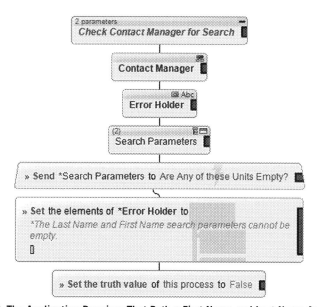

FIGURE 5.88 The Application Requires That Both a First Name and Last Name Are Entered

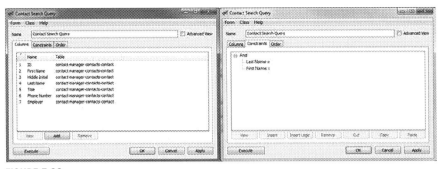

FIGURE 5.89

The Query Manager tool is used to create a template query that will be incorporated into the application and used by the search process. The search process will set the First Name and Last Name entered by the user into the template query's appropriate constraint attributes.

The query tool pictured above is used to define a query. You can define the fields to return as results and the constraints that are applied to the search. It can also execute the query. In this case, however, we do not wish to execute the query from the query tool, but rather we want to insert the query into our application. The class structure shown in Figure 5.90 is the output of the query tool. You can drill down on the Constraint Tree attribute to find the classes representing the constraints.

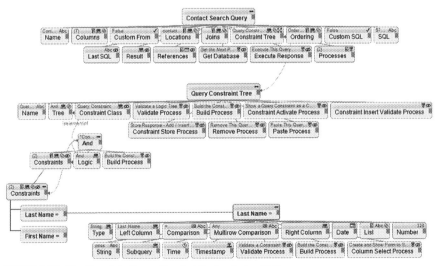

FIGURE 5.90 The Template Query Created By the Query Tool

The image above drills down to identify the classes representing the template query's constraints. The search process will need to set the String attribute of the constraints to the values entered by the user in the First Name and Last Name fields of the application. The model of a Query is very powerful and has several details that are beyond the scope of this discussion.

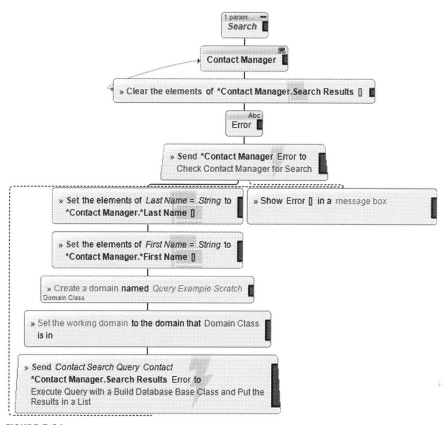

FIGURE 5.91

The Search process sets the constraints' String parameters to the values entered by a user and then executes the query. The results are set right into the Search Results attribute of the application.

The String attribute of the Last Name = class shown in Figure 5.90 holds the actual criterion. It is set to 'Jones' in Figure 5.90. The Search process shown in Figure 5.91 needs to set this attribute (Last Name = .String) to that entered in the Contact Manager form.

SURFACE PLOT CREATOR

The Surface Plot Creator (Fig. 5.92) is an application within the Math package. It creates a 3D surface plot for any expression of two independent variables (Fig. 5.93). There is also a 2D version for expressions of a single independent variable. This application is a fun way to visualize an expression. It also demonstrates reuse of many components of the standard libraries integrated into a single application, for example, expression editor, expression evaluation, GUI creation, and 3D visualization.

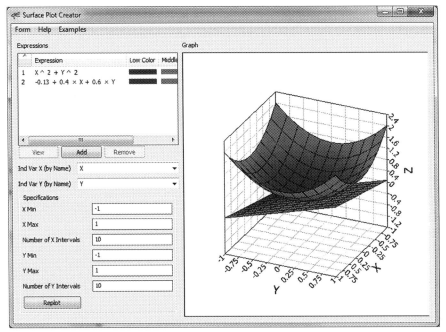

FIGURE 5.92

The Surface Plot Creator application allows a user to enter an arbitrary expression of two independent variables and plot them over user specified limits.

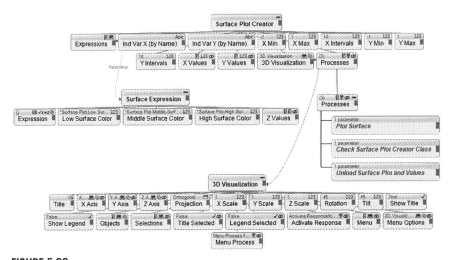

FIGURE 5.93

The 3D Visualization class is analogous to the Graph class when creating a 2D visualization.

MODEL OF A BRIDGE

The following example was developed by Clay Condol as a part of a required project for a Masters in Engineering Management while he was a student at the Rose-Hulman Institute of Technology.

The direct stiffness method (DSM) is a finite element analysis technique often used by structural engineers during design and analysis. This method is the basis for many commercial and free source finite element analysis software. It is a matrix method that is well suited for computer-automated analysis of complex structures including indeterminate structures that cannot be analyzed using static equilibrium equations. This method uses the stiffness (force generated in a member per unit of deflection) of each element in the structure, and compiles those values into a single matrix equation to generate anticipated deflections at the nodes, internal forces of the members, and reaction forces at the supported nodes. For a 2D truss, there are two degrees of freedom associated with every node. The degrees of freedom are a local coordinate system comprised of an x and y-axis for each node. In this model, all forces and deformations are dissolved along these sets of local coordinates (Figs 5.94 to 5.99).

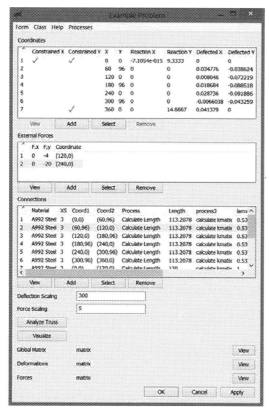

FIGURE 5.94 Model of a Bridge

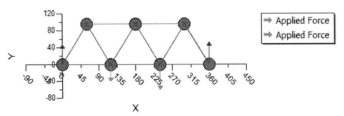

FIGURE 5.95 Visualization of the Bridge Structure and the Applied Forces

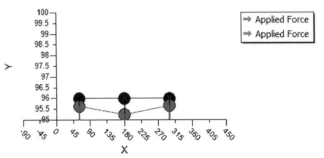

FIGURE 5.96 The Deflection of the Top Three Joints of the Bridge

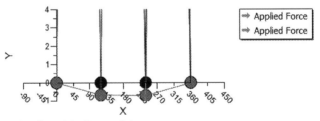

FIGURE 5.97 Deflection of the Bottom Joints

It is difficult to see here that the third joint is actually deflected by a greater distance than the second.

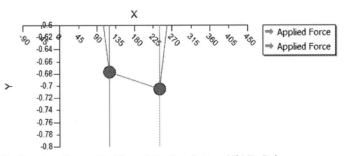

FIGURE 5.98 Here Is a Zoomed-in View of the Two Bottom Middle Points

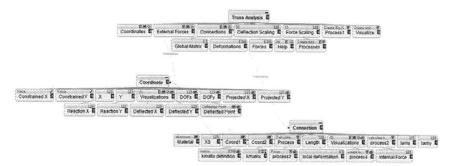

FIGURE 5.99 The Structural Model of the Bridge Application

The functional model and all of the associated processes are not included in this discussion but can be explored in the online examples within the Elsevier Book Examples workspace. See "Exploring an Existing Model" in Part 4 for techniques on how to do this.

Workspaces

6

Workspaces are cloud-based locations that serve three different purposes: they act as a place to codevelop an application, a place to share files of any type, and a place to distribute an application.

Workspaces have an administrator. The administrator controls many factors about how the workspace behaves. In particular, the administrator is able to control who can become a member of the workspace and what happens after a member joins the workspace. Together, these settings define the purpose that the workspace will serve.

There are three types of memberships for a workspace:

1. **Administrators**—Admins control the workspace and all of its settings.
2. **Contributors**—Contributors can access and modify content of the workspace, but cannot change any of the workspace's settings.
3. **Read-only**—These members can view content but cannot modify content. They do not have any of the admin functions.

There are four types of workspaces that define how individuals can become members.

1. **Public**—Anyone can see the existence of this workspace and can choose to become a member.
2. **Public Restricted**—Anyone can see the existence of this workspace, but must request to become a member.
3. **Private with Passphrase**—The administrator will setup a password to join this workspace. It will not be visible to the public. To join the workspace a user will click on a desktop icon "Join workspace with passphrase" and then type in the passphrase.
4. **Private**—Private workspaces are not visible to the public. A user must be invited by the administrator.

Workspaces have five important features:

1. Workspaces have their own file organizer. This is a tool you can use to share files. These files can be of any type including documents, images, spreadsheets, and domain files. Many applications, such as the Analytics Workbench, have Save buttons. The Save button allows you to save the application to a workspace, as well.
2. Workspaces have their own domain manager. Domain management is the Unit Modeler's equivalent to a source code management system. You can check

domains in and check them out. It will keep a history of all checked in files so that you can go back to previous versions if necessary. The domain manager feature also includes a Merge application which will identify differences between versions.

3. Workspaces can be subscription based. If you have put a lot of work into the application, you can designate it as a subscription workspace. In this case, users will have to purchase access before they will be able to become a member.

4. Workspaces have an Announcements tab that will show all of the activity associated with the workspace. The administrator can see who and when they joined the workspace, when files were added to the workspaces.

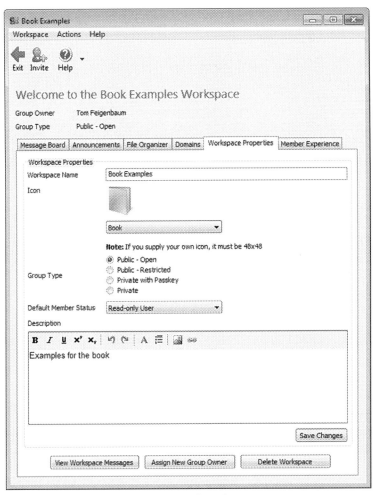

FIGURE 6.1 The Properties Tab of a Workspace Console

5. Workspaces have a message board that allows members to communicate to each other. This is similar to a chat room.

As an example, I formed a workspace to help develop examples for this book. I asked several KeLabs employees to help. In this case, the workspace served as a repository for sharing files. The group type was set to public (Fig. 6.1) so that anybody could find and join the workspace. (We run on a private network so just employees have access. Upon completion of the examples they will be moved to the public network.) The default member status was set to Contributor. This allows members to add files to the workspace.

The main purpose of this workspace was to act as a repository for everybody's examples. The File Organizer (Fig. 6.2) has a tree into which everybody added their domain files.

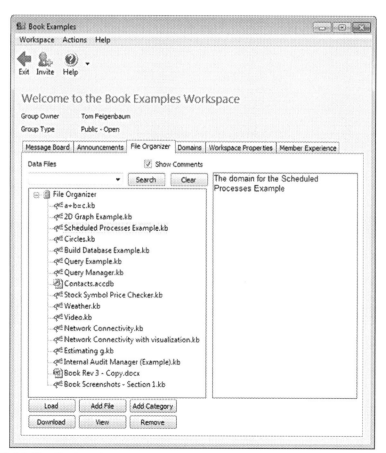

FIGURE 6.2 The File Organizer Tab of a Workspace Console

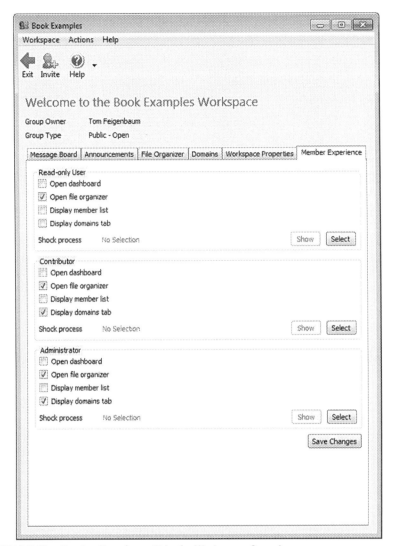

FIGURE 6.3 The Member Experience Tab of a Workspace Console

The Member Experience tab (Fig. 6.3) allows the administrator to define what happens when each type of user joins the workspace. In this example, Read-Only users represent the readers of the book who join the workspace in order to play with the examples. You will not be able to add new files to the workspace's file organizer. Contributors represent the KeLabs employees who will be contributing examples. I was the administrator.

The settings shown in Figure 6.3 are the same for both Read-Only users and Contributors. Upon joining the workspace, the workspace's file organizer will show docked to the left side of the screen. This is what was shown in the Tour of the Unit Modeler section earlier in Part 1 of this book.

The administer will also see the file organizer docked on the left side of the screen, as well as the workspace dashboard, which contains the screens shown above.

An additional option within the Member Experience tab is to identify a process that will be shocked upon joining the workspace. This process can, for example, can show the form of a class in one of the domains. This effectively launches an application. By specifying such a process, the workspace becomes just like an application. When the workspace icon is double clicked on from within a user's desktop, the application will launch. The fact that users are joining a workspace will be transparent to them.

The client software

7

The client software sets up the environment in which any models you create will be run. The client software runs all packages that are a part of the Unit Modeler. In fact, the client software also runs the development package.

The client software is written in C++ and is what loads domains, interprets the units, and ultimately carries out the operators of the units. If a form is shown, for example, the model defines its layout and contents, but it is the client software that actually shows it.

Discussed in this chapter is how to download and install the client software, its initial startup, including login, the desktop, certain features of the forms, controls within the forms and graphs, and other features of the client software, such as the file organizer, access to workspaces, and access to the libraries.

The client software embodies encapsulation. Each operator represents many lines of programming code. This code is structured such that its details are hidden and it is made accessible in a way that it can be reused. The fact that this code is already created is a significant time-saving feature and a significant reason why applications can be developed in a fraction of the time it would take to code from scratch. Much of the work has already been done for you.

DOWNLOADING AND INSTALLING

In order to download and install the client software visit www.kelabs.com and then navigate to the download page. Further instructions will be provided to you there.

JOINING THE ELSEVIER BOOK EXAMPLES WORKSPACE

After installing the software and logging in, your desktop will appear. Double click on the icon labeled 'Join a Private Workspace'. A form will appear asking you for a name and a passkey. Enter the following information:

Name: Elsevier Book Examples
Passkey: elsevier

UPDATES

Updates will be provided periodically. Some updates will only involve domains. When this is the case, the files will be updated automatically. If the domain is a cached domain, then you will see some increase in time to load this domain as it will come from the server this time and then be cached again.

When the Client Executable has to be upgraded then you will be prompted to upgrade. Choosing "yes" will exit you from your current session and restart the application.

LOGIN

Upon loading the client software you will be required to login (Fig. 7.1). You will require a username and a password. Your username will be selected by you when you register for the product at the KeLabs website. If you forget your username or your password, click on the appropriate link from the login form and follow the directions presented to you.

THE DESKTOP

The Desktop (Fig. 7.2) is a convenient feature for accessing all of the resources available to you. A desktop icon can represent many different things; directly load an application, a workspace, a package or even a help article, such as getting started. It can also reference a standard tool of client software, such as personal configurations.

The desktop can be customized by you, but it will initially come up with a set of icons for the available packages and any workspaces that you are a member of.

PERSONAL PREFERENCES

The personal preferences option allows a user to specify several options. Shown in Figure 7.3 is the option to identify a specific workspace to join upon logging in to the Unit Modeler. You can select from all of the Workspaces that you are a member of. By selecting this option, you will not initially see the Desktop.

FIGURE 7.1 The Login Form for the Client Application

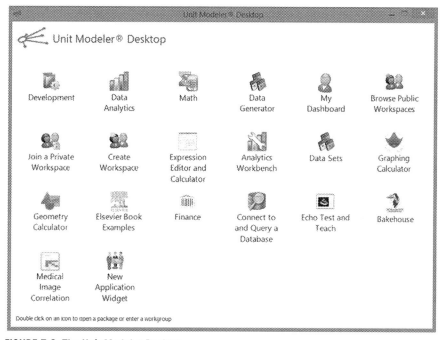

FIGURE 7.2 The Unit Modeler Desktop

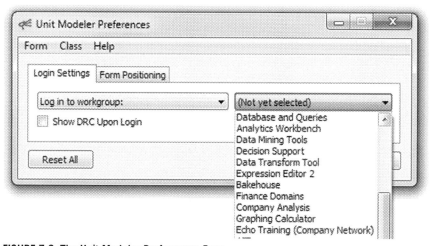

FIGURE 7.3 The Unit Modeler Preferences Form

With this feature you can specify what happens after logging in to the application.

THE FILE ORGANIZER

The file organizer (Figs. 7.4 and 7.5) is a feature of the client software that is much like having a built-in Windows Explorer. It is a convenient way to keep track of various files. You can add all types of files to the file organizer, including spreadsheets, documents, images, and domain files. When you double-click on a file, it will load into its default program type. A spreadsheet file will, for example, open in Excel, if Excel is installed on your computer. A domain file will load as any other domain file. The file organizer allows you to associate a comment with any file that you add to it. You can see these comments by checking the Show Comments Check box at the top of the organizer.

Every workspace also has a file organizer associated with it. If you have joined a workspace, a tab will appear in the file organizer for the workspace. When you load or add a file to a workspace organizer, the system will automatically download or upload that file to/from the server on which the workspace resides.

The Unit Converter Demo in in Figure 7.5 has a domain file and a PowerPoint file. These files were used while initially discussing the concept of this book with Elsevier. They wanted to see a tool that they had created via programming recreated in the Unit Modeler. The Unit Converter tool was recreated in a half-hour in the Unit Model and took about a week via conventional programming.

SPREADSHEETS

List controls are common elements of forms. They are similar to spreadsheets and are often referred to as spreadsheet controls. No matter what form a list control appears in or what data it is displaying, they will all support the same set of features:

- Moving columns
- Selecting items
- Sorting
- Multiple sorting
- Right-click options

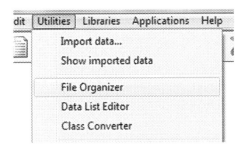

FIGURE 7.4 The File Organizer Is Accessible from the Utilities Menu

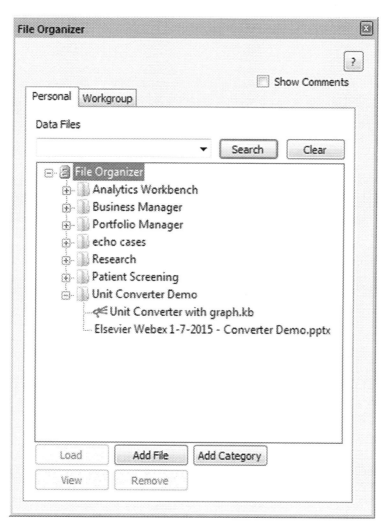

FIGURE 7.5 The File Organizer

You can move a column right or left by clicking on the column header, holding the mouse key down, and dragging it to the desired position.

You can sort a column by left-clicking on a column header. When you apply a sort all of the data in the other columns will also move so that each row is the same before and after sorting.

You can perform a multisort by left-clicking on a column and then holding the control key down on a second column. You can click on as many other columns as you want.

A list control also supports a right-click menu. Right-click menus can be configured individually by a developer. Thus, while every list will have a right-click menu, the menu's contents may differ from list to list.

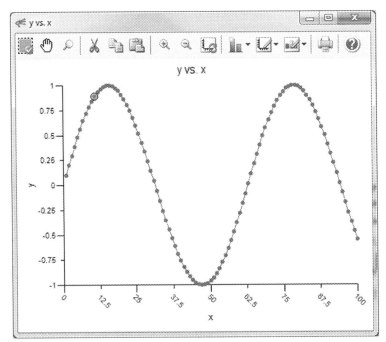

FIGURE 7.6 The Graph Window Has Several Useful Features in Its Toolbar Such as Select, Pan, and Zoom

GRAPHS

The infrastructure for two-dimensional graphs is contained within the Visualization domain. A graph can either be in a stand-alone window with a default custom form, or it can be embedded into an existing class as an attribute of the main class.

The toolbar (Fig. 7.6) on the default display of a graph provides all of the necessary tools for manipulating your graph, adding objects, creating plots, printing, and much more. Graphs that are embedded into an external form will not appear with this toolbar; however all of these tools are accessible through the right-click menus of the graph.

The toolbar buttons are as follows:

- Graph modes
  - —Changes the mode of the graph to Box Select
  - —Changes the mode of the graph to Pan
  - —Changes the mode of the graph to Zoom
- Cut/copy/paste graph objects
  - —Cut selected graph objects
  - —Copy selected graph objects
  - —Paste objects to the graph

- Zooming and reset limits

  ⊕ —Zoom the graph in

  ⊖ —Zoom the graph out

  🔲 —Reset the limits of the graph by setting the limits to automatic
- Edit the graph and graph objects

  📊 —Add a new object or plot to the graph. Provides submenus for adding a new graph object, scatter plot, line plot, and bar chart

  📈 —Edit the graph's axes

  📊 —Edit properties of the graph like the title, legend, and already created graph objects and plots
- Other toolbar buttons

  🖨 —Print the graph

  ❷ —Open the 2D Graphing help article

The first three buttons on the graph toolbar allow you to change the mode of the graph. These modes add means of interactivity so you can manipulate the graph objects and the graph itself. To change the mode of the graph, click one of the mode buttons on the toolbar or right-click in a blank space on the graph and select one of the three mode options. A checkmark (●) on one of the mode buttons in the toolbar signifies the current mode of the graph.

The graph modes are as follows:

- ▦ Box Select mode

  The Box Select mode of a graph allows you to easily select multiple objects and plot items at the same time. While in Box Select mode, you can left-click anywhere on the graph window and drag the cursor while holding the left mouse button to create the selection box. Upon releasing the left mouse button, an object or item that is contained by or intersects with the selection box will become selected. Hold the Ctrl key on the keyboard to keep previously selected items selected as you select new items with the selection box.

- ✋ Pan mode

  When in Pan mode, you are able to pan the view of the graph by left-clicking on a blank space inside the graph limits and dragging the cursor while holding the left mouse button. Upon releasing the left mouse button, the graph's limits attributes will be updated with the new values and the automatic limits attributes will be set to false. To reset the view of the graph, click the Automatic Limits button (🔲) in the toolbar. Clicking this button will set the limits of the graph to automatic, which will set the limits to ensure that all graph objects and plot items are in view.

- 🔍 Zoom mode

  Zoom mode allows you to easily zoom in and out of a graph. While the Zoom In and Zoom Out buttons in the toolbar are always available, Zoom mode enables the ability to zoom in with a selection box and to zoom in and out with the mouse scroll wheel. Zooming with box selection works similar to Box Select mode. Left-click on a blank space within the graph limits and drag the cursor while holding the left mouse button to create the selection box. Upon releasing the left mouse button, the graph will update its limits to dimensions of the selection box and set the automatic limits of the graph to false. Scrolling the mouse wheel forward (away from you) will zoom the graph in toward the center; scrolling the mouse wheel backward (toward you) will zoom the graph away from the center. To reset the view of the graph, click the Automatic Limits button (⊡) in the toolbar. Note: You will not be able to select graph items while in Zoom mode.

Servers

8

The applications we have described so far have all been what are called standalone applications. They load on the user's computer and run there. There is another class of application, also supported by the Unit Modeler technology, called client–server applications (Fig. 8.1). While it is beyond the scope of this book to discuss the development of these types of applications in detail, they are briefly described.

SERVERS VERSUS CLIENTS

The Unit Modeler technology has two primary executable components: Clients and Servers. These executables are nearly identical, but the differences are important. Servers do not create forms or any other type of user interface. If a Show Object Form step was shocked on a server, it will be ignored. Servers are actual Windows Services, meaning they will restart automatically if they shut down for any reason or if the system reboots. There also are other features common to server applications.

USES OF SERVERS

Servers act as central hubs with which multiple clients communicate. This is an important architecture for a large number of applications. These applications are referred to as client–server applications. The server components serve several purposes:

1. To provide a place from which certain domains can be accessed and loaded by many users, whatever type of domains those might be—definition, data, etc.
2. Servers may verify a user's login credentials to determine whether the user has permission to access an application and if so at what level. It can then setup the application environment depending upon the user's level of permission, such as administrator or user. Administrators, for example, may have access to features that users do not. These levels can be defined by a client–server application.
3. Server domains may run queries for applications acting as database frontends.
4. It may host data domains that save a database of data.
5. Servers may act as a repository for files that can be accessed by a client from any computer location.

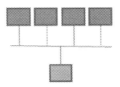

FIGURE 8.1 A Simple Client–Server Network Diagram

6. Servers may perform any other function, such as doing calculations.
7. Multiple servers can be setup to divide large tasks into smaller tasks handled individually by the servers. This is the foundation for big data applications and map-reduce architectures.

HOW DO CLIENT SERVER APPLICATIONS WORK?

Clients and servers work together by speaking to each other. They speak by sending each other data, requesting data, initiating a login process to an application, transferring files, and all sorts of other functions. When you log into the Unit Modeler you will be speaking to a server that will check your username and password, your preferences, and your subscription, and perform other tasks. When you type in a search request to a search engine and send it the search string, you are speaking to a server. It will speak to you by sending back the search results.

While having applications speak to each other may sound straightforward, in practice it is not. Normally, making applications speak to each other is difficult enough, but making them speak over a network introduces even more challenges. The Unit Modeler therefore encapsulated network communications and created operators and assists that make all of the details and complexities transparent to the developer.

There are still other architectural issues associated with developing a client–server application, but you will not need to deal with sockets, authentications, command lists or other details of network communications and client–server development.

ADVANCED ARCHITECTURE

The Shock Server operator is not only used by clients. A server can shock another server. This means that complex architectures can be created that address security, load distribution, and other demanding requirements. Server-side processing can be distributed amongst multiple servers. These servers can be located in many different locations. Therefore servers can be dedicated to certain purposes and further, can be maintained by people dedicated to the content on that server (Fig. 8.2). Ultimately a growing network of servers can be developed.

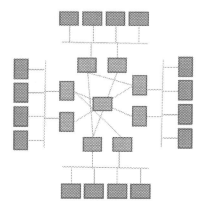

FIGURE 8.2

A Complex Network Architecture Where Servers Speak to Other Servers and Clients Speak with Multiple Servers.

PRIVATE SERVERS

Though much has been discussed about the public library of domains, their benefits do not negate the need for private domains, servers, and networks. The same components that drive the KeLabs central servers can be used to drive a private network running on private hardware and network. With this configuration an organization can have all of the same functionality that is described throughout this book, but only accessible to their own personnel. Administrators of the system can control the experience for their users, the desktop, available applications, permissions and the network's security. Though a private network setup is only accessible to its own personnel, it can still receive regular updates from KeLabs for core domains and executable upgrades.

The Unit Model versus code

9

Whereas a programming language is defined by textual syntax and semantics, the Unit Model has a visual form that permits more concentrated focus on the semantics of the program being built. The Unit Modeler environment positions the Information Unit Model squarely in the dataflow programming paradigm, enabling manipulation via point, click, and drag interactions. However, it should be noted that the open structure of the Unit Model permits a number of programming paradigms, including imperative, object-oriented, functional, and model-driven approaches, and all are widely applied.

Because of their dependence on syntax, programming languages—or more accurately, their compilers or interpreters—are highly sensitive. One missing character can lead to a frustratingly broken program. Modern Integrated Development Environments (IDEs) are well-equipped to point out likely errors, but they are not always able to find the root cause of the problem based on the developer's intentions. The simplistic nature of the Unit Model makes syntactic errors hard to come by.

The Unit Modeler is limited in its scope. Whereas most programming languages abstract machine-level instructions, the Unit Model abstracts a focused and powerful subset of instructions that are especially focused on operations in data analysis and manipulation of information.

The Unit Modeler does implement concepts common to many programming languages, like classes, processes (functions in most programming), and variables, but it also introduces concepts with no obvious parallel in other languages—most notably, the information unit, elements, and paths. Paths allow developers to define relationships between units, and elements comprise the contents of units and can utilize paths on units to define more complex references. Whereas variables in most traditional languages refer to memory interpreted as a specific data type, like binary data representing an integer, units can hold any number of heterogeneous elements.

With reference to executing processes, the Unit Modeler is built as an interpreter of the Unit Modeler. Each step of a process is interpreted when encountered, and the corresponding operation is carried out. Though reflection and runtime structural modifications are possible in some languages (consider JavaScript's object model), the Unit Modeler is built for this type of behavior. Consider two examples:

1. **Finding a class's base class(es):** In a language like Java, you can access a representation of a class's base class by calling the *getClass* function on the object. Note that this is a runtime representation of the class, as the class itself

is defined in code, not as a manipulable object itself. Instantiating an instance of that class dynamically requires knowledge and use of more advanced reflection techniques. Compare the Unit Modeler, wherein a class's base class(es) are destinations of the "isinstanceof" path off of the unit. The actual class structures are referenced, so creating an instance is as simple as creating an instance of a class in any other scenario.

2. **Runtime modifications:** A common question asked about programming languages is whether or not functions are first-class objects. A first-class object can be created, modified, and passed around like a variable. In the Unit Modeler, not only are processes first-class objects, but nearly all entities are first-class objects, including elements, operators, and processes. This means that unit contents can be set to complex elements at runtime, and even the operator of a unit can be modified at runtime. A line like "c = a + b" cannot be dynamically changed to "c = a − b," but in the Unit Modeler, the operator can very simply be changed from the "+" arithmetic operator to the "−" operator.

Programming languages all have variables and structures that can be created to represent something. But there is no direct analog that is equivalent to the Information Unit. Declarations can be made that can represent anything, but these are not consistently used as the only means of representing information, data, or processes. There is no universally general declaration as for a Unit. Everything within a model is viewed as an assemblage of a single data type: the Information Unit. This universality does not exist in any programming language.

Programming languages do implement the same type of flow as in the Unit Model. In the Unit Model a shock (or program execution) will travel down either a true or false path off the step being executed. This path can go to anywhere. There are some features of code that implement some direction of flow, such as *if/then/else* statements and *for* statements.

The Unit Model supports meta programming or the creation of new program components on the fly. A process can create a new process or modify steps within an existing process. Some programming languages also support this ability.

Programming languages have no direct corollary to the concept of a path. While the star (*) feature of the Unit Model is not entirely unique, it becomes much more powerful when combined with the utility of paths. For example, the element *Patients.Weight refers to all patient weights.

In information-based applications, the ability to copy data is pivotal. Copying a complex structure is not always straightforward in a programming language, but the Unit Model exposes a straightforward way to define how components of a model should be copied and moved around via "deep copy." This greatly improves the reuse of existing structures in ways not otherwise possible.

Models are developed and viewed in two-dimensional visual layouts. Insights into the architecture of your application and the interconnectedness of its components are readily understood. You can zoom in and zoom out to see an overview or drill down to see its specifics.

Reuse of previous work is possible in unprecedented ways. Any two models can exist and work together in the same application. The domain libraries and the Development Resource Center make reusable components easy to find, and when referenced, are loaded automatically via a feature called dynamic loading.

Updates occur automatically. Applications built within the Unit Modeler are not just is in a different language, but they are built upon an infrastructure that brings many benefits. One of these benefits is that updates that you may make to your application can automatically be distributed to your users. When an application is built in the Unit Modeler, no new infrastructure or installation program is necessary.

Appendix

GLOSSARY

Attribute A unit that contains information that describes the class to which it belongs (its parent class).

Class An information unit that represents something that has a set of characteristics. Usually a class is general and common to many instances of that class.

Complex Element An element that indirectly references one or more other information units by use of stars (*) and paths on the elements.

Domain Class Every domain has a Domain Class that holds various information about that domain.

Domain Expert A person who has expert knowledge in a particular field.

Domain The term *domain* can refer to two things: (a) a file that created by the Unit Modeler Development Environment that holds a set of information units, and (b) an area of knowledge and information.

Elements A property of an Information Unit. Each information unit can contain any number of elements. Each element is a reference to one or more other information units or text characters.

Encapsulate The act of making something that is complex simple. Encapsulation can be applied to processes, classes, and lists of units.

Form A window that shows information to a user. Forms are used to represent classes in a user-friendly manner.

Information Unit A representation of an individual piece of information. An information unit has an operator, elements, and paths.

Library A set of domains within a particular area of knowledge, e.g., statistics, database.

Model A set of classes, processes, and other information units that constitute an application or serve some other purpose.

Object Objects are Units that represent something that is not a class, a number, or a text string. An object is most often used to represent a list.

Operator A property of an information unit that defines what the information unit does when it is shocked.

Package A set of related applications that are grouped together and made available to a user, usually through a toolbar.

Path A path is a characterization of a relationship between two units. Each path is composed of the following pieces: a source unit, the relation, and a destination unit. A path is drawn as a line on the Whiteboard.

Process A set of units that are connected by > (True) and !> (False) paths that perform a task or set of operations.

Process Unit The top unit in a process. The process unit has an "isa process" path attached to it.

Real Operator An operator that that encapsulates an area of computer technology and the software that controls it.

Relation A description of the relationship between two units.

Simple Element An element that directly references another information unit.

Smart Selection A feature that guides the user toward making selections that are appropriate by highlighting appropriate units and presenting lists of reasonable possibilities.

Step Any unit in a process that is not the process unit.

System Vocabulary A domain that contains vocabulary units that provide a centralized reference point for commonly used concepts.

The Information Unit Model A fundamental and general model for describing knowledge and information. It has two basic entities: Information Units and Paths. Units and paths are assembled to create classes and processes.

Unit Model Operator An operator that only on elements of the unit model.

Unit Modeler A general reference to the entire technology based on the Information Unit Model.

Unit Modeler Class A class that defines the Unit Modeler environment, its menus, toolbars, right-click menus, and many other features.

Unit Modeler Development Environment The name for the package in which a user develops new applications based on the Information Unit Model.

Workspace A cloud-based resource for sharing files, codeveloping applications, and distributing applications.

Subject Index

Printed in the United States
By Bookmasters